The History of Nations

Germany

Other books in the History of Nations series:

China

England

THE HISTORY OF NATIONS

Germany

Annette Dufner, *Book Editor*

Daniel Leone, *President*
Bonnie Szumski, *Publisher*
Scott Barbour, *Managing Editor*
David M. Haugen, *Series Editor*

GREENHAVEN
PRESS ®

San Diego • Detroit • New York • San Francisco • Cleveland
New Haven, Conn. • Waterville, Maine • London • Munich

For more information, contact
Greenhaven Press
27500 Drake Rd.
Farmington Hills, MI 48331-3535
Or you can visit our Internet site at http://www.gale.com

Cover credit: Mountainous landscape with a castle by Cornelius Saftleven, Rafael Valls Gallery, London, UK/Bridgeman Art Library

National Archives, 87

LIBRARY OF CONGRESS CATALOGING-IN-PUBLICATION DATA

Germany / Annette Dufner, book editor.
    p. cm. — (History of nations)
Includes bibliographical references and index.
ISBN 0-7377-1196-5 (alk. paper) — ISBN 0-7377-1195-7 (pbk. : alk. paper)
    1. Germany—History. 2. Germany—Foreign relations. 3. Germany—Ethnic relations. I. Dufner, Annette. II. History of nations (Greenhaven Press)
DD89 .G48 2003
    x—dc21
                                                    2002072463

Contents

Chapter 2: The Bismarck Era and World War I

FOREWORD

I n 1841, the journalist Charles MacKay remarked, "In reading the history of nations, we find that, like individuals, they
have their whims and peculiarities, their seasons of excitement and recklessness." At the time of MacKay's observation,
many of the nations explored in the Greenhaven Press History
of Nations series did not yet exist in their current form. Nonetheless, whether it is old or young, every nation is similar to an
individual, with its own distinct characteristics and unique story.

The History of Nations series is dedicated to exploring these
stories. Each anthology traces the development of one of the
world's nations from its earliest days, when it was perhaps no
more than a promise on a piece of paper or an idea in the mind
of some revolutionary, through to its status in the world today.
Topics discussed include the pivotal political events and power
struggles that shaped the country as well as important social and
cultural movements. Often, certain dramatic themes and events
recur, such as the rise and fall of empires, the flowering and de
cay of cultures, or the heroism and treachery of leaders. As well,
in the history of most countries war, oppression, revolution, and
deep social change feature prominently. Nonetheless, the details
of such events vary greatly, as does their impact on the nation
concerned. For example, England's "Glorious Revolution" of
1688 was a peaceful transfer of power that set the stage for the
emergence of democratic institutions in that nation. On the
other hand, in China, the overthrow of dynastic rule in 1912 led
to years of chaos, civil war, and the eventual emergence of a
Communist regime that used violence as a tool to root out opposition and quell popular protest. Readers of the Greenhaven
Press History of Nations series will learn about the common
challenges nations face and the different paths they take in response to such crises. However a nation's story may have developed, the series strives to present a clear and unbiased view of the
country at hand.

The structure of each volume in the series is designed to help
students deepen their understanding of the events, movements,

and persons that define nations. First, a thematic introduction provides critical background material and helps orient the reader. The chapters themselves are designed to provide an accessible and engaging approach to the study of the history of that nation involved and are arranged either thematically or chronologically, as appropriate. The selections include both primary documents, which convey something of the flavor of the time and place concerned, and secondary material, which includes the wisdom of hindsight and scholarship. Finally, each book closes with a detailed chronology, a comprehensive bibliography of suggestions for further research, and a thorough index.

The countries explored within the series are as old as China and as young as Canada, as distinct in character as Spain and India, as large as Russia, and as compact as Japan. Some are based on ethnic nationalism, the belief in an ethnic group as a distinct people sharing a common destiny, whereas others emphasize civic nationalism, in which what defines citizenship is not ethnicity but commitment to a shared constitution and its values. As human societies become increasingly globalized, knowledge of other nations and of the diversity of their cultures, characteristics, and histories becomes ever more important. This series responds to the challenge by furnishing students with a solid and engaging introduction to the history of the world's nations.

INTRODUCTION

A Brief Overview of German History

Students of American history know that nations are sometimes founded in clear and dramatic moments, as the Declaration of Independence and the American Revolution attest. The births of European nations, however, were seldom so clearly marked. According to scholars, the origins of the German people are located twenty-five hundred years ago in southern Sweden. Given such a long history, it's understandable that it is difficult to say when exactly Germany as a nation came into existence. In fact, it is not much easier to say when Germany as a political unit resembling contemporary Germany came into being, for German peoples have been part of evolving kingdoms and duchies for a long time. Sometimes it is even difficult to say whether a kingdom or duchy should be considered German, as is the case when the rulers of the region are German but the people ruled are not, or when the rulers are not German but the people ruled are. As historian Donald Detwiler put it, "German history began at no specific place or date."[1]

Throughout their history, German peoples moved around within Europe. In approximately A.D. 370, nomadic Hun horsemen penetrated westward into the settling areas of the German tribes and drove some of them into parts of the Roman Empire. Such migrations, which brought Germanic peoples into areas inhabited by other groups, inevitably involved mixing of bloodlines, cultural habits, and practices. As a result, it is difficult, if not impossible, to give an ethnic account of who Germans are. In his 1941 book, *Thus Speaks Germany*, Wladyslaw Wszebór Kulski (writing under the pseudonym W.W. Coole and M.F. Potter) pointed at this ethnic diversity by noting that "the Germans are *par excellence* a nation of mixed origins."[2] The thought that the

13

Germans are one people probably didn't seem very obvious to them at the time, even though they generally shared a common language. Indeed, the idea of a German people probably didn't emerge until as late as the nineteenth century.

A Decisive Defeat

The first reliable documents about Germans date back to the campaigns of the Roman emperor Julius Caesar between 58 and 50 B.C. Caesar's armies, which had conquered much of Europe, managed to push the Germans who had settled west of the Rhine back to the east side of the river. In the historic battle of the Teutoburg Forest in A.D. 9, however, the German military leader Arminius succeeded in halting Roman expansion toward the north. Gaius Velleius Paterculus, a Roman writer, described the monumental Roman loss:

> The circumstances of this most dreadful calamity, than which none more grievous ever befell the Romans in a foreign country since the destruction of Crassus in Parthia, I will endeavor to relate. . . . An army unrivaled in bravery, the flower of the Roman troops in discipline, vigor, and experience in war, was brought, through the supineness of its leader, the perfidy [disloyalty] of the enemy, and the cruelty of Fortune, into a situation utterly desperate and was entirely cut off by those foes whom they had ever before slaughtered like cattle.[3]

The Teutoburg battle wasn't the last time German warriors would thwart the powerful Romans. Centuries later, in A.D. 476, German invasions contributed to the collapse of the Roman Empire.

Clovis and the Spread of Catholicism

In 476, Clovis, the son of the king of the Franks, one of the predominant German peoples, was ten years old. Clovis would become a powerful Frankish leader whose kingdom would dominate much of northern Europe. Although the true character of Clovis has likely been obscured by the mists of myth and legend, there is no doubt that his success as a leader of the Franks depended, at times, on his skills as a warrior. According to one story, Frankish soldiers plundering a church took a certain important vase, which Clovis hoped to claim for himself despite the fact that tradition required that goods captured during war be divided among the army. One soldier who did not want to see Clovis get the vase all to himself split the vase with his battle-ax and said to the king, "Thou shalt receive nothing of this unless a just lot give it to thee." At the time, Clovis didn't react, but he recognized the soldier a year later when he was reviewing his troops and berated him for the poor condition of his weapons. Then he split his skull with an ax and said, "Thus didst thou to the vase at Soissons."[4]

Although Clovis was born a pagan, in time he converted to Christianity, which was the religion of the majority of his subjects. The Frankish kingdom from that point forward represented and defended Catholic interests in Europe. This was a very important development not only in the history of Catholicism but in that of Europe. The powerful kingdom Clovis developed dominated Europe for centuries and eventually gave rise to France, Germany, Belgium, Holland, and Switzerland.

Charlemagne's Empire

Two centuries after the death of Clovis, Charlemagne was born. He would become the king of the Franks and the founder and ruler of the Holy Roman Empire. After assuming the crown in 770, Charlemagne, whose name in English means "Charles the Great," extended the reach of Frankish rule by conquering land in the east. Most important, however, Charlemagne helped Pope Leo III out of trouble, and in return, the pontiff conferred upon Charlemagne the imperial title and he became the emperor of the Holy Roman Empire. Indeed, Charlemagne's reign is particularly noted for developing and consolidating Christian Europe. Charlemagne cannot really be considered a German ruler. As he himself supposedly once said, "To God I speak Spanish, to women Italian, to men French, and to my horse—German."[5] After Charlemagne's death, the empire was divided among his offspring, a development that foreshadowed the dissolution of the Frankish Empire into the present nations of western Europe. Some people argue, in fact, that the beginning of Germany as a nation should be attributed to the beginning of the East Frankish Kingdom under Charlemagne's grandson Louis the German. The kindgom covered an area roughly similar to that of present-day Germany.

Struggles for Power

The large kingdoms ruled by Charlemagne's offspring were threatened by continuous raids. The problems inherent in defending large tracts of land meant that the nobles had to assume more and more of the duties of defense, and, consequently, they gained power. In 962, however, the Saxon Otto I, a man who combined tremendous physical strength with shrewd diplomatic cunning, restored the authority of the monarch and became the Holy Roman Emperor. Indeed, Otto's influence rivaled that of Charlemagne, as the Italian Giorgio Palco noted when he said, "As ruler over the nations, captain of conquering armies, propagator of the faith, director in chief of western policy, Otto impressed himself on the consciousness of the great men of the Empire, on the army and on the people, as in truth a new Charles."[6] Following the Saxons came the important dynasties of the Salian and the Hohenstaufen, which tried to penetrate into Italy. This military campaign weakened their central power in the empire and gave rise to local dukes, whose challenge to imperial power benefited from the emperor's continuous quarrels with the papacy over the leadership of the Catholic Church.

The reign of the Hohenstaufen emperor Frederick I, also known as Barbarossa, helped strengthen the central authority again. He became emperor in 1152 and restored the power of the crown by fighting down the dukes, and along with his successors extended the empire eastward. The death of the last Hohenstaufen emperor, however, caused a period of political confusion that lasted twenty-three years and is referred to as the Great Interregnum. That period of confusion ended when the first ruler of the Habsburg house, Count Rudolph, was voted into power with the support of Pope Gregory X, who wanted an emperor to help with a new Crusade and to balance the power of the king of Sicily. After Rudolph, members of other houses followed as emperors. None of them was able to restore the imperial authority completely, however. The uncertain relationship between the emperor and the various local rulers under him became clearer in 1356, when the Luxembourg emperor Charles IV established rules for the election of emperors and for the power and privileges of the princes who elected them. Albert of Habsburg came into power in 1438, and the Habsburg house kept the throne almost until the Holy Roman Empire dissolved in 1806.

Protestantism and the Thirty Years' War

Although there were countless important events during the centuries of the Habsburg reign, one of the most important was the

Protestant Reformation. Protestantism, so called because it began with the protests of theology professor Martin Luther, quickly spread throughout the German territories, especially the northern parts, and much of northern Europe. In 1517, Luther, a devout Catholic, nailed to the door of his local church in Wittenberg, as an invitation to scholarly debate, ninety-five theses critical of the Catholic Church. Within a few years, in part because of stiff resistance from Catholic authorities, Luther became more radical and openly defied the pope and disputed received Catholic doctrine. It is difficult to overestimate the importance of Luther. As Kurt Reinhardt, a professor at Stanford, remarked, "There are few characters in the history of civilization who have caused such profoundly revolutionary changes in the general outlook of their age and who have determined the destiny of their own nation to such an extent as Martin Luther."[7] Luther's effect, of course, spread far beyond the German borders, for Protestantism shook all of Christendom. Some German states converted to Protestantism along Luther's lines, and Charles V, who was not able to enforce his religious standpoint anymore, declared war against the league of Protestant states. That war finally ended in 1555 with the Peace Treaty of Augsburg, which gave every prince the right to determine the religion practiced within his own territory.

Religious tensions and attempts by the landowning nobles to gain more power continued and cast the spell of the Thirty Years' War over Germany. Between 1618 and 1648, the emperors and the Catholic princes were fighting against Protestant towns and territories, until the Peace of Westphalia granted the princes almost full sovereignty over their territories. Germany now consisted of hundreds of states, ranging in size and importance from the European powers Austria and Prussia to minute abbeys and autonomous villages. During the decades after the Thirty Years' War, Prussia established its role as one of the leading German states. Frederick I named himself king of Prussia, and his son Frederick II greatly enlarged Prussian territory, making Prussia the second most powerful German state after Austria.

The End of the Holy Roman Empire

The final end of the Holy Roman Empire came with Napoléon's intrusion into German territory during the Napoleonic Wars in 1806. Napoléon united some of the many German states and out of sixteen of them created the Confederation of the Rhine. These states adopted a more progressive form of government, inspired by the ideas of the French Revolution, with constitutions and assemblies of voted representatives.

After Napoléon's defeat, the map of Germany was radically redrawn once more at the Congress of Vienna in 1814 and 1815. That congress, which involved representatives from numerous European states, lasted nine months and redrew the map of Europe. It was said, wrote Ernest Henderson, that "at a ball, kingdoms were enlarged or sliced up, at a dinner an indemnity granted, a constitution sketched while hunting; occasionally a *bon mot* [clever saying] or a witty idea brought about an agreement where conferences and notes had failed."[8] Hundreds of German states that

German Confederation, 1815

existed before the Napoleonic Wars were united into thirty-nine states. The two most powerful were Austria and Prussia. Although the Congress of Vienna had a unifying effect, it came at the cost of causing offense to many within the German territories. In addition to upsetting the rulers of the mini-states that had to give up sovereignty, many German nationalist patriots had wanted to see the German empire restored. Still others had hoped for a more liberal form of constitutional government according to the ideals of the French Revolution. Instead of forming a unity, however, the thirty-nine newly created states were a loose confederation with a federal assembly in Frankfurt that seemed rather powerless.

Nonetheless, the potential of the new federation became apparent with the foundation of the Zollverein, a German customs union with the economic power to challenge British supremacy. It soon became clear that unification and a naval fleet large enough to match Britain's could make Germany the most powerful force on the continent. However, Austria, under the conservative leadership of Klemens von Metternich, opposed the idea of German unification.

The German Revolution

Famine and recession characterized the 1840s throughout Europe. The lower classes, which had already suffered under the advance of industrialization, found their situation growing worse. The time for change seemed to have come.

The confederate assembly in Frankfurt, which had previously consisted mostly of representatives who tried to preserve the autonomy of the local rulers who had sent them, started to make real efforts toward uniting Germany and giving it a constitutional government. Southern Germany was a center for advocates of change, given that states there had already adopted constitutions under Napoléon. But the revolutionaries had to confront difficult questions such as "Who is a German?" and "Where should the German borders be?" By the time they had made up their minds about these questions, the tide had already changed again to the advantage of the conservative forces. When Friedrich Wilhelm IV was asked to become the head of a constitutional monarchy in 1849, he rejected the offer, saying that he was not willing to accept the crown from the hands of the people. However, a sense of cultural cohesion and the desire for national unity had spread among the German population.

The Bismarck Era

It was Otto von Bismarck who finally united the German states. He came into power as prime minister of Prussia in 1862 and wanted to strengthen the dominant role of Prussia by unifying with other German states. The new Germany was built on "iron and blood," as Bismarck himself once put it: "The great questions of the time are not decided by speeches and majority decisions ... but by iron and blood."[9] Under his initiative, three brief wars in quick succession determined the borders of the new united Germany. Although Bismarck's critics did not welcome the way Bismarck had commenced these wars, they couldn't help but be dazzled by his success. After the defeat of France, Wilhelm I was proclaimed German emperor in the Hall of Mirrors in Versailles outside of Paris on January 18, 1871.

However, the new Germany was still a very authoritarian state that was not run by the people, which is illustrated by the fact that the emperor was proclaimed by the princes alone and that Bismarck had the final say even though the national liberals, who were generally critical of Bismarck, held far more seats in parliament than Bismarck's supporters. Furthermore, after Bismarck's revolution from above, the nobility was still privileged. Prussian conservatives who wanted Prussia to remain more than merely one province among many ruled by elected representatives successfully held on to the status quo and hindered further democratization. To many, the government system of what had by then become the leading industrial nation on the continent seemed more and more anachronistic.

World War I

After Wilhelm I, his son Wilhelm II became German emperor. It is usually agreed that Wilhelm II's lack of political and diplomatic skill, as well as his rhetoric of war enthusiasm, contributed to the outbreak of the First World War in 1914. The fact that there were plans to build a German navy that would be able to compete with the British Royal Navy also contributed to the international tension at the time. Most important, perhaps, was an unthoughtful promise of military support that the emperor had given to Austria-Hungary in case of war against Russia; on August 1, Germany declared war on Russia in order to honor that pledge of support. After considerable initial success on all fronts, French resistance, the pressure of a British blockade, and finally the U.S. entrance into the war crippled Germany and its allies, Austria-Hungary and Turkey. In 1918, the war was lost.

The resulting Treaty of Versailles imposed harsh conditions and economic hardship on Germany. It is often cited as having contributed to domestic political tensions after the war and even to the rise of Nazism and ultimately the Second World War. Indeed, at the signing ceremony in 1919, the French marshal Ferdinand Foch remarked presciently of the treaty, "This is not a peace treaty; it is a 20-year ceasefire."[10] To many in Germany, it was also not clear that the German surrender had been necessary; consequently, many were suspicious of the parliamentary parties that had approved of the surrender. Dissatisfaction spread when France, in response to Germany's inability to pay its reparations, occupied the industrial border area Rhineland, which was the heart of industrial Europe. Passive resistance and strikes in all of the Rhineland further strained the German economy.

The Weimar Democracy

After the loss of the war, the last German emperor abdicated and left the country to live out the remainder of his days in exile in the Netherlands. Power was handed to the leader of the Social Democratic Party, Friedrich Ebert, but there remained threats to his authority. The Spartacus Revolutionaries tried to seize control of Berlin and occupied the newspaper quarter until they were eventually fought down. Only three months later, a socialist republic was proclaimed in Munich, but this, too, was soon brought down. Trouble returned to Berlin in 1920, when it became the scene of a rightist putsch attempt by parts of the military. Ebert's democratic government had to retreat to the city of Weimar, which is why the democracy that was set up after the First World War is known as the Weimar Republic.

After those turbulent months, the Weimar democracy was able to establish itself in Germany, yet it never enjoyed strong political and social support. Under Chancellor Gustav Stresemann it seemed as if improvement was in sight, but then the Great Depression struck in 1929 and caused mass unemployment. In this difficult situation, Adolf Hitler and his rightist Nazi movement gained influence.

The Rise of Adolf Hitler

Adolf Hitler, who had served in the German army in the First World War, began his political career in the German Workers'

Party in 1919 and became head of propaganda a year later. (The party later became the National Socialist Workers' Party of Germany, or NSDAP, the members of which are referred to as the Nazis.) Hitler soon became president of the party, which at the time was a minor player in the German political scene. While serving nine months in prison for his part in the failed Beer Hall Putsch in Munich in 1923, Hitler began his book *Mein Kampf* (meaning "my struggle"). In *Mein Kampf*, Hitler expresses his hatred of Jews and explains the German need for more "living space," which was to be found in the east. Throughout the 1920s, Hitler and his party gradually became more influential, and in 1933 he became chancellor of Germany. One year later, he made himself the president of Germany, which he referred to as the Third Reich, or third empire. According to his vision, the German people were superior to others, especially to Jewish people, and he wanted to exterminate all Jews and gain more living space for the Germans through a large-scale expansion of the country.

In 1938, *Time* magazine named Hitler "Man of the Year," to reflect the enormous influence he and Nazi Germany held in Europe:

> The figure of Adolf Hitler strode over a cringing Europe with all the swagger of a conqueror. . . . Hitler became in 1938 the greatest threatening force that the democratic, freedom-loving world faces today.[11]

The Nazis under Hitler undermined democracy, suppressed opposition, and launched the Second World War by attacking most of Europe. They were also responsible for the Holocaust, the systematic murder of millions of Jews and other "undesirables" in death camps. Crucial instruments of Hitler's power were the SA, the Nazi Party's paramilitary storm troopers, and the SS, a security squadron that started as a personal bodyguard force for Hitler but later became a huge organization that carried out large-scale executions of Jews, Gypsies, Communists, homosexuals, and other minorities. The Gestapo, the secret state police, also helped to eliminate opposition; they were responsible for the roundup of Jews and others throughout Germany and, later, its territories of occupation.

Hitler's armies enjoyed astounding success in the early days of the Second World War, occupying much of the continent, but the tide began to turn when they failed to crush British resistance. They also suffered enormous military losses on the eastern front when an attempt to invade Russia proved disastrous. As the war progressed, German cities themselves came under attack, and eventually the country was overrun by Allied forces in 1945 and divided into four occupation zones by Great Britain, France, the United States, and Russia.

The Two Postwar Germanies

After disagreements with the Soviet Union, the three Western occupation powers, Britain, France, and the United States, consolidated their zones into the Federal Republic of Germany, also referred to as West Germany. The Soviet-controlled sector became the German Democratic Republic, a socialist country also known as East Germany. Berlin, the former capital of Germany, had also been divided up between the Allied forces. Now, the three Western sectors of Berlin belonged to West Germany although they were surrounded by East German territory.

While West Germany turned toward the Western world and became an economically flourishing country, East Germany was under the influence of Soviet communism and turned into a socialist one-party state with nationally controlled industry and agriculture. West Germany became a member of the North Atlantic Treaty Organization (NATO), a military defense pact between Western democracies. East Germany became a member of the Warsaw Pact, a defense treaty between the Communist and socialist countries of the Soviet-controlled East Bloc. During this time of tension, the so-called Cold War, the United States armed itself for a potential nuclear war against the Soviet Union. Fearing the United States, the Soviet Union did the same. The so-called Iron Curtain, the border that separated those countries who were members of the Warsaw Pact from the western countries in the NATO, ran right through Germany. East Germans were separated from West Germans by one of the most highly guarded borders in the world. Perhaps the most visible symbol of this tension between competing ideologies was the Berlin Wall, which East German Communists built directly through the streets of the city, cutting off the two parts of the city from one another.

Reunification

Konrad Adenauer, the first chancellor of West Germany, had been committed to eventual reunification, even though his policies led West Germany away from the Soviet Bloc countries and toward the West. Adenauer's aim of reuniting Germany became an element of the West German constitution, and he refused to recognize East Germany's legal existence. Later, the West German government tried to come to terms with the existence of its eastern neighbor. After the exchange of ambassadors with the Soviet Union, Germany's second chancellor, Willy Brandt, signed treaties with Poland and the Soviet Union that confirmed existing borders. As *Time* magazine remarked at the time,

> A quarter of a century after World War II, no European peace treaty has been written, and, in a very real sense, the results of the war have not been resolved. Willy Brandt is in effect seeking to end World War II by bringing about a fresh relationship between East and West. He is trying to accept the real situation in Europe, which has lasted for 25 years, but he is also trying

to bring about a new reality in his bold approach to the Soviet Union and the East bloc. [12]

In 1972, the two Germanies finally set up official diplomatic relations, and other Western countries built diplomatic relations with East Germany. In 1973, both countries were admitted into the United Nations.

The time of change arrived when Mikhail Gorbachev came to power in the Soviet Union in 1985 and the Kremlin's influence on its Communist satellite states declined. At the same time, opposition and calls for reforms in East Germany grew. More and more people tried to escape to West Germany through countries like Czechoslovakia and Hungary. Historian Tom Heneghan described two famous details of Gorbachev's 1989 visit to East Germany and its leader Erich Honecker:

> Teenage girls in blue FDJ [the East German organization Free German Youth] shirts and blue jeans squealed "Gorbi! Gorbi!" Other youths echoed dissident slogans. Poland's former Prime Minister Mieczyslaw Rakowski leaned over and asked, "Mikhail Sergeievich, do you understand what they're saying?" Gorbachev nodded, but Rakowski translated the slogans anyway. "They're saying 'Gorbachev, save us.' This is the end.". . . During his East Berlin visit, Gorbachev coined the phrase of the year when he said, "Life punishes those who come too late." It was a warning to Honecker, but he failed to get the message. [13]

Finally, in 1989, with the attendance of regular demonstrations (the legendary Monday Peace Prayers) reaching into the tens of thousands, the East German leadership gave up the attempt to preserve the status quo or issue reforms from above. For the first time in forty years, they allowed free travel into West Berlin and West Germany. On October 9, 1989, thousands climbed onto the Berlin Wall, an act that just hours earlier would have gotten a person shot by border guards, or hacked pieces out of the Wall. Others arrived in West Germany in their small East German cars and were greeted by curious West Germans and a fixed amount of deutsche marks, the West German currency, as a welcome present from the West German government.

A desire for reunification grew on both sides of the border,

and West German chancellor Helmut Kohl, ignoring the immense costs of unifying with the virtually bankrupt East German
economy, introduced the West German currency in the East and
opted for immediate unification. The first elections were held in
both parts of Germany, and on October 3, 1990, West and East
Germany became one country again, for the first time since the
days of Hitler. Soon after, a treaty with Poland was signed that
confirmed the existing western border of Poland.

The Wall in People's Heads

Although the Berlin Wall had fallen, it was commonly said that
there remained a "wall in people's heads." Many "Wessies" had
been hesitant about reunification because of the enormous costs
involved, and sure enough, a new tax had to be introduced to
deal with the outcome of fifty years of dictatorship in East Germany. In the eyes of many "Ossies," on the other hand, snobby
"Wessies" had reduced what was once East Germany into not
much more than a colony. Some difficult moral problems had to
be solved, as well. For example, controversy arose about whether
to open the archives of the Stasi (the *Staatssicherheitsdienst*, or secret police) of the former East Germany. The Stasi had secret files
on a huge number of people, and very often family members, acquaintances, and colleagues had spied on one another, often under coercion. There were also trials of former East German border police who shot people trying to escape over the border to
the West. They had had their orders and had acted according to
East German law, of course, but the state that had given those
commands no longer existed.

Helmut Kohl, the chancellor under whom Germany was re-
unified, had already been reelected once at the time of reunification. He became the chancellor of united Germany two times,
which means he was in power for a total of sixteen years. The
end of his time in office was followed by a scandal regarding
anonymous financial contributions he had accepted for his Christian Democratic Party.

The Center of Europe

Although the integration of East and West Germany has not
been seamless, in recent years focus has shifted away from linger-
ing problems there toward the future of Europe, which itself has
gradually grown more integrated since the Second World War.

A series of agreements and treaties that began in the 1950s culminated in the formation of the European Union in 1993. The original process of integration began between just six countries (Germany, Belgium, France, Italy, Luxembourg, and the Netherlands), but four waves of accessions have enlarged the membership to fifteen countries. There are also plans to enlarge the European Union toward eastern and southeastern Europe. The goal of integration is to promote joint economic and social progress, assert European concerns on the international scene, and develop common security policy. Citizens of member countries are free to live and work in other countries within the European Union, and there are no checkpoints at border crossings. In addition, most of the countries in the European Union now share a common currency, the euro, which Europeans hope will rival the American dollar as a world currency. Although the new currency enjoys support in Germany, many Germans were reluctant to see the end of the German deutsche mark, the rock-solid currency that signaled Germany's postwar economic success. Germany plays a central role in the European Union because it has the largest national economy, and, especially as the organization expands its membership eastward, Germany is situated in the center of the various member states.

As promising as the future is for Germany and the European Union of which it is a crucial part, the country faces challenges. One such challenge is ensuring that the German economy, which traditionally has afforded workers tremendous benefits, high wages, and job security, is able to remain competitive globally. Some fear that the German market is too tightly regulated and inflexible and that the unemployment rate is too high. Another area in which observers believe there is a need for reform is the way in which Germany serves its ethnic minorities, in particular its Turkish minority, which originally arrived after the Second World War when the demand for labor was high. Turkish integration has been incomplete at best, and decades later, most Turks do not have the same educational and career opportunities that ethnic Germans do. Finally, the German military has recently acquired a new role on the international stage. Largely dormant since the Second World War, and indeed required by the German constitution to be used for defense alone, the German armed forces were active in the U.S.-led military campaign in the fall of 2001. Although not everyone was happy with Germany's involvement, some people welcomed the invitation as a sign of Germany's stepping out of the long shadow of the Second World War.

Notes

1. Donald Detwiler, *Germany*. Carbondale: Southern Illinois University Press, 1999, p. 3.

2. W.W. Coole and M.F. Potter, *Thus Speaks Germany*. New York: Harper and Brothers, 1941, p. 130.

3. Gaius Velleius Paterculus, *Roman History*, in *Sallust, Florus, and Velleius Paterculus*, trans. John Selby Watson. New York: Harper and Brothers, 1881, p. 513.

4. Quoted in J.H. Robinson, *Readings in European History*. Boston: Ginn, 1905, pp. 51, 55.

5. Quoted in Philip Dormer Stanhope, *The Letters of Philip Dormer Stanhope, 4th Earl of Chesterfield*, vol. 4, ed. Bonamy Dobrée. London: Eyre and Spottiswoode, 1932, p. 1497.

6. Quoted in Friedrich Heer, *The Holy Roman Empire*, trans. Janet Sandheimer. New York: Frederick A. Praeger, 1968, p. 41.

7. Kurt F. Reinhardt, *Germany: 2000 Years*. Milwaukee: Bruce, 1950, p. 215.

8. Ernest Henderson, *A Short History of Germany, Vol. 2: 1648–1871*. New York: Macmillan, 1902, p. 316.

9. Fürst Bismarck, *Sein politisches Leben und Wirken*, vol. 4, 1878, trans. in *Familiar Quotations: A Collection of Passages, Phrases, and Proverbs Traced to Their Sources in Ancient and Modern Literature*, ed. John Bartlett. Boston: Little, Brown, 1992, p. 474.

10. Quoted in Paul Reynaud, *Mémoires*, vol. 2. Paris: Flammarion, 1963, p. 457.

11. *Time*, "Man of the Year: Adolf Hitler," January 2, 1939.

12. *Time*, "Man of the Year: Willy Brandt," January 4, 1971.

13. Tom Heneghan, *Unchained Eagle: Germany After the Wall*. London: Pearson Education, 2000, pp. 25, 27.

THE HISTORY OF NATIONS
Chapter 1

The Holy Roman Empire

The East Frankish Empire

By Diether Raff

In this article Diether Raff analyzes the development of political forces in ancient and medieval Germany. Raff begins by offering an overview of settlement in ancient times and then discusses the establishment of the Frankish Empire under Clovis and Charlemagne and the later East Frankish or German Empire. It is this empire which later became known as the Holy Roman Empire of the German Nation. Raff also talks about the continuous power struggle between the rulers of the East Frankish Empire and the Catholic Church under the popes. Another major political factor addressed is the tendency of local princes to increase their own influence and thus promote the disintegration of the central imperial power, which eventually led to a total decline of the German Empire. Raff is a history professor at the University of Heidelberg in Germany.

After approximately AD 250, the Franks began to extend their traditional domain between the Lower Rhine and northern Gaul [a region comprising nowadays France and parts of Belgium, Germany, and Northern Italy]. In approximately 500 BC King Clovis of the Merovingian family succeeded in unifying the Franks, defeating the last Roman governor of Gaul, subduing the Alemans and uniting most of the remaining West Germanic tribes in one mighty empire. Reckoned according to present frontiers, this realm incorporated almost all of France, the Rhineland and the region between the Alps and the Central German Uplands. The conciliation of the Germanic peoples and the conquered Roman population was facilitated by Clovis's conversion to Christianity. In the end the Christian faith spread the length and breadth of the Frankish Empire, firmly implanting itself here at the very time when Islam was conquering the formerly Christian provinces of the Roman Empire in Africa and Asia, advancing as far westward as Spain and menacing the West.

The most important of the Frankish kings was Charlemagne (Karl der Große), whom the pope crowned Roman Emperor in the year 800. He ruled over the temporal vestiges of the old Roman Empire and was considered chief protector of the Christian faith.

Charlemagne's empire comprised almost all of present-day France and Italy and the region of central Europe bordered by the Eider, Elbe, Saale, Danube and Drava rivers. When this enormous empire was partitioned among Charlemagne's successors, its unity crumbled and each segment went its own way. Within a century the mighty Carolingian Empire had split into the West Frankish Kingdom, the East Frankish Kingdom and the kingdoms of Burgundy, Provence and Italy. The face of Europe had changed forever and the stage was set for the states of the medieval and modern eras to emerge.

In order to consolidate his hold on power, Charlemagne divided the empire into counties, each ruled by a *Gaugraf*, or count. The count dispensed justice in the name of the king, administered the crown lands, collected taxes and led his troops in battle. The marches created along the borders of Charlemagne's empire protected it against external assault. These margraviates [border countries] were far more extensive than the counties, and the ruling margraves [local rulers of the border countries] more independent of the central authority than the counts, even issuing arriere-bans [a royal proclamation summoning vassals to military service] on their own authority when danger loomed. Charlemagne's emissaries roamed the counties, reviewing the administration of justice and tax receipts, listening to grievances and promulgating imperial laws. They represented the central authority and ensured the unity of the empire. The economy rested of course on the barter system.

The bureaucracy of Roman times was replaced by a nobility sworn to serve the king. In return for this service the nobles were endowed with a fief and certain sovereign rights. As the king's vassals they were required to swear an oath of allegiance to him and to provide military support. The emergence of this feudal system was encouraged by the existence of a class of nobles in all the Germanic peoples.

The power and influence of the feudal lords was magnified

after fiefdoms became hereditary in the ninth century. The might
of these local potentates *vis-à-vis* the central authority increased
further when Charlemagne's weak successors partitioned the empire and proved unable to defend it against invasions of Arabs,
Normans, Slavs and Magyars.

The imperial borders were especially endangered in Austria as
a consequence of its geographic location. In their peril, the Saxons, Lorrains, Franks, Swabians and Bavarians looked to their military leaders, the dukes. In view of the weakness of the central
authority these dukes sought to augment and consolidate their
own power and to ensure peace and security throughout their
own domains.

When the last of the Carolingian monarchs died in 911 the
dukes of the eastern kingdom elected one of their own as the
new king. This election of the Frankish Duke Conrad marks the
split of the Eastern Kingdom from the Frankish Empire as a
whole and the beginning of German history. . . .

The German Empire

In the western half of the Frankish Empire the common folk
spoke largely Old French, while in the eastern half they spoke
deutsch, or German. The word *deutsch* stems from the Old High
German *diot* meaning 'people' and was originally an erudite term
denoting the dialect spoken by the ancient tribes of the east. After the middle of the tenth century this term was customarily applied as well to the land where these people lived: the 'Deutsches
Reich', or German Empire. The English word 'German' is derived from the Latin 'Germanus'.

Conrad I proved unable to establish an effective central authority over the other dukes, but he did succeed in persuading
them to elect as his successor the Saxon Duke Henry. Henry and
his son Otto subsequently met with far greater success in their
attempts to consolidate the young German Empire in the teeth
of both internal and external threats. Like Charlemagne before
him, Otto I relied on the unifying effect of the Christian Church
and on the bishops who were loyal to him. In another step which
recalls Charlemagne Otto betook himself to Rome to be
crowned emperor, 162 years after Charlemagne's journey in the
year 800. Otto then reigned over the eastern portion of Charlemagne's empire and over most of Italy as the temporal leader of
Christianity and defender of the western church. The restoration

of the Roman Empire in the year 800 had raised high hopes for an era of peace, and this second restoration had a similar effect. Fated to endure for eight centuries, this empire later came to be known as the 'Holy Roman Empire of the German Nation'.

Otto I and his Saxon successors did their utmost to expand the might of the empire at the cost of the tribal dukes. No longer content with mere *pro forma* recognition of supreme royal authority, Otto and his successors demanded actual submission. Efforts to reinforce the authority of the king resulted in the transformation of hereditary tribal duchies into non-hereditary duchies and the accordance of temporal powers to ecclesiastics. Bishops and abbots were endowed with such sovereign rights as supreme judicial authority and the power to raise taxes and armies as well as a royal prerogative to establish market towns, collect custom duties and issue coinage. The prelates, their estates and the cities on them were freed from the suzerainty of the dukes or counts. Endowments of land from the royal domains and the transfer of whole counties to ecclesiastical rule placed the German Reich on an entirely new footing.

The Church Gains Influence

The empire was no longer administered by feudal lords, eager to expand their hereditary fiefs and maximise their autonomy, but by bishops bereft of legal heirs. Since the right to invest bishops fell to the king, the danger that royal sovereignty would continue to erode seemed dispelled for the moment. By ensuring that each successive regent of the church domains received his lands and sovereign rights directly from the king, the Saxon rulers made loyal supporters of the bishops and offset the might of the dukes. The secular lords of course had exploited the hereditary system of land tenure in order to gain a large degree of independence from the crown and were always endeavouring to extend their autonomy. The prelates had the further advantage of literacy over most of the secular lords and were therefore better administrators. The taut organisation of the church from one end of the empire to the other helped them in this task.

So long as the king remained competent and able to assert himself against the church, this system proved successful and the unity of the *Reich* was assured. This unity was to be imperilled, however, when the secular overlord, the king, clashed with the spiritual overlord, the pope. Compelled to choose between their oath of fealty to the emperor and the obedience they owed to the pope, the ecclesiastical princes would opt for the spiritual benefits which the church alone could provide.

For the present, however, the empire continued to expand in glory and might under its Salian and Frankish rulers. After the death of Henry II, the last of the Saxon line of emperors, the dukes selected the Frankish duke Conrad, a great-grandson of Otto I, as the new monarch. In contrast to his predecessors, Conrad II viewed his election not as a gift bestowed indirectly by God but as a public mandate requiring that he subordinate his own interests to those of the empire. Conrad II was similar to his predecessors, however, in that he too was forced to contend with dukes eager to increase their autonomy.

In order to bolster the central authority, Conrad awarded the duchies of Bavaria and Swabia to his son, Henry, thus extending the royal domain and strengthening those subvassals whose fiefs were rendered hereditary. In return, this lower level of the gentry entered his service, fulfilling military and administrative functions. Even under Conrad's Saxon successors, literate imperial ministers from this class continued to be the mainstays of the empire.

Not content merely to rein in the dukes, Conrad set out to reestablish the primacy of the empire over the pope and the Church. When he subsequently inherited Romanic Burgundy and incorporated it into the *Reich*, German rule was secured in Italy and the borders of the empire were thrust far to the west. . . .

The Empire and the Papacy

Under Conrad's successors, the ascendancy of the emperor was jeopardised by an ecclesiastical reform movement, the original function of which was to combat the mounting secular influence within the monasteries. This reform movement spread quickly through France, Italy and Germany and soon turned its attention to other offences within the church. Celibacy was re-emphasised and simony was discouraged. In addition, lay investiture came under attack, even though the emperor's right to appoint bishops had become an essential pillar of imperial authority. If he lost this prerogative, he would lose control not only of the church but of much of the empire since the bishops also functioned as territorial lords.

Henry III died young, and under his six-year-old son and further successors, royal authority crumbled. As the power of the empire shrank, the papacy sought to escape its authority by promulgating a new decree which transferred the right to select the pope to a College of Cardinals, thus nullifying the influence of the emperor over the selection.

The church reformers aimed as well to abolish all secular authority over ecclesiastical officials and to establish the precedence of the spiritual realm (*sacerdotium*) over the secular realm (*imperium*). The church, not the empire, was to be the principal supranational authority preordained to lead the concert of nations. In 1075 the pope forbade lay investiture throughout the church and instituted stiff sanctions for any transgressions. This ignited a quarrel that endured almost fifty years before the issue was settled by the Concordat of Worms. Henceforth church functions, imperial domains and the secular justice system were disentangled. The German bishops were elected by ecclesiastics in the presence of the emperor, then invested by him with temporal fiefs and rights and finally consecrated by the church. Thus the bishops retained their worldly possessions and remained secular lords nominally in the service of the monarch, though he lacked all power to control their appointment.

Thus the Ottonic system expired. The emperor's dominion over the church was extinguished and the pope became the recognised overlord of the universal church. The German church was deprived of its unique position and became merely another branch of supranational Christianity as in England or France. At the same time, royal authority within the empire was gravely damaged.

The temporal and spiritual princes of Germany exploited the quarrel between the pope and the emperor to advance their own interests, to expand their possessions and prerogatives at royal expense and to reinstitute an elective monarchy. This increase in the power of the princes had fateful historical consequences, as a dualism of king and princes emerged and eventually the princes established unchallenged dominion. The resultant particularism was to remain the bane of Germany for many centuries to come. . . .

The Free Cities

From the ninth century, more and more strongholds were erected in order to defend the river crossings and passes through which international commerce flowed. Many of these strongholds were subsequently awarded a market charter by the emperor. Armed with such a charter (which after the eleventh century could also be granted by liege lords and lords of the manor), the emerging cities began to escape the orbit of their overlord and to govern themselves according to their own law. The city council and the chief magistrate whom it elected were responsible for defence, the collection of taxes and fees, the protection of crafts and trade, the administration of justice and the care of the sick and the poor. City dwellers were not considered vassals and could freely dispose of their own property. Anyone could win personal freedom by dwelling in a town for a year and a day without raising objection.

The autonomy of the towns fostered the emergence of a new middle class comprising both urban merchants and artisans. The nobility played a role as well in the development and administration of the cities, especially in Italy, Switzerland and the northern and southern sections of the empire. The first city councils were populated by nobles in cooperation with merchants. After 1300 some artisans grew wealthier, organised themselves into guilds and participated as well in town government. The free imperial cities in particular became great centres of wealth thanks to their crafts, commerce and art. The cities gradually expanded by purchasing the surrounding land and, as they waxed in power and autonomy, inevitably came into conflict with territorial princes eager to extend their authority. . . .

The Development of Independent German States

The territorial princes vastly increased their autonomy during the quarrel over investiture and under the reign of Frederick II, the last of the Hohenstaufens. The princes succeeded in appropriating unto themselves the most meaningful of the royal prerogatives: the administration of justice and the right to approve fortifications, grant market charters, issue coinage and impose duties. Thus the feudal lords strengthened their hold over their fiefs at the expense of the emperor and the townsfolk. Around the middle of the thirteenth century they attempted virtually to eliminate the power of the central government by selecting as German kings foreign princes who were too weak to assert their new authority. The outcome was anarchy as the state slithered into lawlessness and private warfare.

This 'frightful time without an emperor' came to an end in 1273 with the election of Count Rudolf von Habsburg. The right to select the king had been transferred in the interim to an electoral college composed of three ecclesiastical princes (the archbishops of Mainz, Cologne and Trier) and four secular princes (the King of Bohemia, the Duke of Saxony, the Margrave of Brandenburg and the Count Palatine of the Rhine). The Archbishop of Mainz presided over the meetings. At first this procedure lacked any legal basis, but was eventually authorised by Emperor Charles IV in the Golden Bull of 1356. Moreover, the electoral principalities were declared henceforward indivisible and inheritable according to the rule of primogeniture. The sovereign rights of the prince-electors were also vested, and royal judicial authority over their territories virtually eliminated. This gave the princes well-nigh absolute authority over their own principalities.

The various principalities thus acquired full legal status, obviating the possibility that a strong central authority would once more impose itself. Before the Golden Bull was promulgated, the princeelectors even defended their right to select the emperor against no less a claimant than the pope. The king they elected would no longer require the approval of the Holy See and would be endowed directly upon election with the title and powers of the Roman emperor. With that the pope's traditional right to crown the emperor lost all legal significance.

The Struggle for Imperial Authority

Henceforth a German emperor would have to rely on the wealth and might of his own house if he hoped to command respect and occupy a powerful position within the empire. The king-emperor's authority over nobles and commoners alike would be rooted in the power of his own family and not in the institutions of the empire, which could no longer confer might and prestige.

The empire of the late middle ages was therefore composed of an emperor struggling to extend the power of his own house, and electors clinging tenaciously to their vested privileges. Legions of prelate princes—archbishops, bishops and abbots—also wielded temporal power. Dukes governed to the east in Silesia, Pomerania and Mecklenburg, though the old tribal duchies in the west had largely shrivelled into counties. Scattered among these larger domains lay over fifty 'free imperial cities' and a host of politically autonomous pigmy states, puny in population but great in imperial lords. . . . Together they comprised the *Reichsstände*, the various states of the empire. Since the early fifteenth century they had shared with their king and emperor in governing the realm and claimed a voice in the *Reichstag*, or Imperial Diet.

This Imperial Diet evolved from court sessions which the emperor convened in various locations and at irregular intervals during the high middle ages. By the late middle ages the *Reichstag* could be convoked by the princes who were now full-fledged members and no longer liege lords participating at the emperor's pleasure. After 1495 the members of the *Reichstag* met in three separate colleges—the College of Electors, the College of Princes and the College of Cities—before gathering to arrive at a joint decision. When a resolution was adopted by a majority vote, it was ratified by the emperor and became an imperial decree. The *Reichstag* was charged with discussing and deciding upon imperial taxes, laws, wars and military expeditions.

The finances of the empire were in a shambles and local wars never ceased, lord against lord, town against prince and knight against town. All aspired not merely to defend their lands and privileges but to augment them. Towards the end of the fifteenth century efforts were undertaken to reform the empire and create a more stable environment. The *Reichskammergericht*, a national court of justice independent of the emperor, was instituted and perpetual land peace proclaimed. States and individuals alike were forbidden to engage in private warfare. Early in the sixteenth century the *Reichstag* divided the empire into ten districts, each ruled by a prince. Attempts to establish a sound financial footing by introducing a head tax, the 'common penny', failed, as did efforts to establish an executive council to oversee imperial policies.

The imperial estates with their array of local interests proved powerful enough to block all reforms of no direct and immediate benefit to them. As the countries of Western Europe grew more capable of united political action, Germany lost her preeminent position in Europe and remained till the second half of the nineteenth century a loose collection of individual states which took note of European affairs only in so far as they impinged directly on their own interests.

The Reformation

BY MARSHALL DILL JR.

*The following piece by Marshall Dill Jr. recounts the Protestant Refor-
mation of Germany, which Martin Luther, a theology professor, initiated
in 1517. Luther wished to draw attention to the Church's excesses, and
nailed ninety-five revolutionary theses onto a church door in Wittenberg
as an invitation to debate. Luther was arrested and called for questioning
in front of the Imperial Diet, where he claimed it was impossible for him
to change his views. His stand inspired the oppressed peasant classes to
rise up against Church and state authority. But expecting Luther to lead
them, the peasants were confounded when Luther sided with local princes
who crushed the rebellion. Although he may have alienated the peasantry, Luther did win religious converts in the aristocracy. With a growing
and influential Protestant minority, hostilities between Protestant and
Catholic plagued Germany in the 1540s and 1550s. They quieted with
the Peace of Augsburg, however, and religious toleration restored calm to
Germany. Marshall Dill Jr. was a history professor at the Dominican
University of California.*

With his useful gift of hindsight, it is no problem for the
historian to see that by 1500 the German world was
on the threshold of momentous events. Alike in the
political, economic, social, religious, and artistic spheres, developments were culminating simultaneously in such a way that an upheaval was almost bound to occur. The fifteenth century had
shown the weakness of the imperial organization; the inert Frederick III had simply emphasized it. Power was certainly slipping
from the head to the members, but the question was which of
the groups of members would receive it: the electoral princes, the
lesser princes, or perhaps the middle-class burghers of the prosperous German towns. The very prosperity of the towns based
on their crafts and their extensive trade served to accentuate the
misery of the peasantry, the overwhelming majority of the Ger-

man population, burdened almost beyond endurance by dues and duties of various sorts levied by both state and church; in years of bad harvest their plight was tragic. To add to their sorrows, the quantity of coined money in Germany increased greatly during these years, bringing with it the evils of inflation. The German peasant was sufficiently wise to know how much better off he might be, an attitude always pregnant with trouble. . . .

The religious revolt centers around the career of Martin Luther (1483–1546). Luther's father, a peasant miner, planned a career in the law for his son; but after a deep religious experience, Martin gave up his legal studies and undertook a religious life, entering an Augustinian monastery. He was ordained a priest in 1508 and sent to the new University of Wittenberg in Saxony as a professor of philosophy. Two years later he went to Rome on church business and was bitterly shocked by the luxury and extravagance he found there in high clerical circles. He was a man of violence, a man burning for God, who lived in fear of eternal damnation and was sure that no deed of his could relieve the penalties of his terrible future in hell. Eventually, from his studies of the Bible he developed the consoling doctrine of justification through faith.

Luther's Ninety-Five Theses

In 1517 a Dominican, John Tetzel, appeared in Wittenberg preaching an indulgence proclaimed by Pope Leo X to collect money to build the new church of St. Peter in Rome. Contributors to the fund, if repentent for their sins, were promised remission of the temporal punishment due for those sins. Luther considered this an intolerable abuse, and on October 31 nailed to the door of the university chapel ninety-five theses, or propositions, concerning the doctrine of indulgences, which he declared himself ready to dispute with any opponent who might present himself. This typically medieval action is generally regarded as the opening event in the history of Protestantism.

It is beyond our scope to enter into the details of the early history of the Protestant movement or to raise the theological problems involved. During the three years after 1517 Luther took part in various public disputes, and his positions were the subject of official inquiries. Gradually, as he attacked the primacy of the pope and later the doctrine of transubstantiation, Luther moved further and further from orthodoxy. . . . By 1520 he had written his major theological tracts. In that year Pope Leo condemned a number of Luther's propositions and threatened excommunication. When this papal ruling (or bull) arrived in Wittenberg, Luther reacted by burning it publicly in the square before the university. Shortly thereafter the excommunication was decreed formally.

At about the same time the new emperor, Charles V, appeared in Germany and called a meeting of the imperial Diet at the city of Worms. The Pope appealed to the emperor to place Luther under the ban of the Empire. The Diet summoned him to Worms under safe-conduct to give him one more chance to recant. In March 1521 Luther appeared twice before the Diet, on the second occasion delivering his famous speech in which he declared himself unable to change his views in any way. He then left Worms and on his way home was spirited away by his friend and patron, Frederick the Wise, Elector of Saxony, to the peaceful seclusion of the castle of the Wartburg, near Eisenach, where he spent almost a year at his translation of the Bible. Aside from its religious importance, this work set the future literary form of the German language. In the meantime the Diet placed Luther under the ban of the Empire.

Luther Gains Influence

After his return from the Wartburg Luther married a former nun and spent most of the rest of his life advising on the formulation of the new doctrines and on the organization of the new churches. Since he could not depend for support on the Empire, Luther based the new institutions on the local territorial princes. Each of these in Lutheran areas became a supreme bishop for his own domain and controlled his own church. This obviously gave a mighty impetus to the growing power of the individual princes and also encouraged the less scrupulous of them to embrace the new faith because they could then seize the possessions and incomes of the old church.

The decade of the 1520s was decisive for the Protestant revolution. In 1521 there was an expectation that Luther could be silenced; by 1530 the breach was complete, a statement of Lutheran beliefs had been drawn up, and Germany was divided spiritually forever. During those years Charles V was not in Germany at all. His major preoccupations were two wars against France, wars which were only peripheral to German history except that they permitted the consolidation of Protestantism without the presence of the emperor to do anything conclusive about it. In fact, in 1522 Charles abdicated further his position in Germany by making his younger brother Ferdinand regent of all the German Hapsburg lands. Ferdinand was married to the heiress of Bohemia and Hungary, lands which fell to him on the death of their king in 1526. As ruler of those eastern territories, Ferdinand's primary concern was to defend them against the Turks. From 1526 to 1532 he waged campaigns in that direction, of which the most serious moment was the first Turkish siege of Vienna in 1529. Both Hapsburg brothers thus were able to give only secondary attention to Germany during this momentous decade....

Luther and the Peasants

The peasants drew up a program called the Twelve Articles, which were both religious and economic, though on the whole limited in their demands. They called for an elective priesthood and the abolition of various oppressive feudal dues. Although some German leaders saw the justice of some of the demands, there was on the whole no sympathy with them, and the peasants decided to resort to force. By the spring of 1525 several hundred thousand peasants were under arms. They conducted a campaign of reprisal against their lords, which rapidly assumed the bloodthirsty character of social wars.

This was a crucial moment for Luther, whom the peasants were hailing as a leader. He had already shown his basic political conservatism in his attitude toward the radicals at Zwickau. He now made his position very clear in a violent and passionate pamphlet entitled *Against the Murderous and Rapacious Hordes of the Peasants.* This was all the propertied classes needed. They organized troops which in the course of several months put down the peasants with appalling brutality. The peasants were crushed, this time permanently, and Luther had placed his future squarely in the hands of the territorial princes.

From this time on Lutheranism ceased to spread among the lower classes. Its attraction was now to the educated, especially the local rulers, who tended to sweep their people along when they themselves became converts. An example is Albert of Hohenzollern, Grand Master of the Teutonic Knights. Lutheran teachings had reached as far as remote Prussia and attracted Albert. He paid a visit to Luther, who advised him to renounce his vows, marry, abolish the Order, and found a dynasty. Albert did exactly that and thus helped to establish the future greatness of the Hohenzollern family. Prussia joined ranks with Saxony, Hesse, and the other Lutheran territories.

A Protestant League Develops

With the creation of more Lutheran states the tendency developed among both Catholics and Lutherans to form leagues based on similarity of belief. While no one wanted civil war or the disruption of the Empire at this time, there is no question that these leagues paved the way for the consolidation of the two groups and eventually for the tragic wars of religion. In 1526 Archduke Ferdinand summoned a Diet of the Empire to meet at Speyer. Ferdinand was intensely concerned with the imminent threat of the Turks and anxious to gain the support of all the German princes in his military efforts. Thus it would clearly not be possible to try to enforce the decisions made at Worms in their full strength. Emperor Charles now believed that a final settlement of the religious problem was not possible until a general council of the church could be convoked. Thus at Speyer a mild resolution was taken providing that, until this council met, the estates "with their subjects, would live, govern, and act in such a way as everyone trusted to justify before God and the Imperial Majesty." Although it was not the intent, this edict seemed to consecrate the religious division in Germany and to make it easier for hesitant princes to embrace the new faith without fear of imperial reprisal.

Three years later the situation had changed a good deal. Charles V and Pope Clement VII had patched up their difficulties; the war with France was brought to a close; the Turkish peril was receding. It seemed possible to Ferdinand to take a stronger line. Accordingly he called another Diet at Speyer (1529) at which he read a message calling for no more religious innovations and announcing the imminent arrival of Charles in Germany and the immediate calling of a church council. The message was approved by the Catholic majority while the Lutherans drew up a "Protest," from which the word Protestant derives.

Charles V Returns

The following year Charles did arrive in Germany for the first time in nine years and called a Diet of the Empire to meet at

Augsburg. It was a splendid affair but ended in failure. It looked like a religious council rather than a political one. There was a full representation of Catholic theologians. The Protestant cause was upheld by Philipp Melanchthon, a young follower of Luther, who hoped that a compromise might be effected between the two parties. He had drawn up a statement of belief, the Augsburg Confession, which blunted some of the sharp edges of Protestantism and which he believed might be a document of conciliation. Although Melanchthon was constantly willing to compromise, there were points beyond which he could not go. No compromise was achieved, and the Diet decreed a return to the very strict prohibition of Lutheran teachings proclaimed at Worms in 1521. The Protestant princes left the Diet, and the *sta-*

THE INVENTION OF THE PRINTING PRESS

Historian David W. Coleman describes the importance of the invention of the printing press. After Johannes Gutenberg produced the first printed book—the Gutenberg Bible—the new technique quickly spread through Europe. The wider availability of books had a tremendous impact on many parts of life.

For an invention that so radically transformed history, we know remarkably little about the early development of the moveable-type printing press. All that can be said for certain is that it was a gradual process that culminated in the German city of Mainz sometime between 1445 and 1450, when several people, including a former goldsmith named Johannes Gutenberg, contributed to the earliest workable prototype. Although it would be an exaggeration to say that Gutenberg "invented" moveable-type printing, it is true that his press was the first to publish a lengthy, substantial printed book, the famous Gutenberg Bible, 1454–1456. From Mainz the printing press spread rapidly, first through Germany and then into other areas of Europe. By 1500 more than one thousand presses had been established across the continent, and they had collectively produced more than nine million

tus quo was hardly changed. The Augsburg Confession has remained a creed for orthodox Lutheranism ever since. The Diet gave the Protestants six months to return to the old faith. The Protestant reply in early 1531 was to found the League of Schmalkalden, which eventually became a firm alliance of the Protestant princes and cities to protect them against Catholic attack. The drift toward open conflict continued.

It looked as if this time the Hapsburgs meant business in their resolve to stamp out Protestantism, but again their attention was diverted by pressing problems elsewhere. Once more the Turkish danger looked ominous. The emperor was forced to agree to the Religious Peace of Nuremberg (1532), a truce which was to continue the *status quo* until a council or the next Diet. In return

---

copies of more than forty thousand separate book titles. Europe's commercial center, Venice, likewise became the continent's capital of printing, as the city alone housed nearly one hundred printing shops.

The cultural impact of the printing press in late-fifteenth-century Europe was enormous. Widespread availability of standard copies of the works of ancient and modern writers alike meant, above all, more rapid transmission and dissemination of ideas than had been possible in previous centuries, when books had been produced and copied only in manuscript form. In addition the explosion in the availability of books made possible by printing responded to and in turn contributed to increasing levels of literacy among the population of Europe. Reacting to the demands of Europe's largely devout reading public, the early book market was dominated by prayer manuals, Bibles, and other religious works. Besides religious books academic readers called for printed copies of the works of ancient Roman and Greek thinkers, including many of those that had only recently been "recovered" by the scholars of the Italian Renaissance.

David W. Coleman, "Background: The Printing Press and the Spread of Ideas (Early American Civilizations and Exploration to 1600)," *American Eras.* 8 vols. Farmington Hills, MI: Gale Research, 1997–98.

the Protestant princes offered Charles help against the Turks. As it developed, this temporary arrangement of 1532 lasted for almost fifteen years. Charles was out of Germany during most of this time. He undertook a campaign against the Turks, two wars with France, and two expeditions to North Africa. It was not until 1544 that he was free to take any important action in Germany. In the meantime the Protestant area in Germany increased enormously. By the mid-forties almost all of north Germany was Protestant and even Austria itself felt the impact of the new doctrines. Among the temporal principalities only Bavaria seemed safe for Rome. A special problem arose in the case of the ecclesiastical territories. If a bishop or abbot decided to turn Protestant, should he secularize the whole territory as Albert of Hohenzollern had done, or should he simply get out of the way himself and permit a new canonical appointment? The solution differed in various places according to the relative strengths involved. In some dioceses secular administrators were appointed to run the affairs of the area while the question remained unanswered. The problem of church lands in secular territories was serious too, especially when one realizes that the church had fulfilled all social and charitable functions. The usual solution was for the prince to confiscate all church property and to assume the responsibility for the church's former duties. The temptation latent in this for avaricious princelings is obvious.

Still another serious problem arose with the introduction of the teachings of John Calvin in Germany. These teachings, far more radical in their opposition to the old faith than those of Luther, spread to southwestern Germany from Calvin's headquarters in Geneva. They made special inroads into the lands of the Elector Palatine. The Lutherans were just as opposed to Calvinism as they were to Catholicism, so the struggle became three-cornered.

The War of Schmalkalden

When Charles V returned to Germany in 1545, he at first appeared to temporize. However, before long it was clear that he was determined to wage war and was trying to win to his side some of the Protestant princes. He was successful in obtaining the help of Duke Maurice of Saxony (not to be confused with his cousin from the other branch of the Saxon line, the elector of Saxony, who was a leader of the League of Schmalkalden).

The War of Schmalkalden broke out in 1546. For some months nothing decisive happened; the Protestants in particular were hesitant and dilatory. In April 1547 Charles won an overwhelming victory over the Saxons at the battle of Mühlberg. The Saxon elector was captured and his dignity transferred to Maurice. It looked as if Charles and Catholicism were triumphant. The following year Charles issued the so-called Augsburg Interim, an attempt at religious peace. It was in fact hardly a compromise, though it did grant a few favors to the Protestants. For instance, they could maintain a married clergy and receive communion in two kinds if they obtained a papal dispensation. There was also an effort to reform some of the abuses of the old church.

Nobody liked the Interim very much. The pope was suspicious because Charles seemed to be arrogating religious decisions to himself, particularly at a time when the Council of Trent was already meeting to deal with the problem. The Protestants were, of course, dissatisfied. Even more significant perhaps was the fact that all the princes, Catholic and Protestant, were worried about the revival of the authority of the emperor—especially an emperor who was primarily a Spaniard. They had enjoyed too long the pleasures of practical independence to be willing to give them up.

The Peace of Augsburg

The situation simmered for several years until in 1552 the Protestant princes revolted against Charles. This time they were led by Maurice, who had changed sides and gone to the length of making an alliance with Charles' bitterest enemy, Henry II of France. This phase of the war was unsuccessful for Charles, who was almost captured at Innsbruck and fled over the Brenner Pass into Italy.

The war continued against France, but in Germany negotiations went on for some time under the direction of Archduke Ferdinand, culminating in the Peace of Augsburg of 1555, a landmark in German history. This treaty settled the religious question with the phrase, *cuius regio eius religio*. This meant that each prince might freely choose between Catholicism and Lutheranism and might require his subjects to conform to his beliefs. An "ecclesiastical reservation" provided that churchmen who henceforth wished to change their religion had to abandon the church property entrusted to them to the Catholic church, which would appoint a new incumbent. All church lands confiscated before 1552 were to remain Protestant; all others were to remain Catholic. The treaty gave no privileges of any sort to the Calvinists. This compromise agreement remained the legal basis of the religious settlement for the next century, though in practice it was often violated.

A few months later Charles V, tired and disgusted, abdicated his titles and functions, and retired to a monastery for the short remainder of his life. His Spanish and Italian possessions went to his son Philip, while his central European holdings went to his brother Ferdinand, who became Emperor Ferdinand I (1556–64). With these events a period in German history came to a close.

The focus of interest in Europe during the second half of the sixteenth century moves away from Germany. It shifts to France, which was on the eve of its long religious struggle; to England and Spain, where the long duel of the reigns of Elizabeth I and Philip II was about to be fought; and to the Netherlands, which was soon to start its war of independence under the house of Orange against Spain. Religiously speaking, the main interest in Germany lies in the loss of ground of Protestantism and the corresponding gains of Catholicism as a result of the Catholic Reformation.

Frederick II and the Rise of Prussia

BY THE *ANNUAL REGISTER*

The following article appeared as an obituary in the British Annual Register of the year 1786. It summarizes the life of Frederick II, also known as Frederick the Great, who turned Prussia into a state that equaled Austria in power. The article focuses on his accomplishments, especially his success at war, and his character traits, which included a strong sense of discipline. The article also claims that the suffering of his old age made Frederick more docile and led him, for instance, to open two hospitals in Berlin for old people of any religion, nationality, and sex. According to the obituary, Frederick's ignorance of literary productions written in German and his admiration for French literature was universally scorned. Consequently, the article says, measures by Frederick's successor that aimed at reducing the influence of the French in many parts of society were accordingly popular.

There was no event that marked the year of which we treat in such striking and indelible colours, as the death of the great Frederick, the illustrious king of Prussia. If he was not the founder of an empire, he accomplished a more arduous task than even that, under its usually concurrent circumstances, has generally proved: for surrounded as he was by great and jealous potentates, possessed of immense standing armies, and at a time when discipline and the art of war were supposed to have been already carried to their ultimate point of perfection, he, merely by the powers of superior genius and ability, raised a scattered, ill-sorted, disjointed dominion, into the first rank of power, glory, and renown; and the newly-founded kingdom of Prussia soon became, under his auspices, the terror or admiration of mankind.

Excerpted from "Obituary of Frederick the Great," *Annual Register*, 1786.

Frederick's Character

But though he must always be considered as one of the greatest
captains and masters of the art of war that ever lived, and as having carried military discipline and field evolution to a degree of
perfection before unthought of, and which is now the great object of imitation with all martial nations; his mind was too comprehensive, and his genius too vast, to be confined to tactics, or
the business of the field; and he shone forth at the same time
with no less ambition of fame, in all the different characters of
legislator, historian, poet, and philosopher.

In the course of his long and exceedingly hard fought wars,
contending against a combination of power which has seldom
been equalled, and with some of the first generals and greatest
nations, he sustained with unfailing constancy, and an uncon-
querable fortitude, the most dismal reverses of fortune that perhaps have ever been experienced and recovered by any commander; he having been repeatedly and suddenly depressed from
the highest pinnacle of success to the lowest extreme of distress
and adversity; insomuch, that even the continuance of his existence as a sovereign was more than once a question sufficiently
dubious. Through a noble perseverance, and the strenuous exertions of his admirable genius, he still surmounted his difficulties
and dangers: fortune again smiled, and seemed only to plunge
him in adversity, that he might rise with brighter glory.

Less Admirable Traits

In estimates of real character we must necessarily take mankind
such as they are, compounds of good and of evil, of great and of
little; we should in vain look for resemblances to those imaginary
heroes, who are represented as so bedizened with virtues, that
nothing like nature or truth can be perceived about them; and
the picture exhibits, as the poet happily observes, "those faultless
monsters which the world ne'er saw." On the contrary, the shades
in Frederick's character were as strongly marked as the bright
parts, and we shall perhaps find that his great qualities had even
more than their due proportion of alloy. There certainly have
been great captains and conquerors, who afforded superior instances of a noble and generous nature to any that he had the fortune of exhibition; who were happily better calculated to excite
the affection as well as the admiration of mankind; and who were
free from many of the defects of his character.—To say that this

ambition was boundless, would be no more than saying that he held the vice common to great situations; but his ambition assorted too much with rapacity to captivate the imagination, as it otherwise might have done; and he looked more to his interest than his fame in the means which he sometimes used for the attainment of his objects. A strict economy, indeed, was indispensably necessary to the peculiarity of his situation, and to the support of such prodigious armies, with means which would have been totally inadequate in any other hands; but he pushed this virtue too far towards the opposite extreme, so as to carry too much the appearance of a degrading parsimony; and it must be acknowledged, by those who pay the greatest respect to his eminent qualities, that he was more fond of gold than corresponds with the established ideas of a great man.

Frederick could brook no opposition to his will either in word or in action; was to the last degree implacable in his resentments; and inheriting from nature, as well as deriving from education and example, a disposition extremely harsh, despotic, and occasionally cruel, it could not be expected that it would have been lessened by the horrors and carnage of war, any more than by the continual personal enforcement in peace of that austere military discipline established by himself, which was as unequalled in its rigour and feverity, as in all other respects; and by which, man being reduced to the state of a living machine, was considered and treated merely as such.

Frederick's Later Days

But the latter part of his life seemed calculated to make amends to mankind for all the ravage and desolation which his ambition had occasioned in the foregoing; to give a new colour to his character; and to cast a softening shade of benignity over all its parts. He became the father as well as the legislator of his subjects; and to them the milk of human nature seemed overflowing in his composition. The extraordinary expences to which he went in peopling and cultivating the sterile or desert wastes which extended over such vast tracts of his dominions, were only limited by the extent and number of the objects to which they were applicable. For though his attention was in a considerable degree directed to almost every branch of improvement, yet agriculture was his great and favourite object; and he accordingly adopted every measure that could render the husmandman easy

and comfortable in his circumstances, and secure in the posses-
sion of his property. And if he deserves praise for having attained
these ends in the latter and more serene parts of his career, it must
surely by considered as the greater glory of his reign, and one pe-
culiar to himself, that when most unfortunate in war, and when
most oppressed by an unequalled combination of hostile power,
yet, that in all the singular distresses to which he was at those seasons reduced, his provident foresight had provided such ample resources for every evil that could ensue, that he never burdened
his subjects with the addition of a single tax, or the demand of a
benevolence; so that his dominions, if it had not been for the
cruel depredations of his numerous enemies, would have borne
the fame appearance as in a season of profound peace. . . .

This great prince departed the present life on the 17th of August, 1786, in the 75th year of his age; a surprising age, whether
we consider it with respect to the greatness, number, and splen-
dour of its actions, the dangers to which it had been exposed, or
the unequalled exertions of body and mind, by which, through
a long reign of more than forty-six years, it had been continually
exhausted.

The King's Physical Decline

His decline had for some time been so rapid, that the event was
easily foreseen; yet, under the joint pressure of an asthma, dropsy,
and lethargy, the former of which had for some time rendered
him incapable of repose in a bed, he displayed in the intervals his
pristine vigour of mind, and all his usual serenity and cheerful-
ness conversation; never uttering the least complaint, nor show-
ing the smallest degree either of regret or impatience at his condition; and on the 15th, only two days before his death, he sent
for his cabinet secretaries at four o'clock in the morning, and
transacted business for three hours with them; but in the evening
of that day the somnolency returned, and he continued nearly in
a state of insensibility until his death.

It was a curious if not singular circumstance, that as the king
began himself personally to feel the infirmities and incommodi-
ties of age, it touched his sympathy so strongly for the distresses
of the unprovided in that calamitous condition, that he immediately founded two hospitals in Berlin for the reception of helpless old age, in all cases whatever, without regard to nation, religion, or sex.

There were numerous other instances of his temper and disposition being greatly softened by age; a circumstance very unusual in mankind, and almost without example in conquerors; who so generally become more rigid, harsh, and oppressive, and too frequently degenerate into absolute cruelty at that season of life.

The attention of all Europe had been long drawn to the contemplation of this expected event, and of its probable or possible consequences. Many apprehended that it would prove the signal for immediate war, and perhaps lead to great political revolution. The character of his nephew and successor, the present king, was not yet much developed; and it was easily seen that a new kingdom which had risen suddenly to such unexampled power and greatness as served to excite the jealousy or apprehension of all its neighbours, merely through the abilities of one man, would require abilities not much inferior to withstand the shocks, to which it might be stable upon the loss of its tutelary guardian and genius. The danger appeared the greater, as its nearest and most potent neighbor [Austria], besides other great political differences, and his finding Prussia almost constantly in his way in the prosecution of his ambitious views, was himself the greatest sufferer by her greatness; and was well known to be of a character not much disposed to forgive or forget to grievous a loss as that of Silesia. [Frederick had seized the Austrian province of Silesia.] . . .

Unpopular Choices

No event or act of the late reign was so universally unpopular throughout Germany, as his predilection for the French language, and the decided preference which he upon all occasions gave to the literature of that nation. The numerous German literati [literary intelligentsia] in particular could not but be grievously affected by it, and indeed every true patriot, from whatever part of that wide empire he derived his existence, must have felt it sensible, as an insult offered, and a glaring contempt shown to his language and country. This predilection the king derived from his early acquaintance and intercourse with French poets and philosophers of the modern stamp, to whom he was likewise indebted for other prejudices and principles still more injurious and unfortunate; particularly that indifference (to call it by the softest name) with respect to religion, which stuck to him through life, and was the great blemish of his character.

It must, however, be remembered, that the German writers in

the late king's earliest days, were of a very different cast and character from those who have since so far advanced literature and science, have done so much honour to their country by their genius and researches, and who by their successful introduction of the poetic muses have used the most effectual means for softening and wearing down the roughness of their native tongue. On the contrary, at and for a considerable time after his accession, laboriousness and fidelity were the chief praises that could be bestowed on the German writers; their works were proverbially verbose and heavy; they had not yet applied with any success to the Belles Lettres [fine, artistic writing]; and their poetry, particularly the dramatic, was barbarous. Early prejudices are with difficulty shaken off, and as life advances, the disposition to that endeavour generally lessens. Frederick had early made himself a party in the affair, by criticisms on, and himself writing against, the German studies and literature. Having thus declared himself, he was too proud and too tenacious of his opinion ever to relinquish it, and would neither observe or examine the wonderful change and improvement which was taking place in both. And so far was he from affording favour or encouragement to the writers who were thus reforming the language and taste of their country, that it is said, he would not even read their productions if in the vernacular tongue.

"Germans We Are"

Nothing then could be more popular, or more generally gratifying, than the new king's declaration in council, that "Germans we are, and Germans I mean we shall continue;" at the same time giving directions that their native language should resume its natural rank and station, from which it had been for near half a century degraded by the usurping French; the latter only having been during that time spoken at court, addressed in letters to the king, used in all public offices and transactions, and even into the academies. Of these the royal academy of sciences was composed almost entirely of Frenchmen; but the king now ordered three Germans to be received in it, and public discourses to be occasionally delivered in the Teutonic. To show his attention to the native literature, he settled a handsome pension for life upon Mr. Ramler, the celebrated German lyric poet; and receive in the most favourable manner the congratulatory verses which were addressed to him by professor Gleim, and other men of learning, who all made it a point to write them in the native language. The late king had likewise placed the collection of the taxes and duties, particularly those on tobacco, almost exclusively in the hands of Frenchmen; but they were now generally, if not universally, replaced by Germans, and the foreigners humanely allowed pensions.

The new king strictly prohibited all publications tending to excite a contempt or indifference for religion: observing that he had marked with great concern the progress of impiety and prophaneness on the one hand, and of enthusiasm on the other, which were making such rapid advances among the people; and which he attributed in a great degree to the multiplicity of these publications. He declared that he would not have his subjects corrupted either by fanatics or atheists; nor madmen to enrich themselves and the booksellers at the expence of religion. He likewise passed a severe law against duelling in all cases whatever; and erected a court or tribunal of honour to take cognizance of those disputes or differences which might lead to that refort.

Upon the whole, every thing that has yet appeared serves to indicate a happy and prosperous reign to that kingdom; and as the monarchy is now thoroughly formed and established, if it should not prove so splendid as the forgoing, it will be so much the better for the people.

THE HISTORY OF NATIONS
Chapter 2

The Bismarck Era and World War I

Unification Under Prussian Dominance

By WILLIAM L. SHIRER

In the following selection, historian and journalist William L. Shirer sketches the developments that led to the founding of Germany in 1871. Decades prior to the event, two rival states—Prussia and Austria—squared off over the issue of unification of German states. Prussia, whose population was ethnically German, was in favor of unifying. Austria, an ethnically diverse state, was against a federation, fearing that without its monarchy, the various ethnic factions within the land would separate and the power of the state as a whole would collapse. The two sides wrangled over power and influence in the other German courts while the unification debate continued.

Prussia's dominance in German affairs became evident, however, when the king of Prussia appointed Otto von Bismarck as head of the government. Bismarck opposed popular sovereignty in the unified states and consolidated Prussian rule by pressuring other German monarchs with Prussia's strong military. In the 1860s, Prussia had swallowed up some smaller states and even invaded Austria. Austria sued for peace in the conflict and begged out of German affairs from then on. This left Bismarck and the Prussians free to reshape the German confederation into a single nation under Prussian rule.

Beyond the Elbe to the east lay Prussia. As the nineteenth century waned, this century which had seen the sorry failure of the confused and timid liberals at Frankfurt in 1848–49 to create a somewhat democratic, unified Germany, Prussia took over the German destiny. For centuries this Germanic state had lain outside the main stream of German histor-

Excerpted from *The Rise and Fall of the Third Reich,* by William L. Shirer (New York: Simon and Schuster, 1988). Copyright © 1959 by William L. Shirer. Reprinted with permission.

ical development and culture. It seemed almost as if it were a freak of history. Prussia had begun as the remote frontier state of Brandenburg on the sandy wastes east of the Elbe which, beginning with the eleventh century, had been slowly conquered from the Slavs. Under Brandenburg's ruling princes, the Hohenzollerns, who were little more than military adventurers, the Slavs, mostly Poles, were gradually pushed back along the Baltic. Those who resisted were either exterminated or made landless serfs. The imperial law of the German Empire forbade the princes from assuming royal titles, but in 1701 the Emperor acquiesced in the Elector Frederick III's being crowned King in Prussia at Koenigsberg.

By this time Prussia had pulled itself up by its own bootstraps to be one of the ranking military powers of Europe. It had none of the resources of the others. Its land was barren and bereft of minerals. The population was small. There were no large towns, no industry and little culture. Even the nobility was poor, and the landless peasants lived like cattle. Yet by a supreme act of will and a genius for organization the Hohenzollerns managed to create a Spartan military state whose well-drilled Army won one victory after another and whose Machiavellian diplomacy of temporary alliances with whatever power seemed the strongest brought constant additions to its territory.

Prussia Was Organized Around Military Force

There thus arose quite artificially a state born of no popular force nor even of an idea except that of conquest, and held together by the absolute power of the ruler, by a narrow-minded bureaucracy which did his bidding and by a ruthlessly disciplined army. Two-thirds and sometimes as much as five-sixths of the annual state revenue was expended on the Army, which became, under the King, the state itself. "Prussia," remarked Mirabeau, "is not a state with an army, but an army with a state." And the state, which was run with the efficiency and soullessness of a factory, became all; the people were little more than cogs in the machinery. Individuals were taught not only by the kings and the drill sergeants but by the philosophers that their role in life was one of obedience, work, sacrifice and duty. Even [philosopher Immanuel] Kant preached that duty demands the suppression of human feeling, and the Prussian poet Willibald Alexis gloried in the enslavement of the people under the Hohen-zollerns. To Lessing, who did not like it, "Prussia was the most slavish country of Europe."

The Junkers [Prussia's landowning nobles], who were to play such a vital role in modern Germany, were also a unique prod-uct of Prussia. They were, as they said, a master race. It was they who occupied the land conquered from the Slavs and who farmed it on large estates worked by these Slavs, who became landless serfs quite different from those in the West. There was an essential difference between the agrarian system in Prussia and that of western Germany and Western Europe. In the latter, the nobles, who owned most of the land, received rents or feudal dues from the peasants, who though often kept in a state of serf-dom had certain rights and privileges and could, and did, gradu-ally acquire their own land and civic freedom. In the West, the peasants formed a solid part of the community; the landlords, for all their drawbacks, developed in their leisure a cultivation which led to, among other things, a civilized quality of life that could be seen in the refinement of manners, of thought and of the arts.

The Prussian Junker was not a man of leisure. He worked hard at managing his large estate, much as a factory manager does today. His landless laborers were treated as virtual slaves. On his large properties he was the absolute lord. There were no large towns nor any substantial middle class, as there were in the West, whose civilizing influence might rub against him. In contrast to the cultivated grand seigneur [great nobleman] in the West, the Junker developed into a rude, domineering, arrogant type of man, without cultivation or culture, aggressive, conceited, ruth-less, narrow-minded and given to a petty profit-seeking that some German historians noted in the private life of Otto von Bis-marck, the most successful of the Junkers.

Under the Prussian Bismarck, Germany Unites

It was this political genius, this apostle of "blood and iron," who between 1866 and 1871 brought an end to a divided Germany which had existed for nearly a thousand years and, by force, re-placed it with Greater Prussia, or what might be called Prussian Germany. Bismarck's unique creation is the Germany we have known in our time, a problem child of Europe and the world for nearly a century, a nation of gifted, vigorous people in which first this remarkable man and then Kaiser Wilhelm II and finally Hitler, aided by a military caste and by many a strange intellectual, succeeded in inculcating a lust for power and domination, a passion for unbridled militarism, a contempt for democracy and individual freedom and a longing for authority, for authoritarianism. . . .

"The great questions of the day," Bismarck declared on becoming Prime Minister of Prussia in 1862, "will not be settled by resolutions and majority votes—that was the mistake of the men of 1848 and 1849—but by blood and iron." That was exactly the way he proceeded to settle them, though it must be said that he added a touch of diplomatic finesse, often of the most deceitful kind. Bismarck's aim was to destroy liberalism, bolster the power of conservatism—that is, of the Junkers, the Army and the crown—and make Prussia, as against Austria, the dominant power not only among the Germans but, if possible, in Europe as well. "Germany looks not to Prussia's liberalism," he told the deputies in the Prussian parliament, "but to her force."

Bismarck first built up the Prussian Army and when the parliament refused to vote the additional credits he merely raised them on his own and finally dissolved the chamber. With a strengthened Army he then struck in three successive wars. The first, against Denmark in 1864, brought the duchies of Schleswig and Holstein under German rule. The second, against Austria in 1866, had far-reaching consequences. Austria, which for centuries had been first among the German states, was finally excluded from German affairs. It was not allowed to join the North German Confederation which Bismarck now proceeded to establish.

"In 1866," the eminent German political scientist Wilhelm Roepke once wrote, "Germany ceased to exist." Prussia annexed outright all the German states north of the Main which had fought against her, except Saxony; these include Hanover, Hesse, Nassau, Frankfurt and the Elbe duchies. All the other states north of the Main were forced into the North German Confederation. Prussia, which now stretched from the Rhine to Koenigsberg, completely dominated it, and within five years, with the defeat of Napoleon III's France, the southern German states, with the considerable kingdom of Bavaria in the lead, would be drawn into Prussian Germany.

Bismarck's crowning achievement, the creation of the Second Reich, came on January 18, 1871, when King Wilhelm I of

Prussia was proclaimed Emperor of Germany in the Hall of Mirrors at Versailles. Germany had been unified by Prussian armed force. It was now the greatest power on the Continent; its only rival in Europe was England.

Yet there was a fatal flaw. The German Empire, as Treitschke said, was in reality but an extension of Prussia. "Prussia," he emphasized, "is the dominant factor. . . . The will of the Empire can be nothing but the will of the Prussian state." This was true, and it was to have disastrous consequences for the Germans themselves. From 1871 to 1933 and indeed to Hitler's end in 1945, the course of German history as a consequence was to run, with the exception of the interim of the Weimar Republic, in a straight line and with utter logic.

Despite the democratic façade put up by the establishment of the Reichstag [Germany's parliament], whose members were elected by universal manhood suffrage, the German Empire was in reality a militarist autocracy ruled by the King of Prussia, who was also Emperor. The Reichstag possessed few powers; it was little more than a debating society where the representatives of the people let off steam or bargained for shoddy benefits for the classes they represented. The throne had the power—by divine right. As late as 1910 Wilhelm II could proclaim that the royal crown had been "granted by God's Grace alone and not by parliaments, popular assemblies and popular decision. . . . Considering myself an instrument of the Lord," he added, "I go my way."

He was not impeded by Parliament. The Chancellor he appointed was responsible to him, not to the Reichstag. The assembly could not overthrow a Chancellor nor keep him in office. That was the prerogative of the monarch. Thus, in contrast to the development in other countries in the West, the idea of democracy, of the people sovereign, of the supremacy of parliament, never got a foothold in Germany, even after the twentieth century began. To be sure, the Social Democrats, after years of persecution by Bismarck and the Emperor, had become the largest single political party in the Reichstag by 1912. They loudly demanded the establishment of a parliamentary democracy. But they were ineffective. And, though the largest party, they were still a minority. The middle classes, grown prosperous by the belated but staggering development of the industrial revolution and dazzled by the success of Bismarck's policy of force and war, had traded for material gain any aspirations for political freedom they may have had. They accepted the Hohenzollern autocracy. They gladly knuckled under to the Junker bureaucracy and they fervently embraced Prussian militarism. Germany's star had risen and they—almost all the people—were eager to do what their masters asked to keep it high.

The Bismarck Era

By Michael Stürmer

In this article, Michael Stürmer presents an overview of Chancellor Otto von Bismarck's political activities under the united Germany's first emperor, Wilhelm I. Stürmer pays close attention to Bismarck's struggle against Catholic political factions that resented his creation of a secular Germany—one that glorified the nation above the Church. At the other end of the spectrum, socialists and the thriving merchant class were balking at Bismarck's centralization of power and his support of the landed gentry. Eventually, foreign politics and a recession would test Bismarck's control of the nation in the 1880s. Stürmer, who is a professor of history and a journalist, has published several books on the history of Germany.

T he industrial revolution in Germany meant that wages rose for the vast majority of the population, beginning in the 1850s. Men and women alike had a chance of living longer and happier lives, and they had a justified expectation that one day their children would fare even better. But what mattered most to the Germans of Bismarck's day was the hope that the era of angst was a thing of the past. Certainly the prevailing mood was one of confidence and optimism, in spite of the many casualties of industrial progress and capitalist transformation and the ensuing resentment, fear of the future and social upheaval. After the Great War, people would refer to the Bismarckian and Wilhelmine past as the good old days—*die gute alte Zeit*—and they grieved for the years when peace and progress seemed the norm.

The Political Landscape

There were various political persuasions within the new Germany after that cold and colorful January day at Versailles, 1871. Enthusiasm for the new turn of events among the liberals was great, almost unlimited, provided that through the Reichstag [name of the German parliament at the time] they could persuade Bismarck to go along with free trade and nation building. They also wished to curb the influence of both major churches and ensure minimal liaison with labor leaders. Unfortunately, the liberals were deeply split. The left wing was composed of 1848ers from Württemberg and the old provinces of Prussia, who had led the charge against royal prerogative. They had tried to squeeze more parliamentary powers out of King William I when he wanted army reform, and they had been the bedrock of opposition against Bismarck ever since 1862 when he assumed office. These liberals saw the constitutional compromise of 1867, when the north German Reichstag had settled scores with Bismarck, merely as a starting point for many more rounds of constitutional wrangling.

Moving distinctly to the right, the National Liberals were by and large a new party. They enthusiastically endorsed the Prussian annexation of the Kingdom of Hanover and the Electorate of Hesse, of Hesse-Nassau and of the Free City of Frankfurt after 1866. They were happy with the Prussian concept of a free-trade oriented economic area, already embodied in the German customs union, with legislation and jurisdiction about to be united throughout Germany together with one currency and one central bank. For the National Liberal leaders and their flock, 1848 was a closed chapter, best forgotten.

However, the conservatives were far from triumphant. They had misgivings about Bismarck's Caesarism, his courting of public opinion, his warmongering against Austria, which was adding oil to the flames of modern nationalism, and his severing of links between throne and altar by taking up the fight for the secular state. To them, the Bismarckian answer to the revolutionary sea change of 1848 had a mephistophelean smell, his alliance with modern nationalism to them was as good as a pact with the Devil. It was only in the course of the 1870s, when the great Prussian agricultural estates east of the Elbe began to suffer under the unforgiving impact of world markets, that the bargain between Prussian conservatives and Bismarck's regime was put on a new, largely economic footing. Neither could afford to do without the other in the common battle against socialists, liberals, the world market and free trade.

Bismarck and Catholicism

A key part of the political spectrum in Bismarck's Germany was the German Center Party, a kind of action committee of political Catholicism. . . . In fact it had been clear ever since 1848 that the clergy, Protestant and Catholic alike, would sooner or later have to be forced to retire into the churches and the universities and lose control of education and charity, except on the margins of society. Throughout German Catholicism, concentrated in the Rhineland, in Silesia and in Bavaria, the battle cry was to unite and set up a political party, to build a bastion against the onslaught of secularism. The Center Party was referred to by its adherents as the *Zentrums-Turm*, the tower. Because of its organizing principle in the Catholic religion, it was the only political party to unite a cross-section of the population, from laborer to aristocrat, from industrialist to bishop. It did not increase the Center Party's popularity among national minded liberals that, in the name of Catholicism, the Poles from Prussia's eastern provinces and the French from the newly acquired . . . Alsace and Lorraine, joined the parliamentary party. The Center Party cut across class barriers and transcended the nation-state. The label "Ultramontane," soon applied to it, was not meant to flatter. It insinuated that its leaders received their guidelines from beyond the Alps—*ultra montes*— that is, from the Vatican. In fact, when one of the first parliamentary initiatives of the Center Party in 1871 was to call upon the German Reich [empire] to send troops to Italy and protect the Pope against the secular Italian state, Bismarck found his worst suspicions of a Europe-wide Catholic conspiracy corroborated. For the next few years, the Catholics were denounced, just as much as the socialists, as *Reichsfeinde*, enemies of the empire. . . .

The Degree of Democracy

The social democrats were not suppressed, let alone persecuted, by the anti-socialist law of 1879 that was introduced as an answer to the assaults on the Kaiser—and also to help Bismarck form a new, pro-government majority. It permitted them to function in the Reichstag, but not to engage in public campaigning. Twelve years later the socialists had risen to more than 25 percent of the popular vote in industrial centers, while the liberals had lost support and declined in numbers and influence. This showed the futility of Bismarck's somewhat half-hearted anti-socialist law and, when he fell, this piece of legislation went too, never to be revived.

The German political system combined elements of both royal absolutism and parliamentary democracy in an uneasy compromise. In its day it was referred to as "German constitutionalism" and was more often than not justified on the grounds of the exposed geostrategic situation of the country in the middle of Europe. There was no *Reichsregierung* [government], as Bismarck once pointedly observed. There was only the *Reichskanzler* [chancellor] taking political responsibility: the Chancellor with his office of a few higher civil servants. Bismarck had seen to it when the constitution was set up that it remained open from whom this responsibility was derived: from the monarch, most likely; from history, most certainly; from the Reichstag let alone the electorate, most certainly not. There were, of course, a number of state secretaries: one for the treasury, one for foreign affairs, one for naval matters, another one for postal services, one for home affairs, one for questions of jurisdiction. But a state secretary answerable to the Reichstag for the largest chunk of the budget, military expenditure, was conspicuous in his absence. The military budget had to be administered through the Prussian Ministry of War, while all matters concerning the royal—not imperial—*Kommandogewalt* [command over the military], the military backbone of the State, rested with the monarch, who, claiming royal prerogative, would handle all matters of military advancement and deployment through the Militärkabinett.

State secretaries could not be members of the Reichstag and that meant that this body had no interlocutor except Bismarck. All important administrative work was done by the Prussian administration and overseen by the Staatsministerium of Prussia, the Prussian cabinet. Prussian ministers were also superior in rank to mere state secretaries of the Reich. Within this construction not only the Reichstag had little influence; even the individual states could not exercise any significant measure of control. It also implied that military absolutism remained almost undiluted except for the army budget, and that was voted not annually, but for many years in advance. As long as Bismarck kept his influence over the King of Prussia and German Emperor, the Iron Chancellor was, in all but name, the ruler of Germany.

However, the German Reichstag, although far from powerless, could not vote a government out of office. Without finding or manufacturing a majority, the government would have found it impossible to function. But, in competition with parliament and political parties, there developed a vast array of organized interests, pressure groups and media claiming a role in that open-ended opera called the German polity. This opera may have been democratic in parts, especially when it came to one-man, one-vote elections. But above all it was functional, translating ever more diverse and indeed controversial interests into a political process as unpredictable as the purest of democracies.

The Iron Chancellor did everything to overcome the consequences of what he, the white revolutionary, had achieved. His domestic policy was carefully crafted to preserve a social balance in which the landed interest was paramount. But this was a losing battle against the growing strength of industry, vital in any case to provide jobs for the rapidly increasing population. The laws curtailing the rights of the social democrats, passed in 1878, had to be compensated for by the introduction, far ahead of other countries, of state insurance against the effects of old age, sickness and accidents, starting in 1883 and soon turning in to a massive system of self-administration overseen by the State. Bismarck's attack on Catholics had to be broken off in order to win their vote. Colonial propaganda was drummed up, but failed to rouse much public enthusiasm. Domestic politics were overshadowed by the great depression of the 1870s and 1880s and the resulting battles between protectionists and free traders: the former, the landed interest and heavy industry; the latter, the export-oriented manufacturers of machine tools and the like, the socialists and the left wing of the liberals.

Bismarck's Foreign Policy

In foreign policy Bismarck preached, time and again, the blessings of peace, equilibrium and the status quo. He had been converted by *le cauchemar des coalitions*—the nightmare of coalitions—to the lost wisdom of the Congress of Vienna, back in 1815. The Austro-Hungarian Emperor Franz-Joseph needed tranquility to keep his multinational empire together. The Tsar needed tranquility to prevent the resurrection of Poland—divided between Russia, Austria and Prussia at the end of the eighteenth century. Bismarck cultivated alliances with both Russia and Austria, but due to the stirrings of the Balkan Slavs against their Turkish overlords, this became increasingly difficult, and the much trumpeted Three Emperors' Alliance of the early years threatened to end in war. There was a strong Pan-Slav movement within Russia, which demanded that the Tsar intervene on behalf of their Balkan cousins, more especially the Serbs. But any increase in Balkan nationalism or interference by other states in the region was highly dangerous for the Austrian Empire. Bismarck had given assurances to the Russians, saying that the whole of the Balkans was "not worth the healthy bones of a Pomeranian musketeer." However, this did not prevent a confrontation between Austria and Russia, caused by the latter's war with Turkey. Consequently, Bismarck had to call a European congress at Berlin in the summer of 1878. In doing so, he saved the face of Austria for the time being and probably prevented a major war between the British Empire and Russia over who would control the eastern Mediterranean. Bismarck claimed to have acted merely as an "honest broker"—his banker, Gerson von Bleichröder, commented that there is no such thing. At any rate, the Russians were ungrateful and disappointed, the Pan-Slavist press began to agitate against Germany, and the Tsar wrote an angry letter to his uncle, the German Emperor, complaining about Bismarck and his support for Britain and Austria.

The "Reinsurance Treaty"

In 1879 the German Reichstag retaliated against a doubling of Russian import duties—the Russians suddenly insisted on payment in gold instead of half-price paper rubles—by introducing protective tariffs for German agriculture, and this economic pressure enhanced the alienation. Only one year after his diplomatic triumph at the Congress of Berlin, Bismarck again tried to mend diplomatic fences, concluding a dual alliance with Austria and then, for balance, a new alliance with Russia. But the latter had to remain a secret because public opinion in both countries would have been opposed to it. In 1887, in the face of much warlike talk, a secret "Reinsurance Treaty" was added, amid growing hostility between Austria and Russia over the Balkans. The treaty, to last for three years, specified that in case of war both Russia and Germany were to observe neutrality: Germany in the case of a war between Russia and Austria, Russia in the case of war with France. Nobody thought that the Reinsurance Treaty was worth very much. But it was to give Germany breathing space if war broke out, and it was also meant to have a sobering effect on Vienna and St. Petersburg, as neither could count on automatic German support.

The Industrial Revolution

Bismarck insisted that Germany was, by now, solely interested in maintaining the status quo, saying, "We are what old Prince Metternich called a saturated power." In reality, Bismarck found himself in the role of the sorcerer's apprentice, who had lost the words of the spell to get the genie back in the bottle. There had been too much upheaval, too much social change, and there had been the industrial revolution.

Germany's industrial revolution had begun on the Lower Rhine and in the Ruhr area during the final decades of the eighteenth century, then in Berlin and Silesia, while the centuries-old industrial centers south of the Main river lagged behind for want of capital, technology, access to markets and, not least, coal to fire the furnaces. In the long run, this would prove to be a blessing in disguise, as southerners had to cultivate their ancient metallurgical skills and apply them to modern machinery. Such was the case of Gottlieb Daimler and Karl Benz in Stuttgart and Mannheim respectively, working on the motor car, or of Robert Bosch who, after a long apprenticeship on the east coast of the United States, supplied the electrical equipment required by the car. But nineteenth-century industrial Germany was built on coal and steel and textiles, on railways and canals, and most of these were to be found in the crescent of prosperity stretching from Aachen in the west via Cologne and Essen to Berlin, and from Berlin to the coal mines and mills of Upper Silesia.

The Economic Boom

Bismarck's revolution from above had coincided with the building of a powerhouse at the heart of the continent. Once most of the main lines were completed, machine tools took over from railways as the leading sector, getting a second wind when, even before the turn of the century, electricity was harnessed to production. A vast building boom gave employment to small-scale manufacturers of household appliances and encouraged many old-style artisans to try their hand in larger undertakings. The textile industry of Krefeld expanded, as did that of northern Bavaria and around Plauen in Saxony. The chemical industry, in the past concentrating almost entirely on raw materials, now found vast markets for fertilizers, pharmaceuticals and artificial dyes. In the 1860s almost overnight Badische Anilin- und Soda-Fabrik (BASF) turned the fishing village of Ludwigshafen, at the confluence of the Neckar and the Rhine, into an industrial landscape of giant proportions. The same was true of Meister Lucius & Brüning in Hoechst on the Main, and of the Bayer works, best known for aspirin, in Leverkusen on the Rhine.

Germany's industrial revolution had started on the principle of free trade and this remained the keynote well into the 1870s. But then the business climate changed throughout the Atlantic world. In May 1873 the Vienna stock exchange collapsed, then Berlin's and Frankfurt's followed suit. For the past fifteen years or so, stocks had been rising with new companies springing up left and right, bringing fortunes to investors, banks and speculators—*Gründungsfieber*, "founding mania," as the conservative Cassandras called it, had become a contagious disease. But now the tide turned inexorably, and no longer could the liberals hope that it would carry them to power. Conservative fundamentalism came into its own, seeing the old Prussia, with its Protestant value system and its rigid social hierarchy, going to ruin. Frustration with the capitalist wealth machine that had suddenly come to a halt gave rise to anti-Semitism, the losers finding the root of all evil in the lust for money and the stock exchange; seeing the new Reich as some giant, godless casino.

Recession

To add to the dark mood of pessimism, German heavy industry began to suffer from British and Belgian competition. The reaction was twofold: pressure on the government to revise trade policy and protect "national work," and the formation of special interest groups to change the mood in the Reichstag, the media and the population at large. The National Liberals proved to be most attentive to the lamentations—and the money—of the barons of heavy industry, while the Fortschrittspartei [Progress Party], the left wing of the liberal movement, represented more the export-oriented machine-tool industry, which saw protectionism as a threat to its booming business with the rest of the world.

An even more serious blow to the social and political equilibrium came from Russia and the United States, which were exporting increasing tonnages of cheap wheat and rye to Germany. The vast prairies of the Midwest, recently connected by railroad to the seaports, especially Baltimore, could produce at very low cost and then ship the grain at cheap rates thanks to the impact of steamers. The landowners and farmers on the north German plains soon became desperate and brought pressure to bear on the Conservative Party and on the government. They received a sympathetic hearing from Bismarck, whose agricultural instincts had easily survived all the free-trade lessons that his banker Gerson Bleichröder might have administered. He immediately understood that here was the material to forge a solid and docile center-right coalition of *Rittergut und Hochofen*, the landed estate and the blast furnace.

Protectionism Versus Free Trade

In 1879 the first protectionist tariff had been passed in the Reichstag, helped by vast unrest over the suspected implication of the social democrats in the two recent attempts on the old Kaiser's life. For Bismarck the new tariff was welcome not only as a means of transforming the Reichstag and securing a loyal majority, but also as a way to increase the revenue of the Reich administration, until then often dependent on transfers from the individual states, especially Prussia. In this, however, he scored only half a victory. The states, led by the Prussian administration, were strong enough to ensure that the money collected at the customs offices went to them first, and only then, if they so wished, to the Reich.

For decades, protectionism versus free trade continued to be the defining issue in the German parliament and in public debate. In 1887 another round of tariffs was added to save the landowners from bankruptcy and the Bismarckian coalition from falling apart. But the cost was high, not only to German industry and the ever-growing number of urban consumers, but also in terms of foreign policy. Tsarist Russia, forever dependent on the German banks to finance its industrialization and infrastructure, was hard hit by the customs duties thrown on the sole product that it could export—wheat from the Ukraine. Close to 30 percent of Russia's imports came from Germany and close to 30 percent of its exports went to Germany. In 1876 the Russian government had imposed double import duties on German machinery and rail equipment, causing an outcry among industry, to which Bismarck was quick to respond. Through the 1880s the language became increasingly threatening, while Bismarck, for internal reasons, found it impossible to give way and grant the Russians the trade treaty and the low tariffs that they kept demanding. He must have known, better than anybody else, that he was putting at risk the vital alliance with Germany's awesome eastern neighbor. In 1887, at the time of the Reinsurance Treaty, Bismarck threw the gauntlet down before the Russians by letting it be known to the board of the Berlin stock exchange that it would be unwise in the future to accept Russian bonds as first-rate securities. This was not only insulting, but also meant higher interest rates for the Russians—and so it gave support to the Franco-Russian alliance that was already in the making.

After more than two decades at the helm of Prussia and Germany, Bismarck's regime began to unravel. In foreign policy his system of alliances showed serious strain: France could no longer be marginalized now that the Paris–St. Petersburg alliance was in the making. On the domestic scene his anti-socialist legislation had not delivered final victory over the enemy, and even his forward looking social legislation had not been effective in curbing the rise of socialism throughout industrial Germany. Both the Catholic center party and the two liberal parties began to question the wisdom and the leadership of the old man. . . . The Emperor with his unquestioning loyalty to Bismarck would not live forever—a change of government was in the offing. Bismarck had become, long before he fell from power, a monument to his own past.

Was Germany Responsible for World War I?

By Hannah Vogt

The Versailles treaty, which ended World War I, assigned blame for all hostilities to the aggressiveness of Germany. Dissatisfied with this simplistic view of European affairs in the era of World War I, Hannah Vogt questions the accuracy of the claim. Although she acknowledges the saber rattling of Germany's Kaiser Wilhelm II, Vogt argues that World War I was instigated by a number of thoughtless diplomatic decisions made by many nations. As a result, the heightened international tension gave rise to a pervasive feeling that war was inevitable. Europe only needed a catalyst—provided in 1914 by the assassination of Archduke Ferdinand of Austria—to spark the continent into open hostility. Vogt, a teacher in Germany, wrote the following selection as part of a book examining the many causes that led the world into its first world war.

I n the Versailles Treaty which concluded the First World War, the victorious powers claimed that Germany and her allies bore the sole responsibility for the recently extinguished conflagration. This claim corresponded in no way with historical truth and has long since been refuted by scholars. Many German historians of the post-war period made it their special task to study the origins of the First World War, and historians in other countries as well made efforts to ascertain the facts. The diplomatic archives were opened; documents and correspondence, treaties and diplomatic notes were published. The result was best summarized by the former British Prime Minister David Lloyd George. Himself one of the *dramatis personae*, he said later that no European statesman of that time had wanted war: "The nations

Excerpted from *The Burden of Guilt: A Short History of Germany, 1914–1945*, by Hannah Vogt, translated by Herbert Strauss (New York: Oxford University Press, 1964). Copyright © 1964 by Oxford University Press. Reprinted with permission.

slithered over the brink into the boiling cauldron of war without any trace of apprehension."

How the First World War originated cannot be explained in a few sentences; and we Germans must certainly avoid turning the argument against the British by saying, perhaps, that it was they who were guilty of secretly causing the war to rid themselves of German economic competition. Assertions of this kind distort reality. Instead, we must realize that many stupidities, wrong decisions, and disastrous errors combined to bring the nations of Europe to the point of believing, in 1914, that only war could resolve their difficulties.

Was the Emperor a Warmonger?

People outside Germany believed that Kaiser [German term for emperor] Wilhelm II was hell-bent on war, and they attributed a great deal of the blame to him. For this reason the Versailles Treaty stipulated that he be surrendered to the Allies and arraigned before a special tribunal "for a supreme offense against international morality and the sanctity of treaties." Was this belief correct?

It cannot be denied that the pre-war German Constitution placed considerable political responsibility upon the Kaiser. He not only had to serve as a symbol and representative of the *Reich* [German state] for the foreigner, he was not merely the embodiment of the national image and the state as a whole (like the English monarch), but he was also the chief executive of the state. He alone had the right to appoint the Chancellor and the cabinet, and through the persons he chose, he also determined to a considerable degree the direction of policy.

There is hardly a figure in recent history who can be judged by his contemporaries and by posterity in such contradictory ways as the last Kaiser. Some see him as the scion of a decadent dynasty, facing tasks above his capabilities, suffering from near-pathological delusions of grandeur. Others admire his astonishing intellectual flexibility, his honesty, his Catholic interests. Contradictions of this sort, arising from the opinions of unprejudiced contemporaries and scholars, cannot be resolved in a universally accepted judgment.

The speeches the Kaiser was prepared to deliver frequently and at the least provocation, gave him the reputation of being warlike and bloodthirsty. He lacked tact, people believed, an opinion

borne out by the comments he wrote in the margins of his ambassadors' reports; and in his speeches this failing led to the worst
kind of *faux pas*, which became known the world over. . . .

Still, it would be wrong to conclude from the Kaiser's speeches
that he wanted war; his deeds were far more moderate. He
wanted no risks, no revolution, no wars. Someone at court once
said in regard to future domestic problems in Germany: "Let him
talk as tough as he pleases, when the trouble really starts and he
must order his soldiers to shoot at Social Democrats, he will draw
back." The same was true of foreign affairs. Although he talked
of "shining armor" and of "keeping the powder dry," he did not
want war. And when finally the peoples of Europe tottered over
the brink into war, the Kaiser was shocked and shaken and knew
no more than his Chancellor Bethmann-Hollweg just how this
could have happened.

Why Was Germany Isolated?

At the outbreak of the First World War, Germany and her ally
Austria-Hungary stood practically alone. How did Germany get
into this situation? Had it been necessary? Was it caused by the
"policy of encirclement" pursued by the other European powers, by British "economic jealousy," as German nationalist literature never tired of repeating? Or was it due to a series of political miscalculations which the German government could have
avoided?

Bismarck had founded the German Empire in the wake of a
war against France. Since then, German policies had to reckon
with France's using the first occasion to undo defeat. France had
managed, in an astonishingly short time, to pay the indemnity of
5 billion francs imposed on her to defray the costs of the war, but
she would never forget Alsace-Lorraine. A statue symbolizing the
lost province was erected in Paris, and it remained draped in black
until 1918. Under these circumstances, the policy of each country was determined by its need to feel secure against the other.

[German chancellor Otto von] Bismarck had sought to guarantee Germany's security through an alliance with Austria-
Hungary (the Dual Alliance of 1879), and a secret neutrality
treaty with Russia (the so-called Re-Insurance Treaty). The possibility that, one day, Russia might come to an understanding
with France over the head of Germany was a constant preoccu-
pation of his, for he knew that this would mean that, in the case

of armed conflict, the German Empire would be threatened with a "two-front war," in the east and the west. Yet, barely two years after Bismarck's dismissal, Russia and France concluded a military agreement, after specialists in the Berlin Foreign Office had advised the Kaiser against renewing the Re-Insurance Treaty. Although Bismarck had succeeded in adding Italy to the Dual Alliance, and thus expanding it to a Triple Alliance, Germany felt isolated, and even more so since she doubted that Italy would keep faith with it.

A Missed Diplomatic Opportunity

In these circumstances, there arose the opportunity of linking the German Empire more closely with England. Since the demise of the Napoleonic Empire, Britain had not entered into alliances with continental European governments. Throughout the nineteenth century, she was most concerned with preserving a balance of power on the continent: no continental nation was to gain hegemony over the others. But her global colonial policies had caused friction with France in North and Central Africa and conflicts of interest with Russia in East Asia. Any of these crises might have led to war, in which case England would need strong support on the continent of Europe. Thus around the turn of the century, English statesmen decided to reverse their previous policy of isolation and to seek *rapprochement* with Germany.

In March 1898, Joseph Chamberlain, then British Colonial Secretary, approached the German ambassador in London with some apposite proposals. But the German Foreign Office did not understand the urgency of the British requests and feared complications. German public opinion had no love for England at the time either; for Germany had taken the Boers' side in the Boer War [from 1899 to 1902 Britain had been at war with the two Boer Republics in South Africa] with great fervor. The English renewed their first proposals three years later in spite of the cool reception they had previously received. This time, however, they hinted that they would seek terms with France and Russia if they were turned down again. Privy Councillor von Holstein, the influential expert in the Foreign Office, considered this hint "an absolute bluff." He was of the opinion that the whale (England) and the bear (Russia) could never unite. Thus, once again, just as in the case of the lapse of the Re-Insurance Treaty, the issue was decided by a man who never faced the limelight of

Europe During World War I

Atlantic Ocean

NORWAY

SWEDEN

DENMARK

NETHERLANDS

BRITAIN

BELGIUM

GERMANY

RUSSIA

LUXEMBOURG

SWITZERLAND

AUSTRIA-HUNGARY

FRANCE

ITALY

ROMANIA

SERBIA

BULGARIA

Black Sea

ALBANIA

PORTUGAL

SPAIN

GREECE

Mediterranean Sea

parliamentary responsibility, but operated behind the scenes. Here again we see a flaw in the German system of government: civil servants functioned almost completely without supervision by parliament. Before very long, events were to prove Holstein's lack of foresight.

During the second round, the negotiations with the English had gone into greater detail. Germany had insisted that England openly join the Triple Alliance. England, on its side, wished for a less formal understanding which would serve to neutralize conflicts of interest, and to defend common concerns. From the very beginning, however, England did not want to get involved in Austrian ambitions in the Balkans. Bismarck once had said: "The Germans always make the mistake of aiming at all or nothing, and of rigidly embracing one single method." It was this mistake which wrecked the negotiations of 1901. England now quickly turned to the very policy she had threatened and which German statesmen had considered an impossibility. England concluded a treaty with Japan, ended existing frictions with France in North Africa, and came to terms with Russia over conflicts in Persia, Afghanistan, and Tibet (1907). State visits by Edward VII to Paris and St. Petersburg further cemented the new, so-called Triple Entente (England, Russia, France)—although no written agreement backed up these very real understandings.

Thus the isolation of Germany grew to the threatening proportions which were to determine the nation's fate in the First World War. Too late, Privy Councillor von Holstein realized (as he was to admit in a letter) that his government had "let slip the opportunity to be friends, both with England and Russia."

The English offer to negotiate a treaty with Germany gives the clear lie to the legend that the powers wished to encircle Germany. It was true that certain economic groups in England favored a weakening of their German competitors, yet British foreign policy before the war was not determined by interests of this type.

Military Arming and War Sentiment

After the treaty negotiations failed, Germany pushed forward its naval building program with great fanfare; as a consequence, Anglo-German relations deteriorated quickly. English and German diplomats repeatedly tried to agree on a limitation of naval strength, but could not overcome the resistance of Admiral von Tirpitz, who refused to give up his naval construction program for which he had the prime responsibility.

Living as we do today, we find the years before 1914 so peaceful and serene that we tend to believe that people in that era must have enjoyed a sense of security, and must have been stunned by the outbreak of the First World War as by an earthquake. In this we are wrong. The world drifted into war because both the statesmen and the people got used to the idea of considering war inevitable. Once people believe in an inevitable fate, reason and patience which could stem the tide retreat, and passion and panic take over.

This mood was encouraged by a series of crises, in which war was repeatedly avoided by a hair's breadth. Many people finally came to feel that the tensions had to be discharged in some violent storm, and they hoped that this would clear the air. Hopes were certainly high that future conflicts could be controlled, but even so fear spread that they might ultimately engulf the world. Under such pressures, all Europe increased its armaments, lengthened terms of military service, and brought armies up to combat strength.

The Assassination of Archduke Ferdinand

Morocco, Turkey, and the Balkans were the critical areas before the war. The Turks had controlled the southeastern part of the

Balkans for centuries. Since the middle of the nineteenth century, the peoples of the Balkans had been engaged in revolutions
and wars for independence, and finally they had succeeded in
ousting the Turks. This created a series of independent states, including the kingdom of Serbia, bordering upon Austria.

As a multi-national state, the Austro-Hungarian dual monarchy was committed to oppose the national aspirations of the
Balkan peoples. Russia, with her desire for an outlet to the
Mediterranean through the Dardanelles, also had a vital stake in
Balkan problems, which further increased tensions. On top of
this, Slavic Russia wished to act as protector to the small Slavic
nations in the Balkans. For all these reasons the Balkans were considered the "powder-keg" or the "fiery wheel" upon which Europe was chained. Any change in status of the Balkans could well
precipitate a European war.

One especially grave event on the road to war was the annexation of Bosnia by Austria-Hungary in 1908. Since the population of this area was ethnically related to the Serbs, Serbia also
laid claim to it, but it was persuaded by the great powers to renounce its claims. Thus the hatred of the Serbian nationalists
against the Danubian monarchy was fanned to white heat.

As early as 1912 and 1913, wars had erupted in the Balkans,
rent as they were by national tensions, but on both occasions it
was still possible to contain the flames. A year later, however, playing with fire led to the long-feared explosion.

In June 1914, Archduke Franz Ferdinand, heir to the Austro-
Hungarian throne and Inspector General of the Army, visited
Austrian troops in Bosnia. Although Austrian officials knew that
secret societies in Bosnia were striving for unification with Serbia at all costs, and even though they had been warned of the
danger to the Archduke's life if he stepped on Bosnian soil, no
special security measures were taken. Thus, when the Archduke
visited the Bosnian capital of Sarajevo, a young Bosnian conspir-
ator managed to jump on the running board of his car and shot
him and his wife dead.

The assassination was political provocation and was regarded
in Vienna as an attack on the Danubian monarchy. Deeper ex-
amination would have shown that it was a problem of domestic
politics; the murderer was a subject of the Austrian Emperor, not
a Serbian national. Nevertheless, Vienna decided, from the outset, to use the murder for a squaring of accounts with Serbia. It

is unclear to this day—in spite of a good deal of research—
whether the Serbian government was really privy to the conspiracy, but certainly at that time no one had any definite proof
of its complicity.

The Emperor's Promise to Austria

Before the Austro-Hungarian foreign minister carried his plans
any further, he inquired in Berlin whether he could count on the
backing of the Kaiser. Wilhelm II answered that "His Majesty
will stand faithfully at Austria-Hungary's side," although he added
his expressed desire that the Austro-Serbian quarrel should be
kept from developing into an international conflict. But with
foolhardy neglect, the conditions under which Germany was to
fulfill her treaty obligations were not clarified. Thus Vienna felt
no need for restraint. Wilhelm II had acted without asking his
diplomatic advisers, thus creating a situation well described by a
late German historian:

> Every German recruit, every German regular, would
> have to march, every German family would have to
> part with its most precious members, if Vienna decided
> that Austria-Hungary's prestige required that the torch
> be put to Europe.

Since Berlin had given the diplomats in Vienna a free hand,
they could now recklessly pursue the alleged interests of the
Danubian monarchy. It goes without saying that they had no intention of unleashing a world war. They allowed themselves
rather to be deluded by the thought that this time—as in the
Balkan crisis of 1908–09—Russia would stand still. Under these
assumptions, the Austro-Hungarian government took its next
steps: on July 23, an ultimatum was handed to Serbia bearing a
time limit of 48 hours. Its demands were so exaggerated that
diplomats all over the world considered them unacceptable. It became apparent that Vienna did not expect Serbia to accept them,
but wanted merely to provoke a rejection, and thus have an excuse for military action. To everybody's surprise, however, the
Serbs "displayed brilliant diplomatic skill" and accepted the Austrian demands with certain reservations. The Serbian government
circularized copies of its note to Austria to all other European
governments, and thereby won their sympathies. Vienna took
two days to comment on the answer, and to declare its content

"unsatisfactory." This was followed by the mobilization of the
Austro-Hungarian army, and, on July 28, by a declaration of war
on Serbia.

Russia Backs the Serbs

Austria-Hungary had consulted her German ally neither in the
drafting of the ultimatum nor the declaration of war. Wilhelm
II, after reading the cleverly worded Serbian reply to the ultimatum, exclaimed with relief: "Now there can be no object in going to war." And even after Austria had declared war on Serbia,
England and Germany worked especially hard to localize the
conflict. During the night of July 29, Chancellor Bethmann-
Hollweg cabled to Vienna: "We are ready to fulfill our treaty
obligations, but we refuse to be drawn into a world conflagration
by a frivolous Vienna which fails to consider our advice."

By then, however, it was too late; the avalanche had gained
momentum. Russia had told Serbia that it could count on Russian support. The empire of the Czars valued "pan-slavism" more
than the solidarity of the monarchs whose inviolability was
threatened by the murder in Sarajevo. Russia ordered a partial
mobilization directed against Austria-Hungary, after she had declared war on Serbia (July 29). The next day the Czar decreed
general mobilization, thus threatening Germany as well.

Germany Enters a Two-Front War

Even at this late hour, Bethmann-Hollweg sought to compromise, but by then purely military considerations began to over-
shadow political policy. Moltke, the German Chief of Staff,
feared that any delay would worsen Germany's military situation.
He therefore intervened in the course of events and, without in-
forming either Kaiser or Chancellor, urged Austrian mobilization against Russia (in a cable to the Austrian General Staff, dated
July 30) and promised German mobilization at the same time.

On July 31, Russia's ally, France, mobilized, too. Germany,
threatened with a two-front war, demanded in an ultimatum that
Russia suspend all military measures against Germany and Austria within twelve hours. The same day, Germany asked France
for assurances of neutrality in case of war. When neither of these
assurances were forthcoming, Germany declared war on Russia
(August 1) and on France (August 3).

At the same time, German soldiers invaded Belgium after that government—as expected—had refused them permission to march through its territory. German action against Belgium was based on the military plans drawn up in 1905 by Field Marshal Alfred Count Schlieffen, then Chief of the General Staff. Although Schlieffen had allowed for a war on two fronts, he wished to maintain a defensive position in the east and obtain a quick result through a concentrated attack in the west. This plan, from its inception, took exaggerated military risks, and it could only be executed by disregarding Belgian neutrality. Militarily everything depended on the quick success of the Schlieffen Plan; but its execution inevitably made Germany's political situation deteriorate.

The violation of Belgian neutrality triggered England's declaration of war. England would have taken this step in any event in order to fulfill her obligations toward France incurred through the Entente Cordiale. But the violation of Belgian neutrality had a decisive effect on the movement of public opinion in England. Now Bethmann-Hollweg—who had been especially active in seeking an understanding with England during the preceding period—saw all his efforts destroyed. "For a scrap of paper you destroy my whole, my only work," he said in anguish to the British ambassador as the latter took his leave. This phrase—the "scrap of paper" which referred to England's guarantee of Belgian neutrality—was to gain notoriety around the world and do much damage as an anti-German propaganda slogan. Yet Bethmann's statement was not intended to question the validity of the old legal principle that "treaties must be kept." Only with Hitler did scruples and morality go completely by the board; for him, indeed, all treaties were mere "scraps of paper."

The British declaration of war completed the line-up of the European powers. The nations of Europe, step by step, had "stumbled into war." Few people of that generation had even the vaguest idea of the full consequences of that event.

The History of Nations
Chapter 3

The Weimar Republic

The Impact of the Versailles Peace Treaty

BY STEPHEN J. LEE

In the following article, Stephen J. Lee gives a brief summary of the conditions of the Versailles peace treaty, which ended World War I. Lee considers whether the terms of the treaty were too harsh on Germany. He proposes that the treaty's severity can be understood in two divergent ways. First, one may conclude that the Allied nations had to implement severe restrictions on Germany to ensure future peace in Europe. Yet, second, one might argue that the harshness of the treaty fostered Germany's economic collapse in the 1920s and 1930s and gave rise to the right-wing parties that blamed the nation's troubles on the treaty and its Allied proponents. Lee is a teacher and author of several books on German history.

Germany signed an armistice with the Allies on 11 November 1918. From this point onwards, negotiations for a peace settlement were carried out between the Allies in Paris, within the format of the Council of Ten. Most of the work was done by President Wilson of the United States, Lloyd George, the British Prime Minister, and Clemenceau, the French Premier. A preliminary draft of the arrangements concerning Germany was sent to the German government, but any attempts made by the new Republic to change the terms were rejected.

The Treaty of Versailles was signed on 28 June 1919. It affirmed, by Article 231, the responsibility of Germany and her Allies for the outbreak of the First World War and accordingly made provision for territorial adjustments, demilitarisation and economic compensation to the victorious Allies for the losses they had incurred. Germany was deprived of Alsace-Lorraine, Eupen

Excerpted from *The Weimar Republic*, by Stephen J. Lee (New York: Routledge, 1998). Copyright © 1998 by Stephen J. Lee. Reprinted with permission.

and Malmédy, Northern Schleswig, Posen, West Prussia, parts of southern Silesia, and all her overseas colonies. Limits were placed upon her naval capacity, her army was restricted to 100,000 volunteers, and the Rhineland was demilitarised. A considerable quantity of rollingstock and merchant shipping was also removed, while France was given exclusive rights to the coal-mines in the Saar region. Finally, provision was made for the payment of reparations by the German government, the total amount eventually being fixed in 1921 at 136,000 million gold marks.

The terms caused considerable resentment within Germany and contributed to the spiralling inflation which undermined the economy between 1921 and 1923. Attempts were made to regularise the payment of reparations by the Dawes Plan (1924) and the Young Plan (1929); the result was to spread the load, extend the deadlines and provide American investments. Following the impact of the Great Depression, most of the reparations were finally cancelled at Lausanne in 1932. The military and territorial terms of the Treaty were undermined by the unilateral action taken by Hitler after 1933.

Whether this was an unwise settlement depends upon the precise wording of the question asked. The first analysis puts forward the view that, in objective terms, the case against the Treaty has been overstated. The second, however, points to the Treaty acting as a catalyst for negative influences within the Weimar Republic itself.

"Carthaginian Peace"?

At the height of the Punic Wars, a Roman senator demanded the complete destruction of Carthage: '*delenda est Carthago.*' The term 'Carthaginian peace' has remained synonymous with the severe and vindictive treatment of a conquered enemy.

The traditional view of the Treaty of Versailles is that it inflicted harsh and unjust terms upon Germany. Foremost among its contemporary critics were [the representative of the UK Treasury at the Versailles Peace Conference John Maynard] Keynes and [British diplomat and representative at the Peace Conference] Harold Nicolson, who expressed disgust with the way in which the terms were drawn up. Some historians adopted a similar view. W.H. Dawson, for example, emphasised that the Treaty cut into German territory in a way which blatantly discriminated in favour of non-German populations. This approach has, however,

been extensively modified, partly by comparison with the settlement after the Second World War and partly as a result of new
perspectives created by revisionist historians. . . . It is therefore
possible to put an altogether more positive interpretation on the
Treaty of Versailles. We should start by not being too dismissive
of the statesmen who drew up the settlement. It is true that they
were accountable to their populations and that they therefore had
to pursue the national interest. But this does not preclude a log-
ical and pragmatic analysis of international needs reinforced by
purely national concerns; this is evident in the settlement as a
whole and especially within the French position. There had to
be three main priorities: to guarantee Europe against the possibility of future German aggression; to revive the economic infrastructure of the Allies; and to ensure the stability of the new
nation states in central and eastern Europe. None of these was
inherently revanchist.

The military provisions of the Treaty may appear harsh. The
army was limited to 100,000 volunteers and the navy to 6 bat-
tleships; the air force was abolished and the Rhineland was demilitarised. Yet these measures need to be seen within the context of the military power of Germany. The combined forces of
Britain, the [British] Empire, France, Russia and Italy had been
insufficient to defeat the Second Reich and it needed the intervention of the United States to guarantee Allied victory. It therefore made sense to limit the base for any future military recovery
by such a formidable opponent. In any case, the argument that
the war had been engineered by Germany, explicitly stated in
Article 231, was not entirely propaganda. A substantial number
of historians, mainly German, have now demonstrated that the
foreign policy of the Second Reich aimed at a war sooner rather
than later as a means of breaking the Franco-Russian alliance and
achieving an early form of Lebensraum in eastern Europe. . . . In
this light, the military provisions were not excessively harsh.
There was only a limited Allied occupation and there was no
zoning, as was to occur in 1945. Germany was also allowed some
means of self-defence. The provision for 100,000 volunteers was
actually in Germany's favour, since it allowed for the development of a professional core upon which subsequent military recovery could be constructed. Finally, it seems that the Allies could
have gone much further. They drew up plans to invade the Reich
should the terms of the Treaty be refused. Yet they did not do so,

even though [Paul von] Hindenburg and [Wilhelm] Groener made it clear to the German government that ultimately nothing could stop them. [Hindenburg and Groener were two German military leaders; Hindenburg later became the German president who appointed Adolf Hitler chancellor.] This shows a degree of restraint and moderation on the part of the Allies not entirely born of warweariness.

The transfer of territory to France, Belgium and Denmark was also limited in scope. The return of Alsace-Lorraine to France, after its conquest by Prussia in 1871, was inevitable. Giving the small industrial regions of Eupen and Malmédy to Belgium was intended to reconstruct the latter's industrial infrastructure, while the incorporation of northern Schleswig into Denmark after plebiscite simply reversed the annexation of the area by Bismarck in 1864. The transfer of resources was more controversial, inviting criticism from J.M. Keynes that the iron and coal provisions were 'inexpedient and disastrous'. German opinion was also incensed by Article 231, the 'War Guilt Clause' which was used to justify reparations. Yet the purpose of this was overstated. Heiber maintains: 'The very fact that this paragraph was not embodied in the preamble or immediately following it, but was given such an

On June 28, 1919, government officials gathered in the Hall of Mirrors to witness the signing of the Treaty of Versailles.

astronomical serial number and almost hidden in the undergrowth of the treaty, suggests that it originally had no programmatic significance.' French revanchism was not, as has so often been suggested, the key factor in the financial provisions; there is a strong argument that they were needed to rebuild the shattered infrastructure of both France and Belgium, whose territory—not Germany's—had borne the destruction of four years of warfare. Germany's industries, by contrast, had remained untouched. [Historian Marc] Trachtenberg argues that the French were far more moderate in their expectations from reparations than were the British, while [historian Jacques] Bariéty maintains that they were seeking not to dismantle or cripple Germany but to establish a Franco-German equilibrium on the Continent: part of the process had to be a greater economic balance between the two powers. . . .

Objectively, the terms of the Treaty of Versailles can largely be justified by the need to safeguard against the very real threat posed by Germany, to rebuild France and Belgium and to give viability to the new democracies of Europe. But the process was complicated by the failure of the Allies to involve the German government at any stage in the Treaty's formulation, and of the League of Nations to carry out its intended moderating role in its fulfilment. Thus, like Carthage, Germany came to see itself as a victim without actually being destroyed. . . .

A Disaster for the Weimar Republic?

It has been argued that the Republic was brought down primarily because of the deep opposition to it engendered by the Treaty of Versailles which made possible the rise of Hitler. [Historian Ludwig] Zimmerman maintained in 1988 that 'Timely revision of the peace treaties would have saved the Weimar Republic and saved the peace'. The pendulum now seems to have swung the other way. [Historian Andreas] Hillgruber argues that the time when the Republic was most vulnerable to the Treaty of Versailles (1919–23) was precisely the time that it survived, whereas the Treaty's importance was 'relatively small by the end of the Stresemann era'. It could certainly be argued that by the time Hitler came to power in 1933 the reparations issue had been resolved by the Lausanne settlement and that, in any case, foreign policy and Versailles were no longer the most important issues in the collapse of the Weimar Republic.

But this has gone too far in the other direction. The impact of

Versailles was important in undermining German democracy—
not because it acted directly in the rise of Hitler but because it
produced several key influences which continued to grow long
after the Treaty itself had ceased to be critical. In this way, the
Treaty was itself a catalyst for, rather than a direct cause of, the
collapse of the Republic. This operated in four ways.

Resentment Against the Treaty

In the first place, Versailles created a deep and widespread resentment throughout the entire population. Germans had already
suffered severely during the closing stages of the war as a direct
result of the British blockade and they assumed that Germany
would have a genuine share of any post-war settlement. Hence,
although they expected to lose Alsace-Lorraine to France, possibly West Prussia to Poland, and even some overseas colonies, they
hoped to gain Austria and the Sudetenland from the now defunct
Austro-Hungarian Empire. The actual terms therefore came as a
profound blow. [President Woodrow] Wilson's principle of national self-determination seemed to operate against Germans
everywhere and in favour of Germans nowhere. Even more resented, however, was Article 231 of the Treaty—the War Guilt
Clause—which provided the justification for the fixing of reparations. The peace delegation under [German diplomat and head
of the German delegation in Versailles Ulrich von] Brockdorff-
Rantzau protested vigorously against this and other terms but was
utterly helpless in the face of Allied intransigence.

Such resentment was increasingly targeted against the Republic for having signed what the media unanimously labelled a
'disgraceful' document. This was actually unjust. [The previous
German chancellor Philipp] Scheidemann's administration had
done everything possible to get the terms revised and had even
questioned Hindenburg about the possibility of military resistance; but, in the end, to save Germany from an Allied invasion,
the Treaty had to be accepted by [German chancellor Gustav]
Bauer's government. The danger was that people of moderate
views would ignore the circumstances and attribute blame, thus
seeing the Republic as tainted at the outset. The government,
quite unintentionally, contributed to this threat. Stung by the perceived injustice of the War Guilt Clause, the Foreign Ministry
employed historians to prove that Germany was not responsible
for the outbreak of the war, and that the destruction was there-

fore a responsibility shared by all the participants. But the side-
effect was to rehabilitate the reputation of the German army, re-
leasing it from any association with aggression and militarism.

Rightist Parties Win Support

This, in turn, revived the cause of the conservative right, which
had a strong attachment to the memory of the Second Reich and
instinctively distrusted the Weimar Republic. The new regime had
provided military conservatism with the sort of logic it needed.
If the German army had not been instrumental in starting the
First World War then it followed that its defeat was a matter for
profound regret. Taken a stage further, this defeat could be seen as
an act of political betrayal by the Republican government. By trying to connect the situation before 1919 with the iniquities of
Versailles in order to disprove German war guilt, the Republic unintentionally gave the conservative right the opportunity to fos-
ter the legend of the 'stab in the back'. This phrase was actually
introduced by Hindenburg in November 1919 before a parliamentary committee of the National Assembly. During his campaign for the Presidency in 1925 Hindenburg sought to justify his
and [General Erich von] Ludendorff's abdication of military responsibility in October 1918 by rewriting history in just this way.
The result is seen by most historians as a serious liability for the
Republic: [Historian Helmut] Heiber goes so far as to say that the
'war guilt lie' became 'a dangerous explosive charge'.

This is especially apt when considering the offensive launched
against the Republic by the Nazis at the end of the 1920s and
the beginning of the 1930s. [Adolf] Hitler's strange amalgam of
fringe ideas was given greater credibility and popular appeal by
his emphasis on two mainstream policies. One was his widespread
use of the 'stab in the back' and the 'Versailles diktat'. These enabled the NSDAP [Nazi party] to collaborate closely with conservative forces within the DNVP [German National People's
Party], the army and business, which enhanced Hitler's reputation at a crucial stage in his party's development. He also pro-
jected the NSDAP as the party which would offer economic salvation to the middle classes suffering under the impact of the
depression after 1929 and, as a result, enormously increased the
NSDAP's electoral support in the elections of 1930 and 1932.

The economic situation which made this possible again had a
connection with Versailles, although the nature of this connec-

tion needs to be precisely identified. Complications over the reparations bill set in accordance with the Treaty of Versailles subsequently led to the establishment of a financial network which eventually collapsed after 1929. It was this system, not the reparations themselves, which proved disastrous for the German economy.

The initial liability was considerable: in April 1921 the Allied Reparations Commission set the reparations bill at 132,000 million gold marks. Tied to this was a condition that 12,000 million would be paid in advance, followed by 2000 million per annum and 26% of the value of Germany's exports. It would be an exaggeration to say that this was the sole cause of the great inflation between 1921 and 1923, but having to ship out substantial capital sums (50% to France, 22% to Britain, 10% to Italy and 8% to Belgium) must have been a major factor in the collapse of the mark. It is true that the government could have limited the extent of the inflation by increasing levels of domestic taxation rather than printing notes, but it very much wanted to avoid this course, which would only further antagonise a population already infuriated by the burden of 'war guilt'. In any case, economic crisis would oblige the Allies to confront reality: that their demands were just too harsh.

The attempt to rationalise reparations led to a new economic order, the Dawes Plan of 1924 setting up a new chain of dependency. By this means, Germany provided reparations payments to Britain, France and Italy who, in turn, were enabled to pay off their war debts to the United States. These returned as loans to Germany. The alternative would have been for Britain and France to have reduced their dependence on German reparations in return for cancellation of the war debts; the United States, however, insisted that these should be paid in full. The famous triangular pattern was therefore firmly set.

Severe Economic Depression

Great damage was to be inflicted on the German economy, not by the continued payment of reparations, but rather by the loans upon which Germany depended in order to sustain an economy capable of paying reparations. At first the role of American investment was highly beneficial. In the period immediately after 1924, Germany received some 16,000 million marks compared with the 7,000 million she actually paid out. This helped to replenish the home market which had been stripped of assets as a result of the inflation. Industrial production expanded, full employment was achieved and there were even salary increases in the public sector. But the problem was that this expansion was highly vulnerable. It did not affect the large-scale consumer industries at home, such as motor vehicles, and it did not have the full infrastructure of export sales. The cycle of dependence therefore remained—and this was dramatically disrupted by the Wall Street Crash in October 1929. From that time onwards the German economy spiralled into depression, resulting in decreased production, foreclosures and 6 million unemployed. The speed with which this happened was linked to the terms of the American loans: they were all short term and subject to repayment on demand. Hence it made little difference that reparations had been extensively rescheduled by the Young Plan in 1929 or virtually cancelled at Lausanne in 1932. Economic catastrophe still occurred, although it was brought about by the loans which reparations had engendered, not by the reparations themselves.

In summary, the terms of the Treaty came as a shock to the people, who blamed the government of the Republic. This condemnation remained with the Republic as a result of the 'stab in the back' myth, which brought collaboration between the conservative right and the radical right. The Republic became particularly vulnerable with the collapse of the economy after 1929. This owed much to the establishment of a new network of dependency to replace the initial problems created by the reparations payments. The Treaty of Versailles therefore set in motion influences which were to prove more damaging to the Republic than the Treaty itself. Its impact was therefore indirect, but real nevertheless.

War, Revolution, and the Birth of Weimar

By Ruth Henig

In this selection from her book The Weimar Republic: 1919–1933, *Ruth Henig discusses the period between the First World War and the founding of the Weimar democracy. She shows how, after initial enthusiasm, Germany was defeated in the war, and she describes tense postwar years when various political parties vied for control of the nation. The Communists under Karl Liebknecht wanted revolution that would bring about a socialist state. But the power of the state was passed to Chancellor Friedrich Ebert, who established a democratic republic. Ebert's control was initially shaky, and he had to call upon the demobilizing German army to back his authority. In January 1919, Ebert had to use military support to eradicate Liebknecht and put down socialist rebellions. This act ensured the future bitterness of German Marxists, but elections soon proved that Ebert had the backing of the national majority. From these elections was born the Weimar Republic. Henig is the head of the history department at Lancaster University in the United Kingdom.*

The German Chancellor, [Theobald von] Bethmann-Hollweg, had worked hard in the weeks after the Sarajevo murders [of Archduke Franz Ferdinand von Hapsburg, the Austro-Hungarian heir to the throne, and his wife, Sophie von Hohenburg] to persuade the German people that Germany had no choice but to fight a defensive war against the encircling Entente Powers [Britain, France, and Russia], and particularly against reactionary, expansionist Russia.

The German population enthusiastically endorsed the government's decision to declare war, and on 4 August, 1914, the representatives of the workers sitting in the Reichstag [name of the German parliament at the time] under the banner of the Social Democratic Party (SPD) voted in favour of war credits. This display of patriotism by the SPD Reichstag deputies had a number of fateful consequences. Committed Marxist members of the party were opposed from the outset to involvement in what they saw as a capitalist war against fellow workers in neighbouring countries. As the war dragged on, those who were ideologically opposed to it were able to gain considerable support for their views, and in 1917 they broke away from the main body of the SPD to form the Independent Social Democratic Party, or USPD. The divisions between the USPD and the SPD grew steadily wider as the war came to an end and added to the political and economic tensions which erupted across the country in the autumn of 1918.

At the beginning of the war, however, unity and patriotism chatacterised the mood of the country. The Kaiser [emperor] was gratified that he saw only Germans, not parties; the socialists, whom he had dismissed as 'unpatriotic fellows' before the war, now appeared to be supporting it as enthusiastically as the rest of the population. This brief outburst of national solidarity and purpose remained strong in people's memories. Though it quickly gave way to stoic endurance and later to increasing social and economic unrest, the myth burned brightly of a *Volksgemeinschaft,* or people's community, bound together in pursuit of a clear set of national objectives. It was reinforced by the experience of soldiers in the trenches, drawn into close comradeship by the hardships and dangers they faced day after day. Throughout the 1920s, the image of a united German people selflessly pursuing a common destiny in war, on the battlefields and in the factories and workshops at home, was repeatedly contrasted with the allegedly shabby political compromises and self-seeking deals of Weimar politicians. It was a contrast that some extreme nationalists, and in particular the former First World War corporal, Adolf Hitler, exploited particularly effectively.

The War Tribute

The scale and duration of the war quickly exceeded all expectations. The failure of the Schlieffen plan to defeat the French army within the first few weeks of combat led to stalemate on the western front, and to fighting on two widely separated battle fronts, in northern France and Belgium, and in Poland and western Russia. This was the military nightmare the German General Staff had sought so desperately to avoid. As the war dragged on, 13 million men in total were called up to serve in the German army, or nearly 20 per cent of Germany's 1914 population. Inevitably, there were large numbers of casualties, around 2 million killed and nearly 5 million wounded. Life in the trenches or on the eastern front took its toll; even those who escaped serious injury suffered gas attacks or severe bouts of frostbite. By 1918, the great German army was beginning to experience significant problems of recruitment and morale. Hundreds of thousands of soldiers tried to buy their way out of combat, or to disappear from view while home on leave.

Throughout the 1920s, the new regime struggled to support the millions of men who could no longer work because of their war injuries, the 600,000 war widows and around 1.2 million children orphaned during the war. These people and their families believed passionately that the sacrifices made during the war should be acknowledged and to some degree recompensed. But in the economic climate of postwar Germany, this was asking for more than governments could afford without heavy tax increases. The economic consequence of the First World War was to impoverish Germany: in 1919, real national income was only two thirds of what it had been in 1913, and industrial production had shrunk to two-fifths.

Poverty and Strikes

To pay for the war, German leaders resorted to heavy borrowing in the confident expectation that victory would enable them to pass on their debts to their defeated enemies. The immediate effect was to trigger off massive inflation. In 1915, prices in Germany rose in one single year by more than they had over the previous forty-five years. By the end of 1918, the German mark had lost about three-quarters of its 1913 value. As price rises and in particular the costs of housing, fuel and food outstripped wage increases, unrest spread, particularly in the urban areas. By the end of the war, with real earnings having declined by between a quarter and a half in value, up to a third of the inhabitants of many major cities were surviving only by means of family support payments from the government, and the food shortages experienced particularly during the winter of 1917–18 drove millions to the edge of starvation.

But the misery was not seen to be equally shared. While millions suffered, a few were still able to afford ostentatiously luxurious holidays at fashionable spas or in elegant Baltic seaside resorts. It was said that 'everything is still available in any amounts at a high price'. By the end of the war, according to [historian Jürgen] Kocka, the 'visible luxury of a few contrasted sharply with the increasing hardship of the masses'. There were other causes of social resentment. The importance of heavy industrial production to a successful war effort enabled union leaders to protect the wages and conditions of their members to a certain extent. Those on fixed incomes, however, who derived their living from rents, investment income or pensions saw an alarming erosion in their wealth by the end of the war.

The "Stab in the Back" Myth

The Russian revolutions of 1917 sent strong shock waves through the industrial centres of Germany. They fanned the flames of worker unrest and contributed to a total of over 550 strikes by the end of the year. In January 1918, more than a million workers were on strike across the country; the response of the military authorities who were now running the war was to redouble efforts to win an outright victory. To Colonel [Max] Bauer, one of [General Gich von] Ludendorff's principal assistants, the choice was clear: victory would bring 'a long and secure peace, with firm, purposeful government at home'. A compromise or negotiated peace, on the other hand, would force Germany 'to drop militarily and politically out of the concert of great powers, decline into economic misery and drift towards a Bolshevik regime ...'.

But with the United States now in the war, victory proved to be beyond Germany's capabilities. Instead of driving on to a glorious triumph, in the course of the summer of 1918 Germany's military leaders [Paul von] Hindenburg [who later became president and appointed Hitler chancellor] and Ludendorff found themselves facing a humiliating defeat. As Germany's allies Bulgaria and Austria-Hungary collapsed, her military options narrowed dramatically. She could fight on to the bitter end, risking invasion and significant territorial losses, or she could sue for the best peace terms available.

Faced with this stark choice, the German military commanders made two crucial decisions which had fateful consequences for their political successors. They decided that the most palatable peace settlement was likely to be gained from American President Woodrow Wilson's Fourteen Points speech of January 1918 which contained proposals which they had previously condemned as a front for 'imperialistic conquest in the guise of peace' and as serving the interests of 'Anglo-Saxon world hegemony'. And secondly they concluded that a civilian-based government would have more chance of securing a relatively lenient peace than a military one. Accordingly, the Reichstag leaders of those parties which had supported a peace resolution in July 1917 were suddenly transformed in late September 1918 from national traitors to responsible ministers, commanded by the desperate military authorities to take over the reins of government under the chancellorship of Prince Max of Baden and to sue for peace on the basis of Wilson's Fourteen Points.

Though the German army had been on the retreat since the late spring of 1918, it was still surviving in reasonable order, and had not yet been forced back into Germany. In handing over responsibility to the political parties at this crucial point in time, Ludendorff proved himself to be far more politically astute than the politicians. He adroitly shifted the blame for defeat onto their shoulders. As he explained to his military staff. 'I have advised His Majesty to bring those groups into the government whom we have in the main to thank for the fact that matters have reached this pass. . . . Let them now conclude the peace that has to be negotiated. Let them eat the broth they have prepared for us.' Thus the highest military authorities in Germany were already accusing the liberal, centre and left-wing party leaders of causing defeat by their demand for a negotiated peace in 1917 and by their refusal to give the army all-out support. It was not long before nationalist groups throughout Germany were elaborating on this 'stab in the back' administered by pacifists and socialists to the valiant army in the field, and asserting that defeat could have been averted, even victory secured, had it not been for the mood of defeatism and the sparks of revolution deliberately fanned by traitors at home.

The German Revolution of 1918–1919
The six months from October 1918 to March 1919 witnessed turbulent revolutionary activity across Germany, fierce struggles between socialists and nationalists and moves to establish a new

constitutional state. This period is referred to as the 'German revolution', but in fact there were three different revolutionary processes in train, each with its own aims and agenda.

There were first of all those seeking far-reaching constitutional changes, initially seeking to reform the monarchy and make it more accountable to Parliament, but then, after the abdication of

THE RED ROSE

This overview traces the life of Rosa Luxemburg, a Polish-born Jew who became the foremost Communist leader during the turbulent years of the Weimar Republic. After supporting a revolutionary riot in Berlin, she was arrested and murdered in January 1919.

Rosa Luxemburg (1871–1919) was a Polish revolutionary and theorist. She led the German workers' uprisings which followed World War I and is considered one of the pioneer activists and foremost martyrs of the international Communist movement.

Rosa Luxemburg was born in Zamo in Russian Poland and brought up in Warsaw. She was the daughter of a middle-class, Polish-speaking Jewish merchant. Dainty, almost tiny, she walked with a limp as the result of a childhood disease.

From her earliest years Rosa possessed "one of the most penetrating analytical minds of her age." In a period when the czarist government was increasing its religious and political oppression in Poland, especially of the Jews, she gained admission to the best girls' high school in Warsaw, usually reserved for Russians. There she joined a revolutionary cell and began a lifelong association with the socialist movement. When she was 18, her activities came to the attention of the Russian secret police, and she fled to Switzerland to avoid arrest.

Luxemburg continued her interests in socialist and revolutionary activities there. She earned a doctorate of laws at the University of Zurich in 1898. Her thesis on industrial

the Kaiser, in early November 1918, pressing for the setting up of a Constitutional Assembly to pave the way for a democratic republic. These were the aims of the Reichstag leaders entrusted with the task of negotiating a peace with President Wilson, broadly supported by the Catholic Centre, Progressive Liberal and Social Democratic parties.

---

development in Poland later served as a basis for the program of the Social Democratic party of Poland. She decided to go to Germany and attach herself to the large, vital, and well-organized Social Democratic party (SPD). In Berlin she obtained German citizenship through a fictitious marriage and quickly became one of the most effective, respected, and even beloved leaders of the international socialist movement. . . .

During World War I Luxemburg, now dubbed the "Red Rose" by police, was imprisoned for her revolutionary activities. Released for a short time in 1916, she helped to found the revolutionary Spartacus Union with Karl Liebknecht. When she again emerged from prison, in 1918, dissatisfied with the failure to effect a thoroughgoing socialist revolution in Germany, she helped to found the German Communist party (KPD) and its newspaper, the *Rote Fahne,* and drafted its program. She and Liebknecht urged revolution against the Ebert government, which came to power after the armistice, and were largely responsible for the wave of strikes, riots, and violence which swept across Germany from the end of 1918 until June 1919.

In January 1919 one of the most violent outbreaks occurred in Berlin. Luxemburg and Liebknecht, in spite of their doubts as to the timing, supported the Berlin workers in their call for revolution. The troops that were called in acted with extreme violence and brutality, crushing the revolt in a few days. On January 15 Liebknecht and Luxemburg were caught and murdered by the soldiers who held them prisoner.

Encyclopaedia of World Biography, 2nd ed. 17 vols. Farmington Hills, MI: Gale Research, 1998.

However, the reluctance of the Kaiser to accept any changes, and an ill-judged attempt by the admiralty to order a last-ditch naval challenge by the High Seas Fleet to the British navy triggered off a second more radical revolutionary process. It seemed to the sailors at Kiel and to the war-weary workers and their families across the country that the authorities were intent on prolonging the war; as the peace negotiations dragged on, there was a mutiny at the big Kiel naval base, which led to the setting up of a sailors' council. Within days, in the first week of November, similar councils appeared at Wilhelmshaven, in Hamburg and Cologne. Soon workers' and soldiers' councils were to be found in towns and cities across Germany, demanding peace and assuming control of local food supplies and services. Some of these bodies were indeed very radical, and modelled themselves closely on the Russian soviets of 1917. Yet others came into being spontaneously in an effort to speed the end of the war and to defend the interests of the local community against unpopular measures ordered by government officials. How great the revolutionary threat of this council or *Räte* movement actually was is still hotly disputed by historians, but the suddenness with which it erupted, and the nation-wide scale and wide scope of its aims appeared very menacing to large sections of the population. Many nationalists, and even those pressing for constitutional reforms, were alarmed by what they perceived as 'Russian solutions' being put forward for German problems and consequently sought to challenge and to undermine the authority of the councils.

The third element of the revolutionary situation was provided by left-wing, avowedly Marxist, socialists who saw in the ending of the war their chance to overthrow the forces of capitalism and to establish a workers' state. They had already broken away from the majority SPD Party in 1917 because of their opposition to the war; now they seized the opportunity to drive forward the workers' revolution in the major cities and in the disaffected regions of Germany, either by harnessing the *Räte* movement to their cause or by directly organising massive strikes and demonstrations by workers. In Bavaria, on 7–8 November, Kurt Eisner and his followers, having seized control of the city of Munich, proclaimed a Bavarian Republic. In Berlin, Karl Liebknecht and Rosa Luxemburg worked to fan the flames of revolution and to gain the support of the disaffected masses for the proclamation of a Marxist state. Having established a left-wing splinter group, the Spartacus League, they were to rename themselves the German Communist Party in January 1919.

Two Proclamations of the Republic

It is perhaps easiest to outline the course of the revolution in three distinct chronological phases. The first phase, from October to 11 November 1919, saw the outbreak of disturbances, as the new Chancellor, Max of Baden, opened negotiations with Woodrow Wilson for a peace settlement based on the Fourteen Points. When Wilson insisted on assurances that those who had been responsible for prosecuting the war would resign and negotiations would be conducted by new civilian leaders, Prince Max sought to persuade an extremely reluctant Kaiser to agree to far-reaching constitutional reforms, and, as mutinies and disorder spread, to abdicate. It was only on 9 November that the Kaiser finally agreed to leave Germany for what he regarded as a temporary flight to Holland—an exile which in fact lasted until his death in 1941.

The same day, Prince Max handed over his powers to the leader of the SPD Party, Friedrich Ebert. An hour later, the SPD leadership proclaimed the establishment of a new democratic republic. But not far away, in the same city of Berlin, Karl Liebknecht was about to proclaim a new socialist republic and to appeal for support from the revolutionary masses. It was not possible for the SPD to exercise effective authority unless they had the backing of at least some of the independent socialists. Thus a Council of People's Commissars was formed, consisting of three SPD leaders and three from the USPD, in a conscious bid to outmanoeuvre the Berlin Revolutionary Shop Stewards who were working to bring about a revolutionary uprising in the capital city. For Ebert, the aim was clear: to stabilise the political situation sufficiently to enable elections to take place as soon as possible for a National Assembly. This body would then be entrusted with the task of drawing up a constitution for the new republic.

In this aim, Ebert had the full support of the government officials, local civil servants and industrialists who had witnessed the onset of revolution with growing horror. But more significantly, a telephone call from General Groener at military headquarters assured him of the full support of the army high command in order to facilitate the orderly retreat and smooth demobilisation of the German army. General Groener correctly surmised that Ebert was as anxious as the army authorities to defeat the Bolshevik challenge which threatened to spread revolution through the major urban centres, of Germany, and that he needed at least some military assistance to restore order. The message of support from the army was swiftly followed by the announcement of peace. That same weekend, on Sunday 11 November, the Armistice was signed between German and allied representatives, and the First World War officially came to an end.

The National Assembly

The second phase of the revolution spanned the period from the signing of the Armistice to the holding of elections for the National Assembly on 19 January 1919. It saw growing tensions between Ebert and the SPD on the one hand, and their USPD partners, who found themselves being continually pulled to the left by the revolutionary activities of the Marxist groups. While Ebert's concern was to ease the transition from war to peace for millions of returning soldiers and try to alleviate some of the economic hardship and food shortages facing large sections of the population, his Marxist rivals were planning street demonstrations and revolutionary uprisings. A demonstration of loyalty to Ebert in Berlin on 6 December was greeted by a counter demonstration organised by the Spartacus League, and in violent street clashes sixteen were killed and twelve seriously wounded. Far more serious clashes took place in January, as the Spartacists unleashed their revolutionary uprising in an attempt to overthrow the government. The uprising was crushed by the army, with the help of *Freikorps* troops, hastily recruited from volunteers organised by individual army commanders. With the situation contained, at least for the time being, *Freikorps* members took the opportunity, on 15 January, to murder both Liebknecht and Luxemburg. This outrage, more than any other event of the German revolution, ensured the implacable hostility of the Marxist left in Germany towards Ebert, the SPD and the new parliamentary republic. The events of January 1919 opened up divisions between the new German Communist Party and the SPD which could never thereafter be bridged. The USPD tried hard to manoeuvre between the two, but before long its members found themselves pulled either to the Communists or to the SPD.

Meanwhile, the soldiers' and workers' councils had held their first nation-wide congress in Berlin, from 16 to 21 December. While their social and economic demands were radical, they shared to a surprising extent Ebert's constitutional aims. Rather than opting to continue *de facto* government through their network of councils, they voted overwhelmingly to support elections to a National Assembly on 19 January. And Ebert's vision of a constitutional workers' republic had received a further boost in a series of far-reaching measures agreed between the leading trade unions and industrial leaders in November. The industrialists agreed that in future they would fully recognise the rights of trade unions to represent their workers, that they would accept legally binding wage agreements and a system of compulsory arbitration to regulate disputes, and that workers' councils should be introduced into all factories and workshops with more than fifty employees. Their most significant concession was to agree to the introduction of the eight-hour working day. The trade union leaders of the SPD thus secured most of the goals they had been pursuing for so long, they and their members were now more concerned to realise the gains they had achieved rather than to engage in further revolutionary activity.

The Elections

The final phase of the revolution started with the elections to the National Assembly on 19 January and ran on until the spring. While workers' demonstrations and revolutionary disturbances continued, particularly in the Ruhr, in Bremen, Hamburg and Munich, they were more sporadic, and increasingly failed to mobilise mass support. Attention switched to the peace negotiations just getting under way in Paris, and to discussions about the new constitution. Above all, the outcome of the elections appeared to indicate widespread support for the political course which Ebert had followed thus far.

For the first time in German history, in the elections to the National Assembly in January 1919, women over 20 were able to vote alongside men for their chosen candidates, who were to be elected by a system of proportional representation. There was a turnout of 83 per cent of those eligible to vote, despite appeals by the Communist Party to workers to boycott the elections. Ebert's SPD Party secured nearly 38 per cent of the vote, with a further 7½ per cent going to the USPD. With the Catholic Centre Party gaining the support of nearly 20 per cent of the electorate, and the German Democratic Party (the former Progressives) securing a further 18½ per cent, there was a resounding majority for the parties whose leaders had agreed to assume the reins of power the previous October. Nationalist and monarchist parties won less than 15 per cent of the votes cast.

The new Assembly delegates gathered in the picturesque southern German town of Weimar which had been home to [the writers Johann Wolfgang von] Goethe, [Friedrich] Schiller and [composer Franz] Liszt. Berlin was considered too dangerous a venue, with revolutionary forces still strongly in evidence, though gradually declining in force. The Assembly opened on 9 February 1919, and two days later Ebert was elected by delegates as the first President of the new republic, gaining 277 votes out of a possible 379. A cabinet was formed, with ministers drawn from the Social Democrat, Catholic Centre and Democrat parties. A constitutional lawyer from the Democrat Party, the Jewish deputy Hugo Preuss, was entrusted with the task of drafting a constitution.

With the acceptance of the constitution by the National Assembly in July, by 262 votes to 75, the German revolution had effectively come to an end. Its constitutional aims had certainly been fully realised, but the more far-reaching social and economic goals of the council movement had not resulted in the wholesale removal of the existing economic or social structures. A Marxist revolution had been prevented, and many left-wing leaders had been murdered, including Kurt Eisner in Bavaria in February. Uprisings continued in militant industrial centres for several months, culminating in a serious disturbance in the Ruhr in 1920 and in communist-led revolts in Hamburg and in central Germany in 1921. But Germany did not succumb to the forces of communism, much to the disappointment of the Bolshevik regime in Russia. On the contrary, the forces of reaction and of strident nationalism made a swift recovery and emerged by 1920 as the most potent enemies of the new republic.

Why Did the Weimar Republic Collapse?

By Joseph W. Bendersky

From the inception of the Weimar, the German republic faced many struggles. In this article, Joseph W. Bendersky analyzes a few of the major obstacles that challenged the Weimar government. He detects a lack of political and social consensus in Weimar society, manifest in strong anti-democratic sentiments amongst both right-wing and left-wing elements. Most administrators and intellectuals did not support the republic, either. Furthermore, the nature of the party system made it hard to form coalition governments. In this unstable environment, conservative party coup attempts and Communist revolts were only barely suppressed by the government. Then, in the 1920s, inflation and perceived foreign insults pushed many Germans to embrace the views of the radical right. Although the republic would survive the decade, its downfall was presaged by the growing strength and influence of the right-wing Nazi Party. Bendersky is director of graduate studies in history at Virginia Commonwealth University.

On November 10, 1918, an obscure German soldier named Adolf Hitler lay grieving on his bunk in a military hospital. He had just learned that the emperor of Germany, Kaiser Wilhelm II, had abdicated and that a republic had been proclaimed in Berlin. What shocked Hitler even more was the news that the war had been lost. The armistice signed the following day was, in fact, tantamount to a German surrender. In Hitler's mind the armistice and the new republic had not resulted from German defeats on the battlefield. They were the work of Jews and Socialists who, out of lack of courage, dis-

Excerpted from *A History of Nazi Germany*, by Joseph W. Bendersky (Chicago: Nelson Hall, 1985). Copyright © 1985 by Joseph W. Bendersky. Reprinted by permission of the publisher.

loyalty, or self-interest, had undermined the government and the war effort. Hitler considered the creation of the republic and the subsequent acceptance of the Treaty of Versailles as political catastrophes for Germany. Thereafter, he blamed most of Germany's economic and political ills on the republic and the treaty. Yet, it was these developments, which Hitler so lamented, that allowed him to emerge from obscurity to become one of the most powerful and infamous dictators in history. Although the roots of the Nazi ideology can be traced back to certain cultural and intellectual currents in the nineteenth century, the rise of Hitler and the Nazis as political forces can be attributed directly to the Versailles Treaty and the crises that plagued the new republic from the very beginning.

The Formation of Weimar

Within two months after the declaration of the republic, Communists incited revolutions in Berlin and several other major cities. Their goal was to establish a Soviet state in Germany similar to the one founded by Lenin in Russia. By April 1919, a Communist republic had also been declared in Munich. These revolts were brutally suppressed by the army and volunteer units, called the Free Corps, but throughout the winter and spring of 1919, Germany remained in a state of civil war. It was under these circumstances that elections took place for a National Assembly that would draft a new constitution. The capital, Berlin, was in such turmoil that the constitutional assembly had to convene in the city of Weimar. As a result, the new democracy became unofficially known as the Weimar Republic.

Despite difficulties, there were initially some encouraging signs that democracy might take root in Germany. In the elections to the constitutional assembly, in which 80 percent of the electorate cast ballots, the supporters of the republic received three-quarters of the vote. A democratic constitution was adopted by an overwhelming majority of the assembly. The Weimar constitution guaranteed all citizens basic civil rights (equality before the law, freedom of speech, press, and religion, and so on) and abolished the privileges of the aristocracy. The Reichstag (parliament) was elected by universal suffrage and was to serve as one of the major institutions of self-government as opposed to the authoritarianism of the former monarchy. The chancellor and his cabinet were directly responsible to the parliament and could remain in office only with the confidence of a majority of the deputies in the Reichstag.

The "Dictatorship Article"

The framers of the Weimar constitution were as concerned about political stability as they were with parliamentary government. Therefore, the constitution also provided for a strong president, who was independent of the Reichstag and directly elected by the people for a seven-year term. The president had broad powers that were intended to provide for strong leadership and a stable government. He controlled the armed forces, directed foreign policy, appointed and removed the chancellor, and could dissolve parliament and call new elections. Equally important, under Article 48 of the constitution he assumed special authority in a state of emergency. In such circumstances, he could temporarily suspend parts of the constitution, institute emergency measures, and intervene with the armed forces to reestablish order and security. Although this clause was later referred to as the "dictatorship article," its purpose was to preserve the existing state and constitution; it was not intended to serve as the basis for a dictatorship. A president could not alter the constitution, and the Reichstag had the right to rescind any emergency decree. Moreover, it was only through decisive executive action under this article that the republic was able to survive as long as it did. On paper, at least, the Germans had finally laid the foundations for a modern and stable democracy.

A Lack of Political and Social Consensus

In practice, the new government had great difficulty in stabilizing the country and getting the democratic system to function properly. At the heart of the problem was the lack of a political and social consensus among the Germans. Before the war, the nation had been ruled from above by an authoritarian regime and as a result, political parties did not learn democratic governmental responsibility and tactics of political compromise. The majority of Germans also lacked political education. These problems were especially acute in Weimar, for no political party acquired a majority in the Reichstag, and it was extremely difficult to form coalition governments from among the various antagonistic parties. Furthermore, many Germans never supported the republic, and many of those who accepted it did not have a real commitment to democracy. The political right associated the republic with defeat, shame, betrayal, and weakness; rightists never accepted the legitimacy of the new government and favored either the restoration of the monarchy or an authoritarian state. The old aristocracy also resented the loss of its special privileges and would not adjust to a democratic government and society. Many middle-class Germans originally voted for the republic not out of sympathy for democracy but because they saw the republic as a bulwark against a Communist revolution. Even this pragmatic support began to erode in less than a year as the middle and lower-middle classes held the republic responsible for their eco-

ONE MILLION MARKS FOR A BREAD LOAF

This article was published in the New York Times *on September 5, 1923. It illustrates the incredible rate of inflation in Germany at the time. According to the article, the first one million mark bread loaf was to be sold in Berlin the next day.*

Paper mark mania is a new form of insanity developing in Germany. Several insane asylums have recently received an increasing number of victims crazed by the sudden plunge into calculations in millions. These inflation victims in many cases are older women of the ruined middle classes, widows with microscopic pensions or fixed incomes which once sufficed for maintaining life but are now hardly enough to buy a piece of bread.

One case of mark insanity took the form of constant figuring, particularly multiplying with zeros.

The mark broke to another record today. After the official rate was fixed at 20,000,000 to the dollar it sank further to 22,500,000.

German pessimism about the paper mark touched bottom, too. It was freely prophesied that the mark would sink to 100,000,000 to the dollar in the next few days or even to absolute zero. A German financial expert commented:
"Today's doings on the foreign exchange market showed

nomic decline. On the other hand, the Communists regarded Weimar as a middle-class capitalist state that had to be over-thrown by revolution; they never ceased in their efforts to desta-bilize the republic. For one reason or another, most segments of German society were disappointed by Weimar.

Weimar was not completely without republican sympathizers. Although most Socialists and workers were disappointed by the limited nature of social and economic reform in Weimar, they enthusiastically supported the new republic. Similarly, Catholics in general and a minority of the middle classes were loyal to the new constitutional order. But these republican sympathizers re-

---

that the brakes cannot be applied any more on the down-ward course. The flight from the paper mark has become universal again."

A wild catastrophe boom sent up all stocks as usual. As the mark fell there was a feeling of panic on the Boerse. Some stocks gained 100,000,000 points and more with the Rhenish Westphalian specialties leading the bull stampede. Bochumer sold up to 3,000,000,000, and Harpener 3,250,000,000.

The Boerse's pessimism was accentuated by credited ru-mors that the Reichsbank would be forced to make further gold shipments abroad.

Greater Berlin beats its first one million mark bread loaf tomorrow. At the same time rolls will cost 50,000 marks. All prices continue to rise fantastically. The eleventh big boost in rail rates will fix the multiplicator at 1,500,000 times for passenger rates, 4,500,000 times for freight rates on the ba-sis of the prewar gold rates. A new big increase in coal prices also is foreshadowed. . . .

In the New York Foreign Exchange Market, the German mark was quoted yesterday at 33,333,333 to the dollar, against less than 16,000,000 the day before end 10,000,000 a week ago.

Cyril Brown, "Figuring in Marks Causes German Insanity; Paper Money Drops to Another Low Record," New York Times, September 5, 1923.

mained in a minority, and in their efforts to make democracy
work, they had to rely upon other segments of society that were
unenthusiastic about, if not hostile to, the republic. Weimar was
not a republic without republicans, as often claimed; it was a republic without a republican majority.

The Political Parties

Another serious problem for Weimar was the political party system itself, which reinforced already existing divisions within German society. German parties were not open associations that developed platforms during elections to attract a broad group of
voters. They were tightly organized and exclusive institutions that
represented the interests of distinct and antagonistic segments of
society, and their programs had little appeal to those outside their
particular social, economic, or ideological group. Many parties
developed their own bureaucracies, social clubs, newspapers, and
auxiliary organizations; in some cases, parties had their own
armies with thousands of members. Not just the political life but
the social life of members as well was centered around the party.
The result was that party members tended to become even more
segregated from other segments of society. In elections, voters did
not vote for a particular candidate but for "party lists" of candidates decided on by each party. The electorate, which had no influence over the selection of these candidates, was forced to accept or reject the entire list. Thus, parties had tremendous control;
until the 1930s, most voters remained loyal to their respective
parties. This control also extended into parliament, where party
discipline was enforced and deputies voted according to the
wishes of their party leadership. The flexibility of these parties
was limited further by the fact that many of them viewed each
other not merely as the parliamentary opposition but as the "enemy," with whom only limited compromises could be made.
Since different party interests conflicted so often, it was difficult
to pass significant legislation; frequently the parliament would be
paralyzed by the intransigence of several parties. Critics of the
republic referred to Weimar as a *Parteienstaat* (party-state). . . .

The failure of Weimar was probably due as much to the nature of this multiparty system as it was to the antirepublican opposition of the radical right and left.

An added burden for Weimar was that important public institutions were staffed with antirepublicans who could not be re-

moved for political reasons, because their rights of tenure were protected by law. Organized and staffed under the monarchy, the bureaucracy remained essentially unchanged after 1919 and was dominated by officials who either detested or, at best, tolerated the new government. They had little loyalty to the government they were sworn to serve; often they favored rightist causes and opposed republican policies. Similarly, university professors, who trained the nation's elites, were usually either apolitical or tended to be conservative nationalists and harsh critics of Weimar. Though a very limited number of professors had a democratic orientation, most relentlessly attacked the Versailles Treaty and the weaknesses of the republic in their lectures and publications, reinforcing the sense of disappointment and the antagonism toward Weimar already felt by their students and the public in general. The army, supposedly the defender of the state and constitution, also displayed little enthusiasm for the republic, preferring an authoritarian state. Weimar governments were never sure if they could count on the army to protect the republic. Certainly there was good reason for such doubt: when the terms of the Versailles Treaty became known, there was serious discussion within the army high command about replacing the republic with a military dictatorship. . . .

Two Attempted Coups

The Versailles Treaty, frustrations with the ineffectiveness of the Weimar government, and pressure by the victors to compel rapid German demobilization set off a series of events in 1920 that almost destroyed the republic within a year after its birth. In March, the so-called Kapp *Putsch* forced President Friedrich Ebert and the legal Weimar government to flee from Berlin. The leaders of this rightist coup, former General Walther von Lüttwitz and a politician named Wolfgang Kapp, were backed by Captain Hermann Ehrhardt, whose Free Corps brigade took over the city. Their goals were to resist the implementation of Versailles and to overthrow the republic. During this first overt challenge to the power and authority of the Weimar political order, the army remained neutral. The republic was saved only by an effective general strike called by the Social Democratic Party (SPD) and labor unions, which brought about a quick collapse of the Kapp government. However, the danger to the republic had not ended. The German Communists exploited this crisis to start a revolution in the Ruhr, the industrial heart of Germany, and by the end of March a Red army of more than fifty thousand had seized control of several major cities. While the army had been reluctant to act against the right to defend the republic, it never hesitated against the left in order to save Germany from communism. A brutal suppression of the Communist revolution followed.

The reaction against the treaty, the turmoil of recent months, and middle-class fear of communism produced further loss of faith in the republic. The June 1920 Reichstag elections signaled a drastic political shift to the right. The parties that constituted the prorepublican Weimar Coalition lost their majority, never to regain it, and the strength of the rightist German National People's Party (DNVP) and German People's Party (DVP) greatly increased. For the rest of Weimar, coalition governments could be formed only with the participation of rightist parties, which were less than sympathetic, often hostile, to democracy.

The return to normalcy and order desired by most Germans did not follow. The gains made by the right did not satisfy the extremists for whom the republic itself symbolized defeat and betrayal. Rightists labeled those associated with the formation of Weimar and the treaty as "November Criminals," because the armistice of November 11, 1918, was considered the beginning of the betrayal of Germany. Certain right-wing extremists took it upon themselves to punish the November Criminals. In August 1921, Matthias Erzberger, a republican leader of the Center party, was assassinated. He had been involved with arranging the armistice. Another prominent republican who favored fulfillment of the treaty, the intellectual and industrialist Walther Rathenau, was assassinated the following June. Rathenau's murder also pointed out the connection between anti-Semitism and antirepublicanism in the minds of the extreme right. Many on the right charged that the republic was created and controlled by Jews to the detriment of "true" Germans. In their propaganda such rightists frequently referred to Weimar as the "Jew Republic."

Economic Troubles

Nineteen twenty-three brought even greater disasters. On the grounds that Germany had failed to meet its reparation obligations, French and Belgian troops occupied the Ruhr in January. The German policy of passive resistance to this action revealed the weakness of the republic and produced an almost complete

collapse of the economy. Shortly thereafter, Germany experienced the most catastrophic inflation in its history. By November 1923, the German mark was worth only one-trillionth of its
1914 value. Middle-class savings and investments became worth-
less; those on fixed incomes and many of the self-employed were
cast into poverty almost overnight. Government deficits reached
close to 99 percent. These problems generated massive unemployment, food riots in certain areas, as well as widespread social
and psychological distress. All of this provided opportunities for
the extreme right and left. Communist strength in several states
increased dramatically, and leftist political violence was just the
prelude to a planned Communist revolution. At the same time
Bavaria had become a hotbed of right-wing radicalism, which
culminated in Hitler's famous Beer Hall *Putsch* of November 8.
The political crisis was so intense and the danger so great that
President Ebert declared a state of emergency under Article 48
of the constitution and authorized the army to restore order. This
decisive executive action was sufficient to counteract these overt
threats, but political and economic conditions remained critical.
The long-range impact of the inflation and disorders of 1923
would affect the entire history of Weimar....

The Middle Class Moves to the Right

Today, most historians agree that the inflation was caused by war
debts inherited from the monarchy and by reparation payments,
two factors beyond the control of the republican government. In
the 1920s, however, the inaccurate explanations of the reactionary
right proved quite convincing to the middle classes. Germans
from all classes, of course, had lost confidence in the government
during the crisis of 1923, but middle-class hostility towards the
republic endured beyond this period. When the next economic
crisis struck in the 1930s, a greatly disproportionate number of
middle- and lower-middle-class citizens would either join or vote
for the Nazi party, which promised them an economic and national rejuvenation. In return for these things, they were quite
willing to sacrifice a democracy in which they had so little faith
and for which they blamed their economic and social decline.

From the early years of the republic, the crisis of Weimar
democracy was also aggravated by Germany's intellectuals.
Weimar granted intellectuals greater freedom and creative opportunities than they had ever known; yet, they reacted to the re-

public with hostility and disdain. Instead of creating enthusiasm for Weimar, intellectuals raised additional doubts and increased popular disillusionment and despair. Some thought their criticism of Weimar's failures and weaknesses would lead to necessary change; but others believed that the republic's problems were inherent in the system itself, and they looked forward to its demise. None of them found the existing situation tolerable, and together they had a devastating psychological impact on Weimar's political climate. . . .

The Stresemann Era

After Weimar weathered the crisis of 1923, antirepublican activities and sentiments subsided dramatically. Between the end of the Great Inflation and the onset of the Great Depression, Weimar experienced its most stable and prosperous interlude. The figure most responsible for this recovery was Gustav Stresemann, leader of the DVP, who served briefly as chancellor in 1923 and thereafter as foreign minister until 1929. Still a monarchist and antirepublican as late as the early 1920s, Stresemann became one of the strongest advocates of the new republic; without his leadership Weimar might not have survived as long as it did. By 1922 he was convinced that the political collapse of Weimar would end in civil war or in a seizure of power by the extreme right or left, and he was determined to prevent these events. As a nationalist, Stresemann wanted Germany to regain its lost position among the great powers of Europe. He realized that this could not be accomplished unless Germany first put its own house in order. Stresemann believed that these objectives could best be achieved by stabilizing the republic rather than by remaining in opposition to it.

Considering that Germany had been at the brink of political and economic collapse, Stresemann's accomplishments were tremendous. Currency and fiscal reform ended the inflation; the Dawes Plan of 1924 set a more reasonable schedule and amount for German reparation payments; and a program of international loans assisted Germany's economic recovery. In foreign policy, Stresemann favored fulfillment of the treaty obligations, because he felt that Germany's recovery at home and of its lost status in international politics could be achieved only through cooperation with the Allies. Stresemann ended the policy of passive resistance and negotiated the withdrawal of the French and Belgians from the Ruhr. By confirming Germany's new frontiers with France and Belgium and by accepting the demilitarization of the Rhineland in the Locarno Treaties of 1925, Stresemann initiated a new era of international cooperation. He brought Germany into the League of Nations in 1926 and arranged a plan for British and French evacuation of the Rhineland. Not only had Stresemann become the dominant political figure in Germany, but he received international recognition as well. In 1926, he was awarded the Nobel Peace Prize. . . .

But events would soon show that, despite these positive developments, Weimar had not overcome its fundamental problems. Very little had changed in the relationships between the various segments of German society. The nation was still deeply divided by class, ideology, and economic interests; the republic had acquired only the toleration, not the enthusiastic support, of the bulk of the German people. In retrospect, it is clear that the years of tranquility and stability were dependent upon the leadership of Stresemann and prosperity. When these crucial factors were removed, Germany would again lapse into political and economic turmoil. Weimar parties would revert to their habitual squabbling, confidence in the republic would quickly disappear, and political radicalization would return.

To a large extent, the early 1930s in Germany would be reminiscent of the first years of the republic. Only this time, a well-organized and dynamic Nazi party would be waiting to exploit the situation.

THE HISTORY OF NATIONS

Chapter 4

The Nazi Era

Hitler's Misconceptions

By Sebastian Haffner

The tenets of the Nazi Party were based on the personal beliefs of its leader, Adolf Hitler. When the Weimar Republic gave way to the Nazi Third Reich, these philosophies guided the actions and policies of the new state. In this selection, drawn from his book The Meaning of Hitler, *Sebastian Haffner analyzes Hitler's theories of race, state, and nation—emphasizing Hitler's belief that nations and races compete in a constant struggle for living space. In doing so, Haffner discovers inconsistencies and flaws in Hitler's views. Haffner lived in Germany during Hitler's rise to power, but he left for England in 1938 and became a distinguished journalist. He returned to his native country in 1954.*

I t is ... worthwhile to take a closer look at Hitler's political concept of the world and to separate what was incorrect from what was correct or at least arguable. Strangely enough, this has scarcely been attempted so far. Prior to 1969, when Eberhard Jäckel produced a synthesis of 'Hitler's Ideology' from the disjointed mass of his ideas scattered among his books and speeches, the literature on Hitler even refused to acknowledge that any such ideology had existed. The prevailing opinion until then may be summed up in the words of Hitler's early English biographer Alan Bullock: 'The only principles of Nazism were power and rule for their own sake.' This point is made in specific contrast to, for instance, Robespierre and Lenin, for whom 'the will to power ... coincided with the triumph of a principle'. Hitler used to be regarded, and is still regarded by many who have failed to investigate the subject in depth, as a pure opportunist. . . .

It certainly is no pleasure to examine Hitler as a political thinker to the point that a critical analysis demands. Nevertheless it seems necessary to do so, and for two opposite reasons.

First, because until it has been done a greater portion of Hitler's theoretical ideas than one might think will survive, and not only among the Germans or among avowed followers of Hitler. Secondly, because until the misconceptions in these ideas are clearly separated from what was more or less correct in them, the correct elements are in danger of being made taboo simply because Hitler also thought so. But two and two still remain four even though Hitler would undoubtedly have agreed.

The latter danger is the greater because the starting points of Hitler's thinking were almost invariably unoriginal. The original element in them, which can be proved almost entirely to have been erroneous, is what he made of them. Just as, in his architectural designs, he started from the conventional neo-classical 'public buildings' style, against which there is little to be said, and subsequently ruined it by exaggerated, ostentatiously provocative proportions, so the basic ideas from which he proceeded in his political thinking were those which he shared with most of his contemporaries. Some of them indeed were such platitudes as 'two and two make four'.

Nation, State, and Race

One such platitude, for instance, is that there are different nations and also, though since Hitler's day one scarcely dares to use the word, different races. An almost universally accepted view in his day and one that still predominates today, was that states and nations should if possible coincide, in other words that states should be national states. Even the idea that wars cannot be ruled out from the life of states became questionable only after Hitler's day, while the question of how they are to be abolished has still not been answered. These are merely cautionary examples to show that what Hitler thought and said need not be rejected as beyond discussion merely because it was he who thought and said it. One should not, with the deadly name 'Hitler', shout down anyone who treats nations and races as the realities they are, or who supports the idea of the national state, or who faces the possibility of war. The fact that Hitler miscalculated does not abolish arithmetic.

Let us now try to present a brief outline of Hitler's historical-political ideology, the theory of 'Hitlerism'. It looks something like this.

The only actors in all historical processes are nations or races, not classes or religions, and strictly speaking not even states. History 'is the description of the course of a nation's struggle for its life'. Or, to pick another: 'Anything that happens in world history is merely the manifestation of the self-preservation of the races.' The state is 'in principle only a means to an end, and sees its end in the preservation of the racial existence of the people'. Or, a little less defensively: 'Its aim rests in the preservation *and promotion* of a community of physically and psychologically homogeneous human beings.' 'Domestic policy must ensure for a nation the inner strength to assert itself in its foreign policy.'

That foreign policy assertion consists in struggle: 'Whoever wants to live must therefore fight, and whoever does not wish to do battle in this world of eternal struggle does not deserve life', and struggle between nations (or races) normally and naturally takes the shape of war. Viewed correctly, 'wars lose the character of separate more or less massive surprises and take their place in a natural and comprehensible system of thorough-going well-founded lasting national development'.

Politics is the art of implementing a nation's vital struggle for its earthly existence. Foreign policy is the art of ensuring for a nation the amount and quality of living space it needs at a given time. Domestic policy is the art of procuring for a nation the power necessary for this, in the form of its racial quality and its numbers.

Nations Struggling for Living Space

In short, politics is war and the preparation for war, and war is mainly about living space. That is universally valid, for all nations and even for all living creatures, because 'their instinct for self-preservation is infinite as is their longing for continued existence, whereas the space within which this entire life process unrolls is finite. In that limitation of living space lies the inevitability of existential struggle.' Specifically valid, for the German nation, is the point that 'it must rally its strength for its advance along that road which, from the nation's present confined living space, leads out to new land and soil'. Its main objective must be 'to remove the discrepancy between our population total and our territory the latter viewed both as a source of nutrition and a power base'.

Secondly, however, wars are about domination and subjection. What the 'aristocratic basic idea of Nature desires is the victory of the strong and the annihilation of the weak or his unconditional subjection'. That is the essence of that 'free interplay of forces which must lead to a continuous improvement of the stock'.

Thirdly, however, and ultimately, the perpetual warlike strug-gle between nations is about world domination. This is expressed most clearly and most briefly in a speech of 13 November 1930: 'Every being strives for expansion and every nation strives for world domination.' And that is a good thing because 'we all feel that in the distant future man will find himself confronted by problems which only a supreme race, as a master nation based upon the resources and facilities of an entire globe, can be called upon to solve'. And right at the end of [Hitler's autobiography] *Mein Kampf* we read, with unambiguous reference to Germany which must 'necessarily gain the position due to it on this earth': 'A state which, in an age of racial poisoning, devotes itself to the cultivation of its best racial elements must one day become mas-ter of the earth.'

The Equation of Race and Nation

So far the ideas are all a little narrow, steep and reckless but they have an inner logic. Things only begin to get confused when one observes Hitler juggling with the concept of the 'race', a key concept in Hitler's thinking ('the racial problem is the key to world history') but never defined by him and often equated with the concept of 'nation'. 'A supreme race as a master nation' shall, according to Hitler, rule the world one day—but which, a race or a nation? The Germans or the 'Aryans'? This is never entirely clear with Hitler. Equally unclear is whom he regards as an Aryan. Only the more or less Germanic nations? Or all Whites except the Jews? This is nowhere clarified by Hitler.

The concept of 'race' is applied, in general usage and also by Hitler, in two quite distinct senses, a value judgment sense and a neutral, descriptive one. 'Superior race', 'to improve the race'— these are value concepts from the sphere of the stockbreeder who, for each particular strain, will exclude inferior examples from breeding and try to improve certain racial characteristics by selective breeding. This is the sense in which Hitler often uses the term when he refers to the 'racial quality' of a nation, to be im-proved, for instance, by the sterilization of the feeble-minded or the killing of the mentally sick. The term 'race' is also applied, in general usage, as a neutral concept distinguishing different vari-ants of the same species, and such variants, of course, exist among human beings as they do among horses or dogs. . . .

All this is in a complete muddle in Hitler's thinking, and

Jäckel, whose praiseworthy account of Hitler's ideology we have so far substantially followed, possibly helps a little by trying to assign to Hitler's racial doctrine a firm and logically unassailable place in the general pattern. That is possible only if one leaves something out. Of course, so long as 'race' is used in the stock-breeding sense, as it sometimes is by Hitler, and one considers that a nation can or should improve its 'racial quality' by 'selective breeding', everything fits. The actors of history, in that case, are the nations, history itself consists of their wars, their rivalry for living space and world domination, and so for that struggle they must be perpetually rearmed; not only militarily and ideologically but also biologically, i.e. by raising their racial quality, by the elimination of the weak and by the deliberate selective breeding of their militarily useful characteristics. All that, of course, is nonsense—a point to which we shall return—but it is consistent within itself. But this is not the whole of Hitler's image of the world but only half of it. The other half is his anti-semitism, and to justify and rationalize that he needs the other meaning of 'race'. Indeed, one might say that he needs an entirely new theory, one that contradicts the former in several respects. . . .

The Struggle Between the Races

This is again an entire theory of its own and would require very elaborate manipulation to make it harmonize with his first theory, which one might call his ethnic theory. According to the former all history consists of the continuous struggle of nations for living space. Now we are suddenly informed that this is not the whole of history after all. Alongside the struggle of nations there is, according to Hitler, yet another permanent feature of history—the racial struggle, by which he means not a struggle between white and black and yellow-skinned people (the real racial differences between white, black and yellow-skinned people did not interest Hitler at all), but a struggle within the white race, namely between the 'Aryans' and the Jews. In other words, between the Jews and all the rest, who might otherwise be in continuous struggle against each other but who, against the Jews, all belong to the same side. This struggle is not about living space, but literally about life; it is a struggle of extermination. 'The Jew' is everybody's enemy: 'His ultimate aim is the de-nationalization, the inter-bastardization of the other nations, the lowering of the racial level of the noblest, as well as domination over that racial jumble through the extermination of the national intelligentsias and their replacement by members of his own nation.' And more than that: 'If the Jew with the aid of his Marxist creed remains victorious over the nations of this world, then his crown will be the wreath on the grave of mankind, then this planet will once more, as millions of years ago, move through the ether devoid of human beings.' The Jews apparently intend to exterminate not only the 'national intelligentsias' but the whole of mankind. If that is so then of course the whole of mankind must unite to ex-

THE NIGHT OF SHATTERED GLASS

On November 9, 1938, when Jews were already excluded from most professions, the Nazi Storm Troopers got the order to commit spontaneous assaults against Jews and their property. During the following night most German synagogues were set on fire, many Jews were murdered and thousands simply arrested. The shattered glass of Jewish shop windows all over the country gave this night its name.

In November 1938 a young Jew, Herszel Grynspan, murdered a member of the German embassy staff in Paris, Ernst Eduard von Rath. By this time Jews had been excluded from most professions, had identity cards, and were forced to bear the names Israel or Sara, but the anti-Semitic campaign was paralyzed—the ministries were expressing certain legal doubts and demanding clarifications, while radicals called for more drastic action.

On 9 November, when Hitler learned of the assassination he discussed it with [Propaganda Minister Joseph] Goebbels, who made an inflammatory speech warning that the German people would seek revenge for the murder. The party and the SA [Nazi Storm Troopers] were ordered 'spontaneously' to express the peoples' outrage at this Jewish crime; the SS was ordered to remain in the background.

The SA took to the streets in uniform and gleefully set to work. On the night of 9–10 November at least ninety-one German Jews were murdered, most synagogues were set on

terminate them in their turn, and in this capacity as extermina-
tor of the Jews Hitler presents himself not as a specifically German politician but as the champion of the whole of mankind:
'By fighting off the Jew I fight for the work of the Lord.' In his
political testament he calls 'international Jewry' the 'world-wide
poisoner of all nations', and his final dictation to [his personal
secretary Martin] Bormann of 2 April 1943 concludes with the
words: 'People will be eternally grateful to National Socialism
that I have extinguished the Jews in Germany and Central Eu-

---

fire, and Jewish property was destroyed. The Gestapo chief,
Heinrich Müller, ordered 20,000–30,000 wealthy Jews to
be arrested and sent to a concentration camp pending expulsion from Germany. Such was the destruction in the cities
and towns on the following day that this appalling pogrom
has been memorialized as *Reichskristallnacht* [Reich crystal
night], a term which trivialised the appalling human suffering involved. The pogrom was far from popular, and everyone knew it had been organized from above. Most Germans
felt it went too far—not so much out of sympathy for Jews,
but rather for fear that the SA's flagrant disregard for private
property might soon affect them.

On 12 November a committee chaired by Hermann
Göring decided that the 250,000 remaining German Jews
should pay a fine of 1,000 million marks and that they were
not eligible for insurance payments for their losses. It was
agreed that Jewish businesses were to be 'Aryanised' and
Jews were forbidden to go to the theatres, cinemas, or swim-
ming pools. German Jews had lost all legal rights and means
of support; the way was now open for genocide. The SS
journal, *The Black Corps,* announced that the Jews would
soon be exterminated. On 30 January 1939 Hitler proclaimed in the *Reichstag* [name of the German parliament at
the time] that if a war broke out in Europe, its Jews would
be destroyed.

Martin Kitchen, *The Cambridge Illustrated History of Germany.* New York:
Cambridge University Press, 1996.

rope.' Here he positively presents himself as an internationalist
and a benefactor of humanity.

Three Remaining Questions

We are not at this point criticizing Hitler's thought (difficult
though it is to present this homicidal nonsense uncritically)—we
are presenting it. But even a mere presentation demands an answer to three questions.

First, what were the Jews in Hitler's eyes? A religion, a nation,
or a race?

Second, what, according to Hitler, were they doing that made
them so dangerous to all other nations that they should deserve
such a terrible fate?

Third, how was Hitler's doctrine of the perpetual struggle between the Jews and everybody else compatible with his doctrine
of the (equally perpetual and equally God-given) struggle of
everybody else against everybody else?

Hitler certainly tried to find answers to these three questions
but all the answers come out somewhat confused and artificial;
here are the frayed margins of Hitler's world of ideas.

On the first question only one thing was clear, to Hitler—that
the Jews were not a religious community. This he repeated in-
defatigably without ever justifying it, although surely it would
need justification. After all it is evident that there is such a thing
as a Jewish religion and that it was this religion which held the
Jews together as Jews throughout nearly 1,900 years of the Di-
aspora. However, to Hitler they were not a religious community.
Whether they were a race or a nation Hitler evidently never
quite decided in his own mind. True, he kept referring to the
Jewish race, moreover in the dual sense of 'distinct race' and also
'inferior race'; but in his second book, which contains the most
careful elaboration of his theory of anti-semitism, he calls them,
probably more accurately, a nation, and even concedes to them
what he concedes to other nations: 'Just as any nation possesses,
as the basic tendency underlying its entire earthly activity, the
longing to preserve itself as a living force, so this is true also of
Jewry.' But he immediately adds: 'However, in line with the fun-
damentally different character of the Aryan nations and of Jewry,
their existential struggle is also different in its forms.'

The Jews—and here we come to Hitler's answer to the second question—were by their very nature international, incapable

of establishing a state. 'Jewish' and 'international' were virtually synonymous to Hitler; anything that was international was Jewish, and in this context Hitler even spoke of a Jewish state: 'The Jewish State has never been limited territorially but has been universal and unlimited in extent; it is, however, confined to one race.' And therefore—here we have it—this 'Jewish state' was 'international world Jewry', the enemy of all other states, against which it was mercilessly fighting with all means at its disposal, in external politics by pacifism and internationalism, capitalism and communism, in domestic politics by parliamentarianism and democracy. All these were tools for the weakening and destruction of the state, all were inventions of the Jews and all aimed at only one thing to disrupt and weaken the 'Aryan' nations in their magnificent struggle for living space (a struggle in which the Jews, cunningly, did not participate) in order thus to ensure their own pernicious world domination.

Hitler: Jews as an Enemy Race

And this brings us to Hitler's answer to the third question. Why did all nations have to unite against the Jews when surely they had their hands full fighting against each other for living space? Answer: they had to unite just *because* they had to fight for their living space, and *in order that* they might devote themselves undisturbed to their pre-ordained struggle. The Jews were the spoilsports in this pleasant game; with their internationalism and pacifism, their (international) capitalism and their (equally international) communism they were diverting the 'Aryan' nations from their main task and their main occupation, and that is why they had to be removed from the world, and not from Germany only. Moreover they had to be removed not like a piece of furniture that is taken away to be put elsewhere, but like a stain that is removed by wiping it out. Nor must they be left with an escape. If they abandoned their religion that meant nothing since they were not a religious community but a race, and if they tried to escape even their race by intermingling with 'Aryans', then that was worse still because they thereby impaired the 'Aryan' race and rendered the nation concerned incapable of its necessary existential struggle. And if they tried to integrate with that nation and become German, French, English or other patriots, then that was the worst thing of all, for their aim would then be 'to push the nations into wars against each other [but surely this was just what,

according to Hitler, the nations were for?] and in that way gradually, with the help of the power of money and propaganda, raise
themselves to being masters over them'. Quite obviously, whatever the Jews did they were always wrong, and in any case they
had to be exterminated.

That, then, is Hitler's second, anti-semitic, theory, which stands
independently alongside the ethnic one and cannot readily be
harmonized with it. The two together make up what may be
called 'Hitlerism', the ideological edifice of Hitler the 'programmatician'—his counterpart, in a sense, to Marxism.

Hitlerism has at least one thing in common with Marxism—
the claim to be able to explain the whole of world history from
one single point of view. 'The history of all society so far is a history of class struggles', we read in the Communist Manifesto, and,
analogously in Hitler, 'All events in world history are merely the
manifestation of the self-preservation drive of the races'. Such
sentences have considerable emotive power. Anyone reading
them has the feeling of suddenly seeing the light; what had been
confused becomes simple, what had been difficult becomes easy.
To those who willingly accept them such statements give an
agreeable sense of enlightenment and knowledge, and they moreover arouse a certain furious impatience with those who do *not*
accept them, since in all such words of command there is a ring
of '. . . and anything else is a lie'. This mixture of swaggering superiority and intolerance is found equally among convinced
Marxists and convinced Hitlerites. . . .

It is, of course, an error that 'all history' is either this or that.
History is a jungle, and no clearing that one cuts into it opens up
the whole forest. History has known class struggles *and* racial
clashes, and also conflicts (indeed more frequently) between states,
nations, faiths, ideologies, and so on. There is no conceivable human community that might not, in certain circumstances, find itself in conflict with another—and, historically, it is hard to find
one which has not at some time been so. . . .

A Fight for Living Space

In Hitler's view of the world, moreover, wars always were wars
of conquest with the aim of gaining living space for the warring
nation, of permanently subjecting (or annihilating) the vanquished, and ultimately, achieving world domination. This was
another misconception on his part. Wars for the sake of living

space had not been waged in Europe, prior to Hitler, since the Migration of the Peoples, that is for roughly one and a half millenia. Europe was settled; its nations were firmly located; and if, as the result of a peace treaty, some province or other changed hands from one state to another, or even if an entire state, as for example Poland, was partitioned among its neighbours, the inhabitants remained where they were. Living space was neither won nor lost: living space was not fought over in Europe. Only Hitler, after an interval of roughly 1,500 years, reintroduced this feature into European history, with terrible consequences for Germany. Expulsion, such as that of the Germans from their former eastern territories, was precisely what Hitler had always preached as the purpose of any war and what he himself had put into practice in conquered Poland.

'Living space' was a misconception also for another reason. The point is that in the twentieth century it no longer pays to fight for living space. If Hitler measured a nation's prosperity and power by the extent of the territory inhabited and farmed by it, if he demanded and pursued a 'territorial policy', then he overlooked, or deliberately ignored, the industrial revolution. Since the industrial revolution prosperity and power have no longer depended on the size of one's territory but on the state of one's technology. And for that, the size of one's living space is irrelevant.

Indeed an excess of 'living space,' that is great territorial expanse with sparse population, can be a positive handicap for a country's technological-industrial development—a fact well known, for instance, to the Soviet Union: it simply cannot manage to open up and develop Siberia, a vast territory rich in raw materials, but too sparsely populated. It is certainly an unmistakable fact that some of the poorest and weakest countries in today's world are enormous, while some of the richest and most secure are minute. Hitler, who certainly was a modern thinker in some areas—such as military technology or the motorization of the masses—was totally and entirely rooted in the pre-industrial age with his living-space theory.

But just that misconception of Hitler's refuses to lie down. Nostalgia for the pre-industrial age and an anxious malaise with the 'inhuman' man-made world we have been bringing upon ourselves ever more rapidly for the past two hundred years, were not only widespread in Hitler's day but are again particularly strong at present. They made Hitler's living-space ideas seem sen-

sible to many of his contemporaries—did not Germany really
look much too small on the map in relation to her strength and
population total? True, if Germany were to become a predomi-
nantly peasant country again—on this point Hitler's thinking
agreed strangely with Morgenthau's—then she really did need
more living space. But only then.

Wars and World Domination

The idea that the wars of the twentieth century were ultimately
about world domination is also older than Hitler and has survived
him. Even before the First World War Kurt Riezler, the adviser
of Reich Chancellor Bethmann-Hollweg, a highly educated
man, wrote: 'In its ideas . . . every nation strives to grow, to spread
itself, to dominate and subjugate without end; it strives to unite
itself ever more firmly and to incorporate ever new elements
into itself, to become an organic unit under its rule.' That is pure
Hitler, except that the language is more unctuous. But it was nevertheless wrong; not every nation has those aims. Or are the Swiss
and the Swedes not nations? Not even the European great powers during the period of European colonial imperialism can be
said, each of them for itself, to have aspired to world domination.
They had learned the lesson too well, over the centuries, that they
could not abolish one another and that any attempt to attain
hegemony even in Europe would inevitably bring about a coalition of the remaining great powers, who would feel threatened
and combine to foil any such attempt. . . .

Germany as a Candidate for World Domination

There is, of course, some truth in the argument that our world,
shrunk through technology and threatened by weapons of mass
destruction, is calling out for unity and that, therefore, the idea of
world rule—world unity, world government, world rule, all these
lie close together—has become topical again in the twentieth
century. Hitler's misconception was not in taking the idea of
world rule up. It was in seeing the German Reich as a serious
candidate for world domination. The Germany of his day undoubtedly was a great power, in fact the strongest in Europe, but
still only one among several, and one that had failed once before
in the attempt to become both the leading power in Europe and
a world power. Only if the union of Europe had been accom-

plished—and that was not to be achieved by wars of conquest and subjugation—might such a united Europe, in which Germany would then have to be absorbed, have had a chance in rivalry for world rule. But the unification of Europe—surely that would have been Jewish internationalism! Hitler instead believed that he was able to achieve his goal with a national Greater Germany alone, by racial policy and anti-semitism—a primitive misconception. A biological rearmament of Germany by racial improvement in the stockbreeding sense would have required several generations, quite apart from all the problems involved; and Hitler wanted to achieve everything he intended in his own lifetime. As for, anti-semitism, Hitler was wrong not only about the Jews but even about the anti-semites.

Anti-Semitism Not a World-Wide Phenomenon

Hitler really believed—this is proved not only by his quoted written and public statements but also by oral and private, remarks made during the war—that his anti-semitism would gain him world-wide sympathy for the German cause, that it would make Germany's cause the cause of mankind. He counted on the existence of anti-semites throughout the world. But Hitler's variety of anti-semitism, demanding extermination, existed nowhere except in eastern Europe, from where he himself had got it; and even there, it must be said to the credit of the Ukrainians, Poles and Lithuanians, it was based not on Hitler's fantasies of a world-wide Jewish conspiracy to enslave or exterminate 'Aryan' humanity, but upon the plain fact that the Jews in those countries were settled as a compact alien people. This was not the case anywhere else, and accordingly anti-semitism elsewhere never aimed at the extermination or the 'removal' of the Jews.

Toward
Dictatorship

BY CRANE BRINTON, JOHN B. CHRISTOPHER,
AND ROBERT LEE WOLFF

*In the late 1920s, while Germany experienced increasing prosperity,
most Germans supported moderate parties such as the Social Democrats.
But as unemployment, poverty, and other severe effects of the Great Depression increased after 1929, the German people began to lean more toward right-wing groups. Among these were the Stahlhelm, or "Steel Helmets," a conservative organization of army veterans, and the Nazis. The
aging president, former general, and war hero Paul von Hindenburg himself leaned increasingly toward the right, believing that more autocratic
rule was needed to alleviate the growing economic emergency, which, of
course, played into the Nazis' hands. In this essay, Crane Brinton and
John B. Christopher of the University of Rochester and Robert Lee
Wolff, the Archibald Cary Coolidge Professor of History at Harvard
University, explain how Hitler took advantage of the changing political
situation and made impressive gains in a series of elections. By making
backroom deals and thereby manipulating Hindenburg and other leading
politicians at the same time, Hitler managed to become chancellor largely
by legal means. Once his position was secure, he could devote his energies
to realizing his ultimate goal, the conquest of Europe.*

D uring . . . [the] middle years of the Weimar Republic,
economic recovery proceeded steadily, until, in 1929,
German industrial output exceeded that of 1913. First-
rate German equipment, coupled with superb technical skill and
a systematic adoption of American methods of mass production,
created a highly efficient industrial machine. . . . The emphasis
was always on heavy industry, which meant that continued prosperity would depend upon a big armaments program.

All through this period, [war] reparations were paid faithfully,
with no damage to the German economy. Indeed, more money

flowed into Germany from foreign, especially American, investment than flowed out from reparations. Dependence on foreign capital, however, which would cease to flow in time of depression, made German prosperity artificial.

In 1925, after President [Friedrich] Ebert died, a presidential election was held in which three candidates competed. The Catholic Center, the Democrats, and the Social Democrats supported the Center leader, Wilhelm Marx. The Nationalists, People's party, and other right-wingers joined in support of Field Marshal Hindenburg, then seventy-seven years old. The communists ran their own candidate and thus contributed to the election of Hindenburg, who won by a small plurality. Abroad, the choice of a man so intimately connected with imperial militarist Germany created dismay; but until 1930 Hindenburg acted entirely in accordance with the constitution, to the distress of most of the nationalist groups. The domestic issues of this period all aroused great heat, but were settled by democratic process. In the elections of 1928, the Social Democrats were returned to power and the Nationalists and Nazis were hard hit. All in all, prosperity encouraged moderation and a return to support of the republic....

The Impact of the Depression

But even before the last achievements of this "period of fulfillment," the depression had begun to knock the foundations out from under prosperity and moderation. Unemployment rose during 1929. After the American stock-market crash in October, foreign credits, on which prosperity had so largely depended, were no longer available to Germany. Short-term loans were not renewed, or else were recalled. Tariff barriers were hurting foreign trade. Hunger reappeared.

Although unemployment insurance cushioned the first shock for the workers, the lower middle classes, painfully recovering from the inflation, had no such barrier between them and destitution. Their desperation helped Hitler, whose fortunes during the years of fulfillment had fallen very low, although he had attracted a number of new followers who were later to be important in his movement....

The Republic in Danger

The government fell in 1930 over a disagreement on a question of unemployment insurance benefits. Hindenburg appointed to the chancellorship Heinrich Bruening, a member of the Catholic Center party. Bruening would have liked to support parliamentary institutions . . . but he was to find it impossible. . . . President Hindenburg, now eighty-two, had fallen more and more under the influence of General Kurt von Schleicher, an ambitious political soldier who had intrigued himself into the president's favor. Hindenburg was now itching to rule by decree, as the constitution authorized him to do in an emergency. By failing to pass Bruening's economic program, the Reichstag gave Hindenburg the opportunity he wanted. Bruening agreed, partly because he felt that a genuine emergency existed, but partly because he was determined to keep his bitter political rivals, the Social Democrats, from replacing him in office.

A presidential decree proclaimed the new budget. When the Reichstag protested, Hindenburg dissolved it and called new elections (September 1930). Nazis and communists fought in the streets, but both gained greatly at the expense of the moderates. The Nazis' Reichstag representation rose from 12 to 107 and the communists' from 54 to 77. Bruening had to carry on against the wishes of the electorate; supported only by Hindenburg, he too now turned authoritarian.

In order to avoid a new government in which Nazis would participate, the Social Democrats decided to support Bruening. When the Reichstag met, Nazis and communists created disorder on the floor, but voted together in opposition to government measures. These measures passed only because the Social Democrats voted for them. . . .

Now Nazis, Nationalists, the veterans organization of the Steel Helmets [and other right-wing groups] . . . formed a coalition against Bruening. This coalition had great financial resources and a mass backing, chiefly Nazi. It had its private armies in the SA, in the Stahlhelm [army veterans], and in other semimilitary organizations. Because the left was split and the communists in effect acted as political allies of the right, nothing stood between this new right-wing coalition and a political victory except the person of Hindenburg, who controlled the army. . . . Early in 1932, the great industrialist Fritz Thyssen invited Hitler to address a meeting of coal and steel magnates. Hitler won their financial support by convincing them that if he came to power he would be their man. Though some of Hitler's followers were now impatient for a new putsch, he curbed them, believing that the Nazis could come to power legally.

In the presidential elections of March 1932, Hitler ran as the candidate of the Nazis, and Hindenburg as the candidate of the Center, Social Democrats, and other moderate parties. The Nationalists nominated a Stahlhelm man, and the communists of course ran their own candidate. Hitler polled 11,338,571 votes, and Hindenburg polled 18,661,736, only four-tenths of a percent short of the required majority. In the run-off election, the Nationalists backed Hitler, whose total rose to 13,400,000 as against Hindenburg's 19,360,000. The eighty-four-year-old marshal reelected as the candidate of the moderates was, however, no longer a moderate himself, but the tool of the ... military.

Although the government now ordered the Nazi SA and SS disbanded, the decree was not enforced. In April 1932 the Nazis scored impressive victories in local elections, especially in all-important Prussia. Bruening was unable to procure in time either an Allied promise to extend the moratorium on reparations payments or permission for Germany to have equality in armaments with France. Schleicher, who was now deeply involved in intrigue against Bruening, worked on Hindenburg to demand Bruening's resignation. This Hindenburg did on May 29, 1932, the first time a president had dismissed a chancellor simply because he had lost personal confidence in him. Bruening's successor was Franz von Papen, a rich Catholic nobleman and a member of the extreme right wing of the center, who installed a cabinet composed of nobles. Papen was Schleicher's man—or so Schleicher thought. The Center disavowed Papen, who had the real support of no political party or group, but whom the Nazis temporarily tolerated because he agreed to remove the ban on the SA and SS. . . .

On July 31, 1932, new elections for the Reichstag took place, called by Papen on the theory that the Nazis had passed their peak, that their vote would decrease, and that they would then be chastened and would cooperate in the government. But the Nazis won 230 seats and became the biggest single party in the Reichstag; the communists gained also, chiefly at the expense of the Social Democrats. The Democrats and the People's party almost disappeared, while the Nationalists suffered, and the Center scored a slight gain. Papen had failed. He now wanted to take some Nazis into the government, but the Nazis demanded the chancellorship, which Hindenburg was determined not to hand over to Hitler. Papen now planned to dissolve the Reichstag and to call new elections. By repeating this process, he hoped to wear down Hitler's strength each time, until he brought Hitler to support him and accept a subordinate place. As Papen put pressure on the industrialists who had been supporting Hitler, the Nazi funds began to dry up, leaving Hitler seriously embarrassed. The elections of November 6, 1932, bore out Papen's expectations. The Nazis fell off from 230 seats to 196. . . .

The Republic Was Doomed

Had Papen been permitted to continue his tactics, it is possible that Hitler might have been kept from power. But Papen resigned as a matter of form because he could not count on majority support in the Reichstag. Angry with Schleicher and sorry to lose Papen, Hindenburg forced Schleicher himself to take the office on December 3, 1932. Now the backstairs general was chancellor, but he had no political support whatever, and had alienated even Hindenburg. He lasted in office only about eight weeks. . . .

Schleicher did [make] . . . every effort to appeal to all shades of opinion except the extreme left. But this attempt in itself alienated the . . . industrialists. The tortuous Papen, eager for revenge, intrigued with these enemies of Schleicher. Early in January 1933 Papen met Hitler at the house of the Cologne banker Baron Kurt von Schroeder. The industrialists, who had temporarily abandoned Hitler, now agreed to pay the Nazis' debts. Hitler, in turn, no longer insisted on the chancellorship. He thus led Papen to hope that he would come back into office with Hitler's backing. Hindenburg, too, was enlisted. When the president refused to give Schleicher the authority to dissolve the Reichstag at its first new session, which would surely have voted him down, Schleicher had no choice; he was forced to resign (January 28, 1933).

But Hitler had now raised the ante, and demanded the chancellorship for himself. Papen consented, provided Hitler undertook to govern in strict accordance with parliamentary procedure. Papen was to be vice-chancellor, and still thought he could dominate the government, since only three of its eleven ministers would be Nazis. He therefore persuaded Hindenburg to accept Hitler as chancellor. But Papen underestimated Hitler. Though Hitler swore to Hindenburg that he would maintain the constitution, he had no intention of keeping his oath. The Weimar Republic was doomed from the moment Hitler came to the chancellor's office on January 30, 1933.

Hitler's War

By Martin Kitchen

In this article, Martin Kitchen outlines the progress of the Second World War. Beginning with the annexation of Austria and the Sudetenland and Germany's initial attack on Poland, Kitchen charts the Nazi successes in numerous military campaigns in Europe and Africa. He then turns to the war with Russia, an enterprise that ultimately held Germany at bay while the other Allied nations gathered enough strength to help turn the tide and secure the Third Reich's final defeat on June 5, 1945. Kitchen is a professor at Simon Fraser University in Vancouver, British Colombia.

German troops crossed the Austrian border on 12 March 1938 and were greeted by a rapturous population. Encouraged by this reception, Hitler decided on annexation. On the following day he addressed the crowds in Vienna and when he announced that Austria was now a German province, their enthusiasm knew no bounds. Hitler was at the height of his popularity; he had realized [former Prussian chancellor Otto von] Bismarck's dream of a greater Germany. In April, 99 per cent of the German electorate voted in favour of the *Anschluss* [a euphemism for the annexation]. Few seemed to be worried by the appalling violence against Austrian Jews and the opposition committed by the German police and SS.

The benefits to Germany were immense. Germany had won more territory than she had lost in 1919 and with it valuable supplies of iron ore and 500,000 unemployed workers who were badly needed in the arms industry. Austria had 1.4 billion marks in gold and foreign currencies in the central bank at a time when the Reichsbank had only 76 million. Czechoslovakia, previously a strategic threat to Germany, was now highly vulnerable to German attack.

The Sudetenland

Two weeks after the *Anschluss* Hitler received the Sudeten German leader Konrad Henlein, and ordered him to make a series of unacceptable demands to the Czech government. One month later he ordered General Keitel to draw up plans for an invasion of Czechoslovakia, code-named Green. The British government made it plain that it would do nothing to help the Czechs, pronouncing that frontier rectifications in Germany's favour were desirable. France was in the middle of yet another political crisis and would not act without British support, while [the Fascist leader of Italy Benito] Mussolini had no objections. On 20 May the Czech government therefore decided to seize the initiative and mobilize its forces. Britain, France, and the Soviet Union were shaken out of their torpor and announced that they fully supported the Czechs' move. War looked imminent.

On 28 May 1938, Hitler gave a three-hour speech to the military and diplomatic leadership in which he expressed his determination to crush Czechoslovakia by means of a decisive four-day Blitzkrieg so as to avoid the intervention of Britain and France. He then intended to deal with France, leaving the way open for his expansionist war in the East. He was still uncertain whether this would involve a war with Britain, but now felt that his Eastern goals could not be achieved without first achieving security in the West.

The Role of Britain and France

Manoeuvres were held on the Czech border in June, while Britain and France urged the Czechs to negotiate. On 13 September the British prime minister Neville Chamberlain visited Hitler at the Berghof. Hitler demanded the immediate annexation of the Sudetenland. Chamberlain replied that he would have to consult the cabinet, and Hitler promised not to use force for the time being. The British and French governments then urged the Czechs to hand over all areas in the Sudetenland in which more than half the population was German. Chamberlain returned to present this suggestion to Hitler at Bad Godesberg, but Hitler blandly announced that 'considering the developments in the last few days this solution is unacceptable'. Chamberlain returned to London and, on 26 September, the British government announced that it would support France in the event of war over Czechoslovakia. Hitler complained that he was being treated 'like a nigger' and in a massive rally in the Palace of Sports in Berlin told the crowds that the Czechs had to decide whether they wanted war or peace.

On 27 September Hitler ordered the army to prepare for an attack on Czechoslovakia. On 28 September, urged by Mussolini, he reluctantly agreed to meet Chamberlain and the French premier Daladier in Munich. Agreement was reached in the early hours of the morning on 30 September. Germany was to get the Sudetenland and, along with Italy, would guarantee the territorial integrity of the rest of Czechoslovakia.

In one sense Munich was a triumph for Hitler. Czechoslovakia was now defenceless and had lost some important industries, along with 3.6 million people. But he had been denied his triumphal entry into Prague, his timetable had been disrupted, and Britain and France had been given a breathing space in which to rearm. Chamberlain had been greeted by the German crowds as a man of peace, confirming Hitler's concern that his people were not enthusiastic about the prospect of a confrontation. He bitterly complained that 'with these people I cannot fight a war!'

Greater Czechoslovakia

On 21 October, Hitler ordered plans to be drawn up for the destruction of Czechoslovakia and the annexation of the Memel— a German province awarded to Lithuania in 1919. In Czechoslovakia the Slovaks demanded their independence, with the support of Berlin. The Czech president Hacha dismissed the Slovak leader Monsignor Tiso and sent troops into Slovakia. Tiso was persuaded to meet Hitler, who warned him that if he did not declare Slovak independence he would support Hungarian claims to his country. On 14 March 1939 the Slovak parliament passed a declaration of independence.

That evening Hacha and his foreign minister travelled to Berlin, where they were treated to one of Hitler's violent monologues on the outrageous behaviour of the Czechs. Hacha was presented with the alternatives of handing over his country to Germany or facing invasion and the bombardment of Prague. Hacha had a heart attack and was revived by an injection from Hitler's doctor so that he could sign a document which placed 'the destiny of the Czech people and their country confidently into the hands of the Fuhrer of the German Reich' in order to secure 'law, order, and peace'. By 9 A.M. German troops had entered the Czech capital. Hitler arrived that evening and announced the formation of the Protectorate of Bohemia and Moravia which turned the Czech lands into a German satellite. His reception in Prague was very different from that in Vienna. The people were silent, grim, and tearful. Few raised their arm in the Nazi salute. On 21 March 1939 Hitler demanded that Lithuania hand over the Memel, and boarded the battleship *Deutschland*. By the time he reached Memel, on 23 March, the Lithuanian government had given way. Hitler suffered badly from sea-sickness but had won another bloodless victory. His attention now focused on Poland.

Poland

Hitler hoped that Poland would be a junior partner in his war of conquest in the East, joining the anti-Bolshevik crusade and providing rear cover for a campaign in the West. He wanted Danzig and an extraterritorial railway and autobahn through the corridor, but was prepared to guarantee Poland's frontiers for twenty-five years. At the same time, on 25 March, he ordered preparations to be made for an attack, Case White, to be launched as early as 1 September 1939.

Poland had no wish to play second fiddle to Germany and was fearful of Soviet reactions. On 26 March, the Polish foreign minister Beck turned down [Hitler's foreign minister Joachim von] Ribbentrop's renewed demand for Danzig, and five days later the British government extended a guarantee to Poland and Romania in response to Hitler's seizure of Bohemia and Moravia. Germany and Poland were now on a collision course, and on 28 April Hitler renounced their 1934 neutrality pact.

Fearful that Britain and France might reach an agreement with the Soviet Union, Hitler cast his ideological scruples aside and agreed to Ribbentrop's proposal for a pact with the devil. [Soviet leader Joseph] Stalin was eager to make a deal which he hoped would give him territorial gains in the Baltic and Poland and he invited Ribbentrop to Moscow. Ribbentrop arrived on 23 August and within three hours an agreement was reached on spheres of influence.

Hitler was now determined to go to war, and nothing could stop him. The British government let it be known that they would support the Poles. On the afternoon of 31 August Hitler issued the order for the attack on Poland to begin at 4.45 A.M.

the following morning. A phoney assault on a German radio station near the border was staged to provide an excuse for the invasion, but few were fooled.

Hitler's War

The German people showed no enthusiasm for war and there was no repeat of the heady days of August 1914. It was not until 3 September that the British and French declared war on Germany. This came as an unpleasant surprise both to Hitler and to his people. Hitler's attempt to fight separate wars in the East and the West and to keep Britain neutral had failed. Hitler promised that he would not take off his 'sacred and treasured' uniform until his final victory, or death.

Germany invaded Poland without declaring war and the campaign was soon over. On 17 September the Red Army annexed eastern Poland the Baltic states later became Soviet socialist republics. On 19 September Hitler gave a speech in Danzig in which he claimed that Poland was destroyed and would never rise again. What remained after the German/Soviet partition became the General Government, a colony subjected to the most brutal exploitation. Both the Soviet Union and Germany systematically liquidated Poland's ruling class. Thousands of Polish officers were

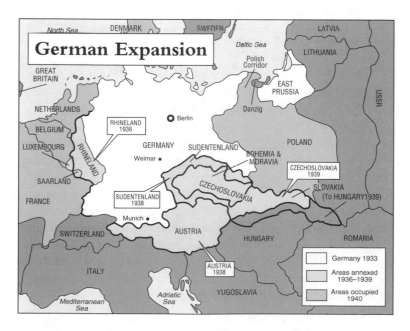

murdered by the NKVD (the Soviet secret police) and buried in mass graves in the forest of Katyn. The Germans were even more thorough: [Chief of SS Security Service Reinhard] Heydrich had prepared five squads of SS special troops (*Verfügungstruppen*) with orders to kill the Polish intelligentsia. Tens of thousands of professionals were slaughtered, and on 27 September Heydrich proudly announced that at most 3 per cent of the Polish leadership was still alive. At the same time the SS herded Polish Jews into ghettos in Warsaw, Cracow, Lemberg, Lublin, and Radom. Some decent soldiers, prominent among them General Blaskowitz, were appalled at the brutality of the SS and protested to their superiors and even to Hitler. The Führer was disgusted at this 'Salvation Army attitude' and Blaskowitz was posted to the western front.

[Heinrich] Himmler, who in October 1939 had appointed himself Reich Commissar for the Strengthening of the German Race, lay down guidelines for German occupation policy in Poland. Poles were to learn 'that it is God's commandment that they obey the Germans, and be honest, industrious and well-behaved.' Children of good blood, and thus capable of becoming Germans, would be educated appropriately. Slav subhumans would provide a 'leaderless work force'. By the summer of 1941 one million Poles had lost their property and been resettled. The land was colonized by Germans on whom fell a terrible retribution in the war's final stages.

France, the Netherlands, Denmark, and Norway

Hitler had won another great victory but Germany's position was far from secure. Italy had declared its neutrality and so had Japan, the armaments industry was not yet on a war footing and Germany was still dependent on imports of strategic raw materials. Most serious of all, the country depended heavily on the Soviet Union, without whose help it could not mount a campaign against France. In this awkward situation Hitler decided to strike a soon as possible. France was to be defeated swiftly. Britain would be excluded from the continent and might agree to the division of the world which Hitler had repeatedly offered. He would then be free to complete his great historical task of carving out an empire in the East.

The offensive was delayed twenty-nine times, the military arguing that the weather conditions were too poor in order to postpone a campaign about which they had serious misgivings. On 9 April 1940 Germany attacked Denmark and Norway, securing supplies of Swedish iron ore and strengthening its strategic position against Britain. The campaign in the West began in May, when Holland was defeated in a brilliant operation lasting five days. The main offensive from the Ardennes to the Channel then trapped the British and Belgian armies and much of the French. The British and some French were able to escape from Dunkirk when Hitler ordered the German tanks to halt. Their left flank was dangerously exposed, with supply lines overextended, the troops weary and tanks in need of repair. On 14 June the Germans entered Paris, and on 21 June Hitler sat in Marshal Foch's chair in the same railway carriage in which the 1918 armistice had been signed, dictating his peace terms.

A new French state under the aged defender of Verdun, Marshal Petain, was created in the south, with its administrative capital in Vichy. Germany took Alsace and Lorraine, although the provinces were not formally annexed. Italy, which against Hitler's wishes had declared war on 10 June, received a small frontier strip. Northern France was placed under military occupation.

Britain

Hitler still hoped to come to an arrangement with Britain, but Winston Churchill, who became prime minister in May 1940, steeled his countrymen to continue the fight. On 16 July Hitler ordered preparations for an invasion of the British Isles, codenamed Sea-lion. Three days later he made his 'appeal to reason' in a speech in the Reichstag in which he called upon the British government to end hostilities. The air war over England began on 13 August but by 16 September the offensive was halted by heavy losses and bad weather. Hitler, who uncharacteristically had shown no interest in the invasion plan details, realized that air superiority was essential and pressed ahead at the beginning of July with his plans for the invasion of the Soviet Union.

On 19 July President Roosevelt indicated that he would not stand idly by and let Britain be defeated. Hitler now insisted that the Soviet Union had to be conquered in the spring of 1941. With Germany in command of the continent the British would have to abandon the fight, the United States would not have time to rearm, and would face a greatly strengthened Japan. The first step was the three-power pact between Germany, Italy, and Japan signed on 27 September. This amounted to very little. The Japanese remained neutral and had no intention of coordinating their strategy with the Germans. The most that Hitler could hope for was that this racially dubious *Volk* [people], which were proclaimed to be Aryan until further notice, would keep the Americans occupied in the Pacific. Attempts to bring France and Spain into the bloc also failed. [Henri-Philippe] Petain wanted guarantees specified in a formal peace treaty, and [Francisco] Franco sensibly remained aloof. . . .

The War Against the Soviet Union

The attack on the Soviet Union began on 22 June 1941 and went like clockwork. On 15 July Himmler unveiled his General Plan East which envisaged the expulsion of thirty-one million people to Siberia, German colonization in the East and the 'waste disposal' (*Verschrotten*) of the racially undesirable; he was put in charge of the realization of Germany's eastern empire. On 21 July Hitler told the Croatian defence minister Kvaternik that he intended to destroy the European Jews, first in the Soviet Union, then in the rest of Europe. If any European state harboured Jews, Hitler warned, they would act as 'incubators for destructive bacteria'. On 31 July Heydrich received orders from [Reichsmarschall Hermann] Göring to make the necessary preparations for the 'general solution of the Jewish question in Europe'. Goring explained that he was acting on Hitler's orders.

By the end of July the German offensive was running out of steam and in December the Soviets launched a successful counteroffensive in front of Moscow. Hitler dismissed most of his commanders in order to run the war himself. By now, some among the Nazi leadership were convinced that the war was lost. Even Hitler saw the writing on the wall and said: 'If the German people are not strong enough and are not prepared to sacrifice their own blood for their continued existence, then they should vanish and be destroyed by another, stronger power.' To this he added that he would not waste a single tear for his fellow Germans.

Hitler planned a major offensive in the south-eastern sector for 1942, but failed in the summer to encircle the Red Army. He at once ordered Army Group B to take Stalingrad and advance to the Caspian, and Army Group A to push on to Baku. In the northern sector Leningrad was to be seized and destroyed. On 23

October Montgomery launched his offensive at El Alamein which was to lead to the defeat of the Axis troops in North Africa. On 19 November the Soviet counter-offensive began north of Stalingrad and General Paulus' 6 Army was soon cut off. Hitler ordered Stalingrad to be held at all costs. On 2 February 1943 the remains of Paulus' army surrendered and 90,000 men were taken prisoner; few of them survived. Although Hitler's decision to fight on in Stalingrad was strategically correct, allowing the bulk of the German forces to be extricated from the Caucasus so that they could launch a counter-attack on 20 February, Stalingrad was a crushing defeat and Hitler was no longer seen by all as an invincible leader. At home the Hitler myth was beginning to fade and terror was beginning to take its place. . . .

Defeat

By now the war could not possibly be won. On the eastern front Army Group Centre had suffered a crushing defeat in June 1944 and it was now only a matter of time before the entire front collapsed. At the same time the Allies [American, British, and Canadian armies] had landed in Normandy and were advancing. The allied air offensive had reached a new level of intensity. 'Fortress Europe' no longer had a roof and Germany's beautiful cities were reduced to piles of rubble. Half a million civilians died in the raids and four million homes were destroyed, but it was not until the summer of 1944 that the bombing had a serious impact on transport and industrial production. . . .

Hitler retreated into a fantasy world in which he imagined the Allies falling out, and the British joining him against the Soviets. He announced that his new 'miracle weapons', the V1 and V2 rockets, would bring victory. In a desperate gamble he ordered an offensive through the Ardennes to Antwerp and Brussels. The Ardennes attack badly weakened the eastern front and came to a halt after four days of heavy fighting and losses. The Soviet Union's offensive began on 12 January 1945 and the Red Army was soon on the Oder [River], driving before it millions of terrified refugees who tried to flee the bestial orgy of murder, rape and plunder in which the Soviets wrought their revenge. They meted out similar treatment to the hapless folk they 'liberated' in Poland, Romania and Hungary.

On 16 January Hitler returned to his bunker in the Berlin chancellory, over twenty feet below ground, isolated from the world in a fantasy twilight. The Nazi grandees rejoiced in the senseless destruction of Germany's cities: [propaganda minister Josef] Goebbels' press proclaimed that the 'so-called achievements of the bourgeois nineteenth century had finally been buried', making way for a revolutionary new National Socialist society. Hitler told [Nazi architect Albert] Speer that the Allies were doing useful work preparing the way for the rebuilding of the cities according to the plans they had drawn up together. On 19 March Hitler issued his 'Nero Order' calling for a scorched earth policy that would leave the Allies nothing, while Speer did all he could to ensure the Gauleiters did not carry it out.

On 20 April 1945 Hitler celebrated his fifty-sixth birthday with Goring, Goebbels, Himmler, [Hitler's secretary Martin] Bormann, Speer, Ribbentrop, [Nazi official Dr. Robert] Ley and some senior commanders. His mistress Eva Braun travelled to Berlin for the occasion. Two days later Hitler held his last conference. The Russians were already in the suburbs. He screamed at his generals, accusing them of treason, cowardice and insubordination, and then collapsed weeping, muttering that the war was lost and that he would shoot himself. On 29 April he married Eva Braun and wrote his political testament, appointing Admiral Dönitz president and minister of war and Goebbels chancellor. The newlyweds committed suicide the following day and their bodies were burnt. Goebbels and his wife committed suicide, having first murdered their six children. Bormann was killed escaping from the chancellory, his body found many years later. Dönitz prolonged the war as long as possible, enabling three million of his countrymen to escape the clutches of the Soviets. On 9 May the fighting ceased. On 23 May Dönitz was arrested, and on 5 June the Allies formally took control of a vanquished Germany.

The Holocaust

By Mary Fulbrook

In this piece, Mary Fulbrook gives an overview of the Nazi attempt to exterminate the entire Jewish population of Europe, which came to be known after the war as the Holocaust of European Jewry. She shows how Nazis tried several methods of killing their victims before settling upon special extermination camps with gas chambers. In such camps, Fulbrook notes, the Nazis were able to kill as many as nine thousand people a day. After giving an answer to the question of how many Germans must have known about or even facilitated the Holocaust, Fulbrook summarizes some of the most famous German attempts to resist Hitler and his Nazi regime. Mary Fulbrook is a lecturer in German history at University College London.

Hitler's basic aims had been two-fold: to achieve *Lebensraum* [living space] for the German race; and to rid that race of what he saw as a pollutant, a bacterium, poisoning and infecting the healthy 'Aryan' stock: the Jews. Slowly, during the period after 1933, Jews had been identified, stigmatised, and excluded from the 'national community', the *Volksgemeinschaft*. Measures had been adopted to give Jews an outcaste status, and many Jews, realising they had little future in Germany, had already fled for more welcoming shores. While there had been acts of violence and discrimination against Jews, there had however been no systematic policy for totally ridding Germany of the Jewish population. In war-time, things changed. For one thing, with the conquest of territories in which there were far larger Jewish communities (particularly in the east), the 'Jewish problem' assumed new proportions. For another, more extreme circumstances suggested and promoted more radical solutions. Hitler let it be known that he wanted the expanded Reich to be 'cleansed of Jews' (*Judenrein*). Initially, schemes were actively considered for the mass deportation of Jews to a reservation in

Madagascar, and Jews were even sent to southern France in preparation for shipment. In eastern Europe, there were plans for a Jewish reservation in the area around Lublin in southeastern Poland. After the invasion of Russia in the summer of 1941, the 'final solution' became altogether more sinister.

Mass Shootings and Death Vans

No written Hitler-order for the extermination of the Jews has ever been found; nor, given Hitler's style of government, is such an order likely ever to have existed. But he let his wishes be known and fostered a climate in which the policy of extermination could be effected. There is some disagreement among historians as to whether the extermination programme which actually took place was the direct consequence of a pre-determined plan, or whether it developed in a more ad hoc, haphazard manner as a result of local initiatives which were later co-ordinated. Whatever the interpretation, the broad outline of facts is clear. The first mass killings of Jews were undertaken by specialist so-called *Einsatzgruppen* [special command groups] who arrived in Russia in the wake of the invading German troops. Jews were rounded up and taken out to forests where they dug mass graves, were lined up naked, and were then shot into the graves. This technique had serious disadvantages from the Nazi point of view: killings were relatively public and easily witnessed by passers-by, allowing the news to filter back to Germany; and those doing the shooting—which included shooting young women cuddling babies in their arms—often, despite the SS suppression of human emotions and inculcation of obedience and brutality, found themselves physically incapable of undertaking such cold-blooded murder without first imbibing copious quantities of vodka. Meanwhile, in the ghettoes in Poland, overcrowding and disease were becoming ever more serious, as more and more Jews were transported from occupied territories. From the point of view of those in charge of the Warsaw and Lodz ghettoes, some means would have to be found sooner rather than later of dealing with the increasing numbers of Jews, whether by halting the influx or disposing of those already there. The means chosen was death: immediate death by inhalation of gas, rather than shooting. Jews from the Lodz Ghetto were rounded up, from December 1941, and driven out to Chelmno (Kulmhof), about forty miles north-west of Lodz, where they were driven around in vans which had the exhaust pipes redirected to pump the exhaust fumes back inside the body of the vehicle. When the screams of those packed inside had died down, the drivers stopped and the bodies were dumped in mass graves in the forest. This too, however, proved to be a relatively 'inefficient' means of killing: it could—and did—kill tens of thousands, but could not dispose of millions.

The Concentration Camps

In January 1942, a conference was called at Wannsee, in the beautiful lakeland surroundings on the west of Berlin, to co-ordinate the 'final solution' which was already taking place, under the general direction of SS-leader Heinrich Himmler. In Poland, specially designed extermination camps were opened at Belzec, Sobibor and Treblinka. Under the so-called 'Reinhard Action' (named after Reinhard Heydrich, who was assassinated in Prague in May 1942), these camps effected the liquidation of the vast majority of Polish Jews. They made use of the expertise and personnel of the now-terminated 'euthanasia' programme. The most infamous of the camps, the name of which has come to epitomise evil and suffering, was however not tucked away out of sight in eastern Poland, but was in fact within the borders of the greater German Reich: Auschwitz. Auschwitz (Oswiecim) was a major industrial centre on the main west-east railway line in Upper Silesia. The Auschwitz complex spread over several square kilometres, in and around the town, straddling both sides of the main railway line (with an extra side-line built specifically to allow trains to go directly into the extermination centre at Birkenau). Auschwitz I, an already existing prison and labour camp largely for political prisoners, was the scene of horrific 'medical' experiments under Josef Mengele; it was also the place where the use of Zyklon B gas was first tried [in gas chambers]. Auschwitz II, or Auschwitz-Birkenau, was established a few kilometres away, as a specifically designed factory for mass murder. Whole train-loads could be 'processed', the trains cleaned and readied for their empty return to the west, within three or four hours. When all the gas chambers and crematoria at Auschwitz-Birkenau were in full operation, it was possible to kill up to 9,000 people within twenty-four hours. Also in the town of Auschwitz was the Monowitz camp, whose inmates worked for I.G. Farben's new Buna plant at Dwory. The Auschwitz complex also supplied labour for a number of other German firms such as Krupp, Borsig and Siemens. This was no isolated, hidden concentration camp, but rather a vast enterprise of which large numbers of Poles and Germans were perfectly well aware. Complicity in the functioning of the Third Reich extends far beyond a small band of Nazi thugs and criminals.

The bureaucratically organised, technologically perfected and efficiently executed mass murder of over 6 million Jews, as well as the almost complete annihilation of Europe's gypsy population, and the killing of numerous political opponents of Nazism or others deemed 'unworthy of life', from a whole range of cultural, political and national backgrounds, including communists, Social Democrats, Conservatives, Protestants, Catholics, Jeho-

vah's Witnesses and others—this mass killing, undertaken by members of that highly cultured nation which had produced the music of [Johann Sebastian] Bach and the poetry of [Johann Wolfgang von] Goethe, raises questions almost impossible to contemplate, let alone answer. But that does not mean that the phenomenon should be elevated to a plane of unique reprehension, abstracted from real historical explanation, above causality and the focus solely of horror and shame. This reaction, which is quite understandable, nevertheless evades the real questions of responsibility and guilt. Hitler created the climate and provided the impetus for mass murder—which even conflicted with other central aims of the regime, such as the need for slave labour in the war effort—but he cannot be held to be the only guilty man, as certain explanations which concentrate on the takeover of Germany by a uniquely evil individual imply. Nor can responsibility be placed solely on a small band of fanatics around Hitler. Hitler did not come to power by accident; nor was his regime simply maintained by terror and coercion. Many Germans, in different capacities, facilitated the Holocaust by their actions or permitted it to continue by their inaction. By the end of 1943 at the latest, a considerable percentage of Germans—amounting to several million—knew that the Jews who were being rounded up and shipped off to the east would, directly or indirectly (via transit camps such as Theresienstadt), ultimately end up in a place not of 'resettlement' but of death. This was known, too, by governments of neutral countries and of Hitler's enemies; but powers such as Britain and the USA, for whatever range of reasons, good and bad, chose to ignore the question and concentrated rather on the military effort of defeating Germany in war.

Attempts of Resistance

Whatever the extent to which people 'knew' about the evils of the Nazi regime, most Germans preferred to ignore or disbelieve what did not concern them directly. Their intimations were better suppressed. There were some courageous groups and individuals in Nazi Germany who made attempts to oppose Hitler and terminate his rule. These included many clandestine leftwing opposition groups in the 1930s who continued to meet, discuss and organise, despite the flight of the SPD [Social Democratic Party of Germany] leadership into exile and the disper-

sal of KPD [Communist Party of Germany] members to
Moscow as well as the west. There were also many who had little hope of doing more than expressing their dissent in symbolic
ways, like the dissident youth groups such as the 'Edelweiss Pi-
rates' or the swing culture. For many who refused to assent or
conform to the regime, there was little that simply keeping faith
with like-minded souls could hope to achieve. Attempts by
better-placed individuals who moved in elite circles and could
hope to influence foreign opinion or alter the course of events,
such as Adam von Trott, were for a variety of reasons unsuccessful. A few individuals were simply unlucky. Hitler had extraordinary good fortune in escaping assassination attempts, as when the
Swabian carpenter Georg Elser single-handedly succeeded in hol-
lowing out a pillar in the Munich Beer Hall and installing a
bomb timed to go off when Hitler would be giving his speech
commemorating the 1923 putsch. Unfortunately for Elser's plans,
on the particular night of 9–10 November 1939, it was foggy in
Munich; Hitler decided at the last minute not to fly back to
Berlin as planned, but rather to leave early and take the overnight
train. He thus had left the hall when the bomb exploded. Elser
was arrested crossing the border to Switzerland. After detention
in concentration camps throughout the war, he was finally shot
in Dachau in April 1945. A group of Catholic students in Munich, known as the 'White Rose' group led by Hans and Sophie
Scholl, were equally courageous in their printing and distribu-
tion of leaflets criticising the regime. Their attempts to rouse
public opinion, and to connect with other resistance groups in
positions to affect the regime, could do little more than keep a
flame of morality burning among the prevailing self-centredness,
conformity and apathy. They were caught and executed, still in
their early twenties. Many others too paid with their lives.

The July Plot
The resistance which received most public attention in West Germany after the war was the so-called July Plot of 1944. This constituted, however, a somewhat ambiguous legacy for West German democracy. Many individuals associated with the July Plot
had earlier helped the Nazi regime to power and sustained it in
the 1930s. Conservative nationalists had shared many of the revisionist foreign policy goals of Hitler, and for many doubts had
begun to grow only after 1938. Hopes of toppling Hitler and re-

placing him by a conservative regime were faced with a number of difficulties, including the oath of obedience sworn to Hitler by the army, as well as the early successes of the war which made circumstances less propitious for a coup attempt. By the summer of 1944, Germany's eventual defeat was becoming increasingly inevitable, and the accusation can be levelled against the military resistance that they simply wanted to salvage Germany from total destruction and occupation. Moreover, even taking into account differences of opinion among nationalist resistance circles about the form a post-Hitler regime should take, most of them were essentially anti-democratic in outlook. They wanted an authoritarian government by elites, and not a return to the sort of constitution embodied in the Weimar Republic; they disliked the idea of mass participation in government, and had little conception of any need for popular legitimation of a new government. In the event, their conceptions of alternative government could never be realised. The attempt by [Claus von] Stauffenberg to kill Hitler failed. A briefcase containing a bomb was placed by Stauffenberg under the large table in the Wolf's Lair where Hitler and others were engaged in military planning. The bomb successfully went off, and Stauffenberg, seeing the explosion after leaving the building, returned to Berlin reporting success. But the weighty table, under which the briefcase had been pushed, shielded Hitler from the full blast of the explosion, and he survived relatively unscathed. In the wake of the July Plot the reign of terror was intensified to an extraordinary degree. Not only were the main participants in the plot arrested and killed in the most gruesome manner, but thousands more were also rounded up, imprisoned, tortured and in many cases put to death. Penalties for even the most minor 'crimes against the regime' in the winter of 1944–5 were increased, so that thousands of ordinary Germans were executed for such offences as listening to foreign radio broadcasts or making political jokes, as the many agonising detailed case-histories in Berlin's Plotzensee jail testify.

THE HISTORY OF NATIONS
Chapter 5

Divided Postwar Germany and Reunification

Occupation and Denazification

BY MARY FULBROOK

After the defeat of Germany in World War II, the Allies (England, France, Russia, and the United States) divided the nation into four zones of occupation. Mary Fulbrook, a professor of German history at University College in London, examines in the following selection some of the problems Germany faced during its occupation. Besides issues of war reparations and establishing new borders, Fulbrook discusses the challenges that "denazification" posed to the occupation powers as well as to the Germans themselves. Assigning blame for the atrocities of war at the Nuremberg Trials as well as later trials against Nazis served to restore the rule of law to Germany. But, as Fulbrook argues, such public finger-pointing also raised the uncomfortable—and largely avoided—question of how guilty each German citizen was of supporting the Nazi regime and its heinous crimes.

When Germany was defeated in May 1945, a demoralized population was living among ruins. The big cities that had suffered bombardment from the air were reduced to piles of rubble between gaunt, hollow shells of bombed out buildings, lone walls with empty windows forming a jagged skyline, the occasional intact building standing out starkly amidst the ruins. People eked out an uncomfortable existence in cellars. In towns and villages which had escaped the worst attacks of the Allies, conditions were nevertheless comparably demoralizing, as women worried about husbands and sons at the front, and about the need for food and clothing for the children and old people at home. Enthusiasm for Hitler, and for his war, had been waning steadily since the turn of the war's fortunes with the Russian campaign, and faith in the omnipotent Führer had given way to weariness and a longing for the end of war. Yet there was no knowing exactly what the post-war period would bring. Some Germans longed for 'liberation' and the possibility of a radical transformation of Germany; others felt fear and ambivalence about future retribution. When hostilities ceased in May 1945, few could have predicted what the future would bring. Yet in the following four years patterns were developed and set which were to stamp their mark on the next four decades of German—and international—history.

The Allies and the Framework of Political Life

Initially the Allies themselves were not at all certain what to do with post-war Germany. There were differences of opinion both between the Allies—particularly between the Soviet Union and the Western powers—and within each Allied regime. In practice, the developments following the defeat of Germany laid the foundations for the double transformation that subsequently occurred: the establishment of a divided nation, with a relatively conservative, arguably 'restorationist' state in the West, and a hardline communist state in the East. In neither Germany was the 'Third Way' taken, for which many democratic, anti-fascist Germans had hoped—the transformation which would combine democracy and socialism, while also permitting German unity and neutrality. While the division and remilitarization of the two Germanies—and their relative 'conservatism', although of differing political complexions—only became crystallized in the course of the 1950s, the initial steps in this bifurcation can be seen even in the very early stages of the occupation period.

The Division into Four Zones

During the war, a range of options for the future of Germany—pending what all agreed should be an unconditional surrender—were mooted. Some advocated relatively mild treatment, others harsh and punitive handling; some sought the retention of a relatively centralized, if federal, state, others radical dismemberment and division into a number of smaller countries which could pose no threat to the balance of power in central Europe. There were differences of opinion between, for example, American President Roosevelt and his State Department; British Prime Minister Churchill and the British Military and the British Foreign Office; as well as, more obviously, between the Soviet Union, the Americans and the British. One of the few decisions which emerged from wartime planning which was however to have decisive long-term significance was the agreement on zones of occupation. A map (emanating from the Post-Hostilities Planning Subcommittee in September 1943) was put before the European Advisory Committee in London in January 1944, and accepted by the Soviets in February 1944. This proposed three zones of occupation—and in the event drew the line of what was subsequently to become the East-West division of Europe and the international system. In September 1944 it was agreed that Berlin should be under four-power control, and a little later a Control Commission for the co-ordination of Allied occupation policies was decided upon.

At [conferences in] Tehran (28 November–1 December 1943) and Yalta (4–11 February 1945) there was vague and general agreement in principle on the need to demilitarize, denazify and democratize Germany. It was also agreed at Yalta that France should have a zone of occupation. There was by now some friction and unease over this question: the original zones had been drawn to give rough parity of population numbers in each of the British, American and Soviet zones—thus in effect giving the Soviets a much larger land area, since much of their zone was less densely populated agricultural land. The early agreement over zones had been facilitated by Western fears that the Red Army might in fact have overrun most or all of Germany by the end of the war, and would then be committed or forced to retreat to its previously determined occupation zone. However, in fact by the war's end it was the western allies who had advanced deeper into Germany than they had expected; and it was western troops who eventually had to withdraw from areas that were to form part of the Soviet zone. By the spring of 1945, this position had become clearer, and the western powers hoped that France would gain her zone at the expense of the Soviets. This was however opposed, and France's zone was carved out of western territory in south-west Germany. Disagreements between the Allies also continued over questions concerning the form and level reparations should take, the eastern boundaries of Germany with Poland, and the future shape of Germany itself.

These problems continued to bedevil the Potsdam Conference of 17 July–2 August 1945. Although the war was over, with the surrender of German troops to the Allies on 7–8 May 1945, there could be no Peace Treaty since there was no German government with which to conclude one. The eventual Protocol of Proceedings emanating from the Potsdam Conference was a vaguely worded compromise—again assenting to broad and laudable aims, such as demilitarization, denazification, and democratization—which left many areas open to a variety of interpretations. . . .

Denazification

The problems facing the Allies in 1945 were immensely complex. They had to administer a war-torn country, attempt to get basic transport and communications functioning again, feed and house the hundreds of thousands—eventually millions—of refugees fleeing or expelled from former eastern homelands, and combat problems of homelessness, malnutrition and disease among the native population. At the same time, they had to be extremely suspicious of those Germans who were in a position to help administer affairs; they had to deal with the problem of taking over a society which had been run by Nazis and immersed in Nazism for over a decade.

Along with democratization, denazification was an agreed aim of all the occupying powers. It was generally accepted that in some way Germany must be cleansed of Nazis, that those guilty of sustaining Nazi rule must be punished, and that it was essential, if future peace was to be secured, that Germans should be convinced of the error of Nazi views and persuaded to assent to more democratic and peaceful values. Yet it was not at all clear how these various goals should be effected. In practice, the Allies in different ways stumbled through a series of changing conceptualizations and policies which produced their own quite curious and frequently wayward effects. Neither the negative tasks relating to denazification, nor the more positive programmes of re-education, could be said to amount to a straightforward success story in either the western or eastern zones.

The Nuremberg Trials

The only part of these processes in which all the Allies collaborated was that of the Nuremberg Trials of the major war criminals. These lasted from 20 November 1945 to 1 October 1946. The war guilt of individuals was investigated, as well as that of the German government, the General Staff of the Army, the SA, the SS, the SD [Nazi paramilitary organizations], the Gestapo [Nazi secret police], and leaders of the [National Socialist Party]

(NSDAP). The government and the Army General Staff were cleared in general terms, but the other organizations mentioned were declared to be criminal....

The Nuremberg trials raised a host of questions, legal, moral and political. To what extent could people be punished for actions which were not at the time a crime? Had war atrocities only been committed on the German side, and was it not simply a case of 'might makes right', with the victors claiming a spurious moral superiority over the vanquished? Would the German public not simply gain sympathy with their leaders who were on trial, and not really believe—or become immune to—the evidence of the atrocities that had been committed in their name? Despite initial war-time discussions about possible vengeance on a mass scale, the Allies finally agreed that it was important to restore a sense of the rule of law and justice in Germany; but in some respects the Nuremberg trials did not adequately fulfill these tasks. Nevertheless, these and succeeding war crimes trials did serve to raise a host of questions about the nature of guilt in Nazi Germany, such as that concerning the relative importance of giving orders from behind a desk far removed from the actual scene of the crime, or the implications of following orders and committing acts of the utmost inhumanity under threat and duress.

Later Trials

Individuals continued to be investigated and tried for alleged war crimes by the Germans and other affected governments for decades after the end of the war. The German statute of limitations, which set a limit of twenty years in prosecutions for murder, was lifted in 1969 to allow continued prosecutions for war crimes. Many criticisms have been raised about the Nazi war crimes trials. At first, it seemed that the Germans were less than energetic in pursuing prosecutions. A Central Office of *Land* [State] Justice Departments was established at Ludwigsburg, near Stuttgart, in 1958 to co-ordinate investigations. By the end of 1964—two decades after the end of the war—it had just over seven hundred cases in hand, leading to the trials of the later 1960s. Much of the credit for tracking down former Nazis must be given to the Simon Wiesenthal Centre, set up by a Jew who was determined neither to let the perpetrators of atrocities retire into happy civilian life nor to leave the nature of their crimes unrecorded. In the process of acquiring testimonies and accumulat-

ing evidence of the post-war fates and whereabouts of former
Nazis, uncomfortable facts were discovered about the Allies' own
treatment of some of them after the war. In particular, certain
Nazis had been found very useful by the US government in its efforts to combat Communism in the Cold War, and had therefore
been protected and aided in their disappearance in the post-war
period. But despite both this sort of revelation, and the mounting
and perpetually disturbing evidence of Nazi atrocities, later war
trials gave rise to a range of criticisms. Elderly, pathetic figures were
being brought to account for deeds committed in their youth, and
while it could be fairly said that the disturbance to their health,
reputation, tranquil retirement or family life was totally incom-
mensurable with the appalling deeds for which they were being
tried, legal aspects of some of the trials gave rise to concern. War
crimes trials were increasingly hampered, too, by such problems as
the reliability and availability of eye-witness testimony and of
other evidence, decades after the events which were alleged to have
occurred. They could however be justified in a number of ways,
including the importance of educating a younger generation.

How to Rebuild Society

In the immediate post-war period, trials of individual war criminals could hardly help to deal with the far broader question of
what to do with, and how to transform, a society which had been
imbued with Nazism at all sorts of levels and in a variety of ways.
At the more general level, that of the transformation of German
society, what denazification meant in detail depended on a variety of factors: on theories of the nature and roots of Nazism as
a sociopolitical system; on assumptions about German society,
about the bases of certain beliefs and behaviour, and the social
determination or social location of political guilt; and on considerations about the exigencies of post-war reconstruction. 'The
major difference was between the Soviet interpretation of
Nazism as rooted in certain socio-economic conditions, with the
correlate that the eradication of Nazism required major struc-
tural change, and the more individualistic, psychological western
interpretations of the problem.

Who Was Guilty?

Even within the western camp there were considerable differences of interpretation. Some held the extreme view that all Ger-

mans were bad Germans, and endorsed the notion of 'collective guilt'—which initially informed at least American policy in Germany. Others wished to distinguish between real Nazis, nominal Nazis, and non- and anti-Nazi Germans. Once the principle of distinction was accepted, the problem arose of the criteria by which people could be thus classified. Left-wing and Marxist-influenced intellectuals in Britain and America held the view that certain prominent social groups bore a greater burden of responsibility than others. But, in practice, after the initial period when automatic arrest categories were employed (for example, for SS personnel), the question was refocused at the individual level, and the task became one of trying to find appropriate external indices or evidence for internal predispositions and states of mind. The complications proved to be immense. For example, Party membership might indicate commitment to Nazi ideals; it might indicate (as for those joining after it became compulsory for certain professional groups in 1937) a desire to support one's family by retaining one's job; it might even indicate a desire to work against Nazism from within, or to fill a position for fear of replacement by someone worse. More problematic, membership could subsequently be represented as having been motivated by the highest ideals, there being no real means of checking claims about inner state against ambiguous external evidence. Most people could in any case persuade themselves of the acceptability and justifiability of their actions, and produce appropriate testimonies to their character, forgetting the ambivalence, the compromises, and the baser considerations of the past. Important, too, were the practical problems of implementation, the unintended effects, and the other considerations which arose to alter the subsequent course of denazification. In no zone did denazification present a simple, clear, consistent story.

Konrad Adenauer: "We Belong to the West"

BY *TIME*

Time magazine nominated Konrad Adenauer, the first chancellor of West Germany, "man of the year" for 1953. The following article appeared in the first Time issue of that year. It describes Adenauer as the man who helped turn West Germany into one of the most powerful European countries shortly after the crippling defeat in World War II. He is also portrayed as the one responsible for West Germany's turn toward the Western Allies, giving up on the people's wish for immediate reunification with Communist East Germany. Adenauer feared reunification could have turned all of Germany into a satellite of the Soviet Union.

On a mild morning last April, a band of dignitaries gathered before the Tomb of the Unknown Soldier in Arlington National Cemetery. In the place of honor stood a tall old man whose somber mask of a face looked stiffly ahead. Before him, stretching to the hilltop, was an array of granite pillars, blocks and crosses—the graves of Americans who had died in two wars with Germany. Behind him fluttered the black, red and gold flag of the Federal Republic of Germany.

The U.S. Army band sounded "The Star-Spangled Banner." Then it broke into the measured strains of "Deutschland über alles" [the German national anthem]. "This," murmured the old man, "is a turning point in history."

More dramatically than headline or speech or essay, the music symbolized an amazing story. In 1953, only eight years after the shame, horror and impotence of defeat in mankind's bloodiest war, Germany came back. It was a world power once more. More than any other, the person who brought this about was the stolid old man who stood in Arlington, visibly moved by the strains of his national anthem echoing among the tombstones. He was Konrad Adenauer, Chancellor of the West German Republic, apostle of United Europe, 1953's Man of the Year.

Konrad Adenauer had already guided the hated land of the Hun [disparaging term for Germans during WWI] and the Nazi back to moral respectability and had earned himself a seat in the highest councils of the Western powers. Though she still lacked a formal peace treaty, and the Iron Curtain fenced her off from half her land and from 18 million countrymen, Konrad Adenauer's West Germany last year emerged as the strongest country on the Continent save Soviet Russia.

Her conquerors wooed her for her favors. Neighbors who had helped defeat her so short a time ago talked fearfully once more of her new strength and her even greater potential. Her economy glowed with health. Her products cascaded into the world's markets. In September came an election which the whole world nervously watched, to see whether the oil of democracy could mix with the vinegar of German authoritarianism. The West German voters swept all their Communists and Nazis out of national office and overwhelmingly put their faith in the dedicated, firm-handed democrat, Konrad Adenauer. No longer the passive object of other forces, Germany in 1953 was again one of the formidable forces of history and Konrad Adenauer one of history's makers.

"This year," said the Man of the Year, "is the year in which the re-emergence of Germany . . . changed the world picture." . . .

Creatures of Destiny

It was a year in which the so-called big powers, Eastern and Western alike, seemed less the shapers of destiny than its creatures. The change in the hands which governed the two greatest powers brought a strange sense of indecisiveness to world affairs. The strain of the cold war brought hesitations and serious arguments to the Western Alliance. The dawning of the thermonuclear age, with its talk of megaton bombs (equal to 1,000,000 tons of TNT), cast great and sudden doubt on the validity of the thinking and the plans of statesmen and diplomats and soldiers. Both sides were caught in a sort of pause, to re-examine and to retool. It was in this atmosphere of confusion, holding back and reassessment that the unhesitant, unconfused, unswerving re-emergence of West Germany made its mark on 1953.

Energy, Ambition, Work

Like so many turning points, it was a long time in the reaching, but it was a shorter time than even the most sanguine German had a right to expect when he crawled from the smoking rubble one day in 1945 to learn that the Nazi Reich was no more. And, as with most great, historic turns, it was made possible by countless events. There was the decay of the wartime Alliance, Russia's shortsighted intransigence in the German occupation. There was the West's decision to form one unified country of West Germany without waiting for a peace treaty. There was the Berlin blockade, which jolted the West into the urgency of rearmament; the Korean war, which shocked it into the decision that it needed German troops as well. There was some $3.3 billion in U.S. aid to Germany. There was the privilege of concentrating on building industries and markets while West Germany's conquerors bent to the ordeal of arming themselves. There were the uprisings in East Germany. Above all, there was the happy combination of energy, ambition, and respect for work which distinguishes the German.

In this mixture of happenstance, deliberate policy, improvised decisions and national persistence can be found the explanation for the speed of West Germany's comeback. But the ideas and leadership of Konrad Adenauer explain, more than anything else, the character of the comeback.

When the Western Allies stumbled upon him right after V-E Day [Victory in Europe Day, May 8, 1945], Konrad Adenauer was just an old man in a high, starched collar, stern and vigorous and proud, already well into the twilight of his life. In his three-score-and-ten, his homeland had soared and sunk through two great historical phases and entered a third. Two of these phases Konrad Adenauer had lived out in a routine of efficient ordinariness and relative obscurity. He was born (Jan. 5, 1876) in the age of [Prussian chancellor Otto von] Bismarck; he was already 42 when the Kaiser fell. Through the sad days of the Weimar Republic and the ugly early days of Naziism he was respected as veteran mayor of Cologne and a wily politician, until he was forced out of office by the Nazis, for whom he showed nothing but flinty scorn. Had he died at 70, he would not have rated a paragraph in most U.S. newspapers.

He lived not only to see a third phase of German history, but to mold it.

He Will Have It

"I remember a meeting of the Cologne municipal council in 1918," Adenauer wrote recently. "As mayor, I wanted to see the old fortifications circling the city replaced not by factories or houses crowded together, but by a refreshing green girdle of parks. No one on the council agreed. I began to feel that I would have to capitulate. Then ... I went all the way in marshaling my data. ... After I had presented the facts at several meetings, all the councilmen but one were convinced. Finally, that one rose and said: 'Let him have his way—he will have it anyhow!'"

Germans, Western occupiers and Russian antagonists have all since learned to know how that lone Cologne holdout felt. To the occupiers, Adenauer has proved a rugged bargainer—tireless, insistent, all but immovable. "We are not an African tribe," he snapped one day, "but a Central European nation proud of its country." On another occasion: "It was the German army and not the German people that capitulated, and this the world had better remember." One day in 1949, when Adenauer visited U.S. High Commissioner John J. McCloy, the two men fell into a Gaston & Alphonse routine at the door. "After you, Chancellor," said McCloy, "I'm at home here." A chill smile flickered on Adenauer's flat, leathery face. "No, no," said he, "after you, Mr. McCloy."

To Germans he also talked sternly. When they complained of occupation pressures, or of the slowness of Allied decontrol, he stopped them with one indignant question: "Who do you think won the war?" He preached: "We must part with concepts of the past. When you fall from the heights as we Germans have, you realize it is necessary to break with what has been. We cannot live fruitfully with lost illusions. I do not believe in fairy tales."

Christians Hold Together

What Adenauer does believe is the key to the strategy he has followed to reconstruct Germany and to promote the construction of Europe. He believes that:

- A Christian civilization must hold together politically or perish before Communism.
- West Germany would be swallowed up as a Red satellite if

it tried to remain neutral and play Russia against the West.

- West Germany must some day be reunited with the German land east of the Iron Curtain, but that day will come only when the Western world stands strong enough to force—without war—a Soviet withdrawal from Central Europe. He refuses to recognize the Oder-Neisse frontier, but is ready to promise not to cross it with troops.
- West Germany must earn the West's trust and confidence by demonstrating that its lesson has been learned in the two disastrous German adventures of the 20th century.
- Germany still cannot be trusted to rearm by itself. "It is no secret," said a close associate, "that he considers Prussians savage and dangerous."
- Nevertheless, the rearmament of Germany is inevitable; if it is not armed as a part of a supranational army, with controls on its size and use, then it will be armed with a new national *Wehrmacht* [German army].
- Far greater than the need for German troops is Europe's need to unite—politically, militarily and psychologically—those historic antagonists in war, Germany and France.

"I deem it false . . . to speak of German rearmament," Adenauer said not long ago. "This is an expression which has no place in those new forms toward which we are striving. We want nothing of the old. We do not want to restore a national army."

By "those new forms," Adenauer means the European Defense Community (EDC). The idea came, providentially, from France. Germans could not propose it without risking the impression that it was simply a cunning maneuver to unlock the occupation shackles and revive the *Wehrmacht*. But when the enemy from across the Rhine proposed it in 1950, Konrad Adenauer could more easily champion it.

The Dream Fades

The U.S. made EDC the core of its European policy. Britain supported it. Italy could hardly wait to approve it. The Benelux [Belgium, Netherlands, and Luxembourg] countries got behind it.

But by 1953, the clear dream had clouded over. The sharp-beaked vagaries of politics tore at the men who did most to shape and promote the EDC idea. First, down went Good European Robert Schuman, France's longtime Foreign Minister. He was thrown aside because France, tortured by division and illusion, turned in confusion and fear from its own brain child. Next went Good European [Italian prime minister] Alcide de Gasperi, and Italy's ratification became questionable. The death of [Soviet leader Joseph] Stalin, and [British prime minister Winston] Churchill's insistence on sounding out the dictator's successor, gave the French more opportunity to haggle and hesitate. The EDC idea was close to dying.

Then came West Germany's time to decide. EDC meant several unpalatable things to Germans. Two disasters in half a century had been enough; thousands wanted never to bear arms again. On the other side, Nationalists balked at joining hands with the French, and oldtime professional soldiers seethed at the "disgrace" of banning for good the *Wehrmacht* and General Staff. Joining in with the West, they argued, might turn the East-West German boundary into a 38th parallel and Germany into another Korea. It might seal off forever the Communist-held lands to the East. Would it not be smarter, more comfortable, less dangerous, to stay uncommitted and play off the fears of both sides?

Across West Germany, tireless, graven-faced Konrad Adenauer campaigned bluntly on the issue of United Europe. His main opponents, the socialists, bluntly campaigned against it. Germans had a clear-cut choice. "Our country," said Adenauer, "is the point of tension between two world blocs . . . Long ago I made a great decision: we belong to the West and not to the East . . . Isolation is an idea created by fools. It would mean that the U.S. would withdraw its troops from Europe. Ladies and gentlemen, the moment that happens, Germany will become a satellite."

On Sept. 6, the people of West Germany walked up to two doors to the future. Which would they choose? Western diplomats, disheartened by the fall of Schuman and De Gasperi, guessed timidly that Adenauer and the dream of Europe would squeak through—but barely. But the old man in the high, starched collar simply rode up to his Rhondorf home, went off to Sunday Mass, left order not to be disturbed, and at day's end turned in for a long night's sleep.

The Flag of Europe

The results astounded even composed Konrad Adenauer. From the historic election, no party was left strong enough to challenge Konrad Adenauer's Christian Democrats, and no person or bloc within the Christian Democrats was left strong enough to chal-

lenge Konrad Adenauer. When his followers gathered at the
Chancellery steps next morning to salute him, Adenauer smiled
his thoughtful, deep-frozen smile. "Perhaps," said he, "we have
won by a little too much."

Adenauer's victory was a victory for Europe, and the West's
big cold-war success of 1953. When the striped German flag was
raised in post-election triumph above the Chancellor's Palais
Schaumburg, the green and white flag of European unity was
run up alongside it. "The elections," said Konrad Adenauer, "have
decided that Europe will come about, that the EDC will come
about, and that the cold war is lost for Russia."

By 1953's end, his certainty was not so widely shared. France
might or might not ratify EDC. But Germany's vote had saved it
from death in 1953, and kept alive the hope that in 1954, Europe
might yet be born.

If the European dream does come true, Adenauer will go
down in history as one of its creators. If it fails, his efforts will
still have served Germany well. He has won her respectability.

At the Big Three's [France, Britain, and the United States]
Bermuda conference, the absent, uninvited Chancellor of West
Germany was even more a participant than France's ailing Premier, who spoke scarcely a word. Before dispatching to Moscow
their agreement to a Big Four conference in Berlin, the Big
Three leaders solicited Adenauer's approval. When Prime Minister Churchill suggested it might be wise to consider some alternative to EDC for Germany's rearmament, President Eisenhower dismissed the proposal with a wave of his hand. The U.S.
will not consider alternatives, said the President, and besides,
"EDC is what Adenauer wants."

Decisive Events

West Germany has won this place at the council table despite the
fact that it is still nominally an occupied country, and has yet to
arm a single soldier, build a plane or roll out a tank.

Seated one day last week in his huge office in the Palais
Schaumburg, Chacellor Adenauer made a temple of his fingers
and, chatting with *Time* correspondent Frank White, allowed
himself the luxury of some mild self-satisfaction. "I cannot
avoid smiling a little when, as chief of an occupied country, I
sit down with the leaders of the occupying nations, such as Mr.
Eden and M. Bidault. In spite of the fact that Germany hasn't

yet full sovereignty, its economic and political impact is fully felt in world affairs."

Adenauer had his own list of "the decisive events" of the year: "The clear and determined attitude" of the U.S. to take the lead in the struggle against Communism, the uprisings in East Germany, his own election victory, and President Eisenhower's atomic pool proposal, which Adenauer believes "may well be the beginning of real understanding between East and West." Stalin's death, he says, was "not a factor of major importance." It did not increase the chances for peace. "Stalin had the power and prestige to alter the course of Kremlin foreign policy. His successors have not."

Adenauer has some advance worries for 1954: "There is wind in the air, and the sky is not without clouds." Biggest clouds: indecision in France, the approaching four-power conference on Germany, the state of mind of the U.S. Congress.

As for France: ". . . The French people have a much clearer conception [of EDC] than does the French Parliament . . . I am convinced the French will finally agree to the formation of an integrated Europe."

On four-power negotiations: "The hope that the Soviets have altered their course is unfounded. Their strategy for the Berlin conference is mainly that of delay . . . The three [Western] ministers must maintain an undivided front. Russia will attempt to weaken the French will to ratify EDC. If successful . . . it would be Russia's greatest triumph."

On Congress: "I fully understand that there should be impatience. I confidently hope, however, that as much as they dislike what happens, they will be wise enough not to stop giving [moral] assistance and [financial] support at this critical moment, when final success is in sight."

"The first six months of 1954 will be decisive."

Near the Heart

As far as it went, the story of Germany's rise in 1953 was good for the democracies and bad for Communism. But other years and other men will determine whether there will be a happy ending. Konrad Adenauer is 78 this month. In the frost of his rigid, imperious command over machinery of both party and government, few sprouts of leadership have been able to grow. "How long I can hold my present office no one can tell," he said.

"Even I cannot. My health and strength are excellent. Nothing, however, is nearer my heart than that before I go . . . I shall have brought Germany securely into the community of free and democratic peoples of the Christian West . . ."

The question mark of the future intrudes like a brooding outsider on the encouraging spectacle of a West Germany healthily revived, strongly and democratically led, dedicated by its electorate to a United Europe as well as to a new Germany. "We never question Adenauer's sincerity when he talks of Franco-German agreement," said a top French diplomat. "He is truly European . . . But we don't forget another German, Stresemann, who wanted good relations with France. Six months after he died [1929], what happened? His party and policy collapsed."

Konrad Adenauer himself has also seen the brooding outsider. If the dream of Europe collapses, there is, he fears, the possibility of a revival of German militarism. "I never minimize this possibility if Europe fails," said he last week. "If France refuses to accept reconciliation with her former enemy, how we would accept the effect of such a reversal I do not know . . . The whole population would be affected. We cannot say what would happen. But we have had experience in the past."

"Perhaps I had better not die yet awhile," said Konrad Adenauer. "There is still too much to do."

The Soviet Union and Its East German Ally

By Jeffrey Gedmin

In the following article, Jeffrey Gedmin discusses the relationship between the Soviet Union and occupied East Germany, which became known as the German Democratic Republic (GDR) in 1949. In the course of his analysis, Gedmin concludes that the Soviet occupation force had not been in favor of the creation of a German republic, preferring instead to simply extend Soviet rule into the German state. As Gedmin sees it, the East German Communists desired to build their own nation, constantly struggling for sovereignty and recognition from the occupation force. Gedmin is a resident scholar at the American Enterprise Institute.

The German Democratic Republic is forever and irrevocably allied with the Union of Soviet Socialist Republics.

> —Article Six of the GDR's
> 1974 amended constitution

The closer the friendship with the Soviet Union, the better socialism in one's own country develops.... We adhere to the well-established principle that the attitude toward the CPSU [Communist Party of the Soviet Union] and the USSR is a touchstone of faithfulness to Marxism-Leninism and to the revolutionary cause of the working class.

> —Erich Honecker (leader of the GDR
> from 1976 to 1989), *The German Democratic
> Republic: Pillar of Peace and Socialism,* 1979

East German leaders had always understood that their very existence depended on the presence of Soviet troops on GDR soil. In the years before [Soviet premier] Mikhail Gorbachev's ascendancy to power in March 1985, the Soviet Union's relationship with the GDR was characterized by immensely profitable cooperation in a number of ways.

Ideologically, the GDR had established itself as the most loyal of Moscow's East European client states, a model of orthodox communism. The fact that Moscow had concentrated in East Germany its greatest number of troops outside the boundaries of the USSR underscored the country's strategic importance. Economically, since the 1960s the GDR had been the Soviet Union's most important trading partner (providing 10 percent of Soviet trade) and a major supplier of chemical products and industrial equipment. In the international arena, the East German state had become, next to Cuba, Moscow's most important proxy in providing economic, military, and security assistance to Communist allies from the Sandinistas in Nicaragua to Marxist movements and regimes across Africa and Asia.

Nevertheless, the GDR's position of relative security in its relationship with the Soviet Union had not come easily. And after four decades of political and economic consolidation, the longevity of an East German Communist state still precariously depended on the good offices of Soviet interest and power. Honecker never lost sight of the unshakable fact that the GDR's friendship with the Soviet Union was, as he put it, "decisive for the foundation of our existence," a "vital necessity." Thus more than anywhere else in Eastern Europe, as [historian] Timothy Garton Ash later observed, in East Germany Gorbachev's effect was most critical.

Should There Be One or Two Germanys?

Even before the end of World War II, Soviet officials had been engaged in laying the groundwork for a Communist administration in the Soviet zone of occupation in Germany. The country's division was by no means a self-evident tenet of Moscow's initial postwar policy on Europe, as Soviet authorities first sought to project their power across the entire country. Even once the sovereignty of the GDR appeared ensured by the mid-1950, East Berlin's relationship with Moscow was subsequently marked at times by suspicion, distrust, and ambiguity.

At the Potsdam conference held in July and August 1945, the United States, Great Britain, and the Soviet Union agreed to treat Germany as an economic whole and to administer it jointly. For the course of an interim period of unstipulated length, five or more central departments were to administer the Allied Control Council's policies. During this time within the Soviet leadership two schools of thought on the future of Germany soon became evident.

One faction within the Soviet leadership, represented by Politburo [the highest committee in the CPSU] member Andrei Zhdanov and Sergei Tiul'panov, chief of the information bureau of the Soviet Military Administration in the occupation zone from 1945 to 1949, advocated vigorous and rapid communization of the Soviet-occupied territory. They believed that Soviet security interests would be best served by two Germanys, not one, no matter the conditions.

A second faction was represented by Vladimir S. Semenov, political adviser to the supreme commander and military governor of the zone, and USSR secret service (KGB) chief Lavrenti Beria (later, posthumously, accused by [Nikita] Khrushchev [premier of the Soviet Union from 1958 to 1964] at the Twentieth Party Congress of the CPSU of attempting to sell out the GDR). They favored a less confrontational policy that appeared to leave open the possibility of a unified but neutralized Germany that would secure a dominant Soviet influence in Europe, minimally through a Rapallo type of agreement [a pact guided by Germany's desire for friendly political, military, and economic relations with the Soviet Union] and maximally through the communization of a united German state.

After the war the Semenov-Beria faction sought to exploit fertile ground in the western zones for the idea of Germany's neutralization. The Social Democratic party's leader, Kurt Schumacher, though a virulent anti-Communist, was nonetheless a determined advocate of a united, neutral Germany and represented a prospective partner for this Soviet group. Even members of what eventually became [West German chancellor] Konrad Adenauer's Christian Democratic Union—chief advocate of Western integration—were initially sympathetic to the idea of a neutral German government as a bridge between East and West.

Precisely because these competing views within the Soviet leadership were becoming increasingly evident, the East German

Communists learned from the beginning that a sense of insecurity was neither paranoid nor overreactive. Just seventeen months after the founding of the Socialist Unity party (in April of 1946), the East German Communists were treated to their first hint of Moscow's ambivalence. The Soviets stung their East German

THE BERLIN AIRLIFT

On June 24, 1948, the Soviet occupation force under Joseph Stalin cut off all supply routes into West Berlin, which was held by the Western allies. West Berlin was encircled, but the Americans came up with the bold plan to build an air bridge in order to bring food and medication into the city.

When Germany surrendered in 1945, the victorious Allies divided the country into four occupation zones according to the terms of the Potsdam agreement. The Soviet Union occupied the eastern portion of Germany and the eastern sector of Berlin, while Britain, France, and the United States took control of the western zones of Germany and the rest of Berlin. The non-Soviet sectors of Berlin lay 110 miles within the Soviet zone, connected to the Anglo-American-French zones of occupied Germany by highway, railroad, and three air corridors.

On June 18, 1948, the United States, Britain, and France announced plans to create a unified West German currency. Objecting to the unified West German state implied by the currency as well as the circulation of the currency in western Berlin, Soviet premier Joseph Stalin cut land routes between western Germany and Berlin on June 24. The blockade separated two million West Berliners from their normal sources of supply.

The Western powers had four options: they could abandon Berlin, cancel the currency reform, force an armored column through the Soviet zone and risk war, or airlift supplies to Berlin until the crisis could be solved diplomatically. They chose the last option Both the U.S. Air Force and the Royal

comrades when they not only failed to invite them to the first meeting of the Cominform [executive committee of the Eastern Block] in September 1947, a meeting to which even the French and Italian Communists were invited, but also neglected to inform them that the meeting was scheduled to take place.

Air Force (RAF) participated, with the Americans calling the operation "Vittles" and the British calling it "Plain Fare."

Rarely in history had airlift alone saved a large encircled population. Western economic experts estimated that western Berlin would need at least 4,500 tons of coal and food per day to survive the Soviet blockade. . . .

Operation Vittles exceeded expectations. On April 16, 1949, U.S. and British aircraft delivered a record 12,941 tons of coal and food to Berlin. First Lieutenant Gail S. Halvorsen supplemented the regular airlift by dropping candy attached to handkerchief parachutes to the children of Berlin, a practice which was dubbed "Operation Little Vittles." Such success stories reinforced Western support for the airlift and eventually reached beyond the Iron Curtain.

Finally convinced that the Berlin blockade was not achieving its goals, the Soviets reopened land routes between western Germany and Berlin on May 12, 1949. . . .

The Berlin Airlift, the largest humanitarian airlift operation in history, was militarily and diplomatically significant. Operation Vittles proved above all that airlift could sustain a large population surrounded by hostile forces. The non-Soviet sectors of Berlin escaped absorption by the communist zone, while the western zones of Germany continued moving toward unified democratic statehood. Demonstrating the commitment of the United States to contain Soviet expansion, the Berlin Airlift saved the city without war. It exemplified the ability of the western Allies to work together against a common enemy, and the North Atlantic Treaty Organization (NATO) was born during the airlift.

Daniel L. Haulman, *The United States Air Force and Humanitarian Airlift Operations, 1947–1994.* Washington, DC: U.S. Government Printing Office, 1998.

Even two weeks before the GDR's founding on October 11, a delegation comprising the East German Communists' top leadership—Walter Ulbricht, Otto Grotewohl, Wilhelm Pieck, and Fred Oelssner—made a secret twelve-day visit to Moscow. During this time the East Germans may well have worked to gain assurances that Moscow was firmly committed to East Germany's sovereignty.

When the German Democratic Republic was finally founded on October 11, 1949, "Stalin sent the GDR a telegram of congratulations," writes British historian David Childs, "but not much else." It is true that Stalin praised the founding of the East German state as a "turning point in the history of Europe," whose existence along with that of the Soviet Union excluded "the possibilities of new wars in Europe." But that Soviet diplomatic representatives still kept the door open for some form of German unity, however, at least suggests that the Soviets had not fully decided on one Germany or two.

The historian Norman M. Naimark argues that both before and after Stalin's famous proposal of March 10, 1952, to the Allied Powers for the creation of a neutral, demilitarized, united Germany, the Soviet Union may have been prepared "under the appropriate circumstances to cashier its East German partner in exchange for a neutral Germany." Indeed, in the early years of its existence, the GDR appeared to serve the Soviet Union principally as a source of desperately needed war reparations and as an instrument of political leverage in shaping the landscape of the new Europe. Interestingly, only after 1955 did the Soviets, long after having formalized their relations with the other East bloc states, sign a state treaty with the GDR.

In this atmosphere of uncertainty the East German Communists had felt compelled to work all the more intensely to win the favor and confidence of their Soviet patrons to justify their existence. Since the 1948 rupture between the Soviet Union and Yugoslavia, Ulbricht had vigorously purged the party to decimate internal opposition but also to assure the Soviets of the unconditional loyalty and reliability of the East German Communist regime in the Socialist camp. According to the East German party's own accounts, although party membership was on the rise, some 150,696 unreliable individuals, either party members or candidates for party membership, were expelled from the ranks between 1948 and 1952.

Stalin's Death

[Former Soviet premier] Stalin's death on March 5, 1953, triggered a new episode in Soviet East German relations. Ulbricht responded to the death of "the greatest human being of our epoch" with a flurry of publications of the writings and speeches of Stalin. From Mecklenburg to Saxony, new monuments were erected, and bleak and sparsely supplied East German shops became inundated with souvenir busts and other memorabilia of the great Soviet leader. GDR authorities changed the name of the city Eisenhüttenstadt, near the Polish border, to Stalinstadt (it was later renamed Eisenhüttenstadt).

The difficulty was, though, at the same time Ulbricht was raising the Soviet dictator's personality cult in the GDR to new heights, a power struggle had broken out within the Soviet leaderships. The faction of the Soviet Communists that advocated a more moderate German policy, a course that would endanger the security of hard-liner Ulbricht (perhaps even the GDR itself), was maneuvering to gain advantage. And indeed this Soviet faction, by no means averse to meddling in the internal politics of the East German party, had already found a compatible group within its leadership. The Soviet Semenov-Beria group began to offer direct support to Ulbricht's rivals, Rudolf Herrnstadt and Wilhelm Zaisser, editor in chief of *Neues Deutschland* and minister of state security, respectively, who were also committed to slowing the GDR's increasingly rapid march to socialism. It is in fact "tempting," as [historian] Martin McCauley has observed, to see the work of these Soviet East German collaborators as devoted to "a plan to prepare the way for a united Germany."

Of even greater, more immediate concern was the charge of Ulbricht's critics that East Berlin's overly aggressive industrialization policies, first announced at the Second Party Congress in July 1952, were destabilizing the country. Evidence of this, anti-Ulbricht forces argued, was the rising number of East Germans fleeing to the West, depleting an already listless, debilitated work force. In 1951, 165,648 East German refugees were registered by West German authorities. Despite efforts by the Communist regime to secure the internal German border in the summer of 1952, the number still rose by the end of the year to 182,393— over half the refugees were under twenty-five years of age. In 1953, 331,390 East Germans were received in the West, though many thousands more undoubtedly entered West Germany without bothering to register with refugee officials.

The June Uprising

During the spring of 1953, the Soviet "moderate" line, seizing opportunities afforded by Stalin's death in March, was inching toward greater leverage in Moscow. At this time, the Soviet faction led by KGB chief Beria began to exert pressure on East Berlin to "halt [its] accelerated construction of socialism." A New Course, announced by the East German Communists in June, conceded party and government errors and promised amnesty for those who had left the GDR illegally. East Berlin suggested a softening of the policies of forced collectivization of agriculture and nationalization of artisans and small businesses, price increases were withdrawn, and persecuted members of the intelligentsia had ration cards returned to them. In this sudden shift, East Germany's "moderate" Communists were bolstered, while Ulbricht's position seemed to hang in the balance.

East German workers, however, starting what at first appeared to be a series of small strikes in East Berlin on June 15, provided the catalyst for large-scale antigovernment demonstrations, which within forty-eight hours had spread to over 270 cities and towns throughout the GDR. Whether in East Berlin or Leipzig, demonstrators demanded a far-reaching program of change, including everything from reduced work norms to free elections. This spontaneous anti-Communist eruption proved more than the party and its security organs could handle, forcing Moscow to use Soviet forces stationed in the GDR to crush the uprising. Twenty-one demonstrators were reported killed, seven later executed, and as many as a thousand imprisoned.

Ironically, the June uprising may have helped save Ulbricht's career. If the Soviet leadership—itself still enmeshed in its own power struggle—had replaced Ulbricht at the time, that decision could have been viewed only as a victory for East Germany's restive populace. Rather than risk further destabilization, the Soviets chose to back off, allowing Ulbricht time and maneuvering room to consolidate his position.

On May 14, 1955, the GDR was admitted to the Warsaw Pact [a mutual defense agreement between European Communist states; West Germany joined NATO—the Western counterpart—the same year], and in September of the same year the first treaty between the Soviet Union and the GDR was signed. The Soviet occupation troops were converted, semantically, into allied forces, and the GDR received by Soviet definition its full sovereignty. The Soviet Union did retain the right to fulfill its international obligations regarding "Germany as a whole," in particular regarding the special status of Berlin. And although the GDR was granted permission to manage civilian transit between Berlin and West Germany, the Soviets continued to oversee air traffic in the three corridors between West Germany and Berlin as well as Western allied–related traffic. Nevertheless, the self-image of the GDR's leadership soared. For the first time East Germany felt confident enough to consider itself on equal terms with the other Communist states of the region. The power of the new state was consummated on January 18, 1956, when the National People's Army was founded. . . .

Millions Flee to the West

From a certain point of view economic conditions in East Germany should have improved in the 1950s. Reparations [for damages to the Allies during WWII] ended in 1954, occupation costs ceased to be levied after 1959, and food rationing ended in 1958. But the command economy—although the most productive in the bloc—could only sputter, and while West Germany's system had begun to generate wealth, East Germans were left behind, their portion of the country mired in poverty. During the latter half of the decade a steady stream of East German citizens continued to flow westward in search of political freedom and economic opportunity.

Between 1949 and 1961 over 2½ million East Germans fled to the West, draining the GDR's work force. Nearly 50 percent of the refugees were under twenty-five years of age; only 10 percent were retired. Communist authorities tensely watched the number swell during the three years before the construction of the Berlin Wall. In 1959, 144,000 East Germans emigrated from the GDR; in 1960 the number reached 199,000. In the first half of 1961, 207,000 East Germans left for West Germany.

Rumors had begun to emerge in the West that the Communist regime was preparing to undertake a violent response to the mass flight of its citizens, and in fact the Western allied powers had received intelligence early in the summer of 1961 indicating that the GDR might intervene to abate the flow of refugees. On

June 15,1961, East Germany's Communist party daily, *Neues Deutschland*, printed a statement given by Walter Ulbricht in East Berlin in response to the rumors circulating in the West:

> As I understand your question, there are people in West Germany who wish that we mobilize the construction workers of the capital of the GDR in order to build a wall. I have no knowledge that such an intention exists. The construction workers of our capital are occupied with building apartments, and this takes their entire energy. No one has the intention of erecting a wall.

Refugees continued to pour out. During the first two weeks of August alone, over 47,000 fled. Ulbricht had indeed organized a contingency plan to stem the GDR's hemorrhaging. In the early hours of the morning on August 13 East German construction workers under the supervision of the People's Police and the National People's Army began to seal off passage to the West as they laid the foundation of the Berlin Wall. The West expressed indignation but mustered little else. West Berlin's mayor, Willy Brandt, desperately appealed to U.S. President John F. Kennedy to guarantee the territorial integrity of West Berlin, which remained precariously embedded in the heart of East Germany.

Ulbricht's sealing of the East–West Berlin border crushed much of the spirit of dissent inside the GDR. And as the flow of refugees began to subside, the GDR's economy showed signs of stabilizing. Beyond its domestic effect, Ulbricht's action in Berlin brought about a kind of redemption in the eyes of the Soviets. Times had changed since the Soviet Union had been forced to intervene on behalf of the East German Communist regime to crush the uprising in 1953. Now the East Germans were able to demonstrate their own competence and capability in the handling of their internal affairs.

Indeed, Moscow seemed to approve. In 1964, the first Treaty of Friendship, Mutual Assistance and Cooperation between East Berlin and Moscow was signed (again, long after friendship treaties had been signed by Moscow and the other East European states). The Soviet-GDR treaty acted as a military supplement to the Warsaw Pact, guaranteeing among other things that the GDR's borders would henceforth be considered "inviolable and a basic factor of European security." For Ulbricht the treaty had the double function of strengthening his position within the East bloc and further building the GDR's case for international legitimacy.

The Berlin Wall

By Eleanor Lansing Dulles

East German authorities erected the Berlin Wall in 1961 to stem the tide of refugees fleeing to West Berlin, where British-, American-, and French-controlled sections of the city offered sanctuary. Even after the wall went up, East Berliners still devised ingenious, if desperate, methods to overcome the barrier. In this selection from her book Berlin: The Wall Is Not Forever, *Eleanor Lansing Dulles cites a few of the attempts East Berliners made to escape their side of the city. As Dulles sadly notes, however, not all attempts to outwit the wall and the East German guards who patrolled it were successful. Many escapees were shot while fleeing to the West. Their deaths remain a testament to a captive people's desire to be free.*

The tragedy of August 17, 1962, when Peter Fechter hung on the barbed wire with no one to help, marks a low point of despair and of disillusion for many. This episode has been referred to as marking a serious change in the Berlin attitude toward Americans. . . . Many of the accounts of this incident, which were repeated to me over and over by the younger residents of Berlin, have developed out of deep emotion more than out of a knowledge of all the facts. The legend that has gained credence and is often told, and which is even more shocking than the actual story, is that the boy hung bleeding for six hours while the American authorities consulted Washington as to what to do. They speak with bitterness of a cold indifference, of hesitating bureaucrats who do not understand the human suffering resulting from the division of Germany. This has now, for the rebellious, provided a focal point for criticism of foreign weakness and German irresolution which could be fanned into hostility.

Two Feet from Freedom

Pierre Galante, in his book on the Berlin Wall, vividly describes the attempt by Helmut Kulbeik and Peter Fechter to gain free-

dom in West Berlin. On August 17, the two young men started
out for work in the morning, eating an early lunch of bacon and
potatoes together. When the other men went back to work, they
strolled over to a sawmill near the building site on Ernst-
Thälmannplatz. "On the first floor they wrestled with the barbed
wire and boards at the window, wrenched out the nails and sta-
ples, and pulled the barbed wire down. They took off their shoes
and hid them among the rubble and bits of rubbish." Then they
crossed the wasteland between the building and the barbed wire
on the East side of the Wall.

They were near Checkpoint Charlie where newsmen and
other observers are almost always gathered to watch the crossing
into East Berlin and where a museum now stands to record the
story of many dramatic escapes.

They slipped into the sandy roadway of the Zimmerstrasse.
They did not know that above them at firing slits in bricked-up
windows of the sawmill there were three Grepos (East Border
police). The boys reached the Wall and climbed to where it was
topped by barbed wire. There were two more feet of wire above
them. Helmut was ahead. Looking back he saw Peter paralyzed
by the fear of a Grepo standing a few feet away from him. Helmut was over the Wall in a moment, while Peter was felled by a
burst of several shots from a tommy-gun. Wounded, he tried to
climb but could not pull himself up to reach the top. The East
Berlin police were close to him at the foot of the Wall as he fell
back on the cement on the wrong side. He lay with his hand out-
stretched and bleeding.

The West Berliners had watched his desperate climb, and hundreds of them rushed to the Wall. There was no possibility of
saving Peter. Newspaper reporters and photographers arrived in
a matter of minutes. Some futilely tried to climb the Wall, but
the police were there with guns poised. The Vopos [East German
police officers] threw a tear gas bomb over into West Berlin as
American military police came up. It was almost forty minutes
before steel-helmeted Grepos carried him away without waiting
for a stretcher. Peter Fechter, only eighteen years old, was the fifti-
eth victim.

Reactions in the West
Although some aspects of this tragic event are obscure, it is not
generally known that the action took place beyond the Wall and

under the poised and smoking guns of the East Germans. The American military police, who came to the West side of the Wall within a few minutes after the fatal shots, were under orders not to cross the line into East Berlin while on duty. Because of the shocking nature of the event, however, they had immediately sent word to American authorities at Military Headquarters.

On this day, Charles Hulick, the Acting Head of the U.S. Mission in Berlin, was in conference with the U.S. Commandant in the General's office on Clay Allee. The first report that reached them during their morning conference on various matters was that a Vopo had been shot at the Berlin Wall near Checkpoint Charlie and was hanging bleeding on the wire. This report obviously raised problems, but it was still hearsay. They sent officers immediately to the scene to determine exactly what happened. It was approximately twenty minutes later that they learned that the man who was wounded on the East side of the Wall was an escaping East Berliner and that an angry crowd was gathered on the West side of the Wall. Before the American officers could reach the scene, some eight or ten miles from headquarters, the young man had been carried away. In a short time, a sign was held up at a window in the East sector, "He is dead." Pictures of this event are grim reminders at the spot where Peter died. . . .

The Tunnels

The story of the tunnels is one of the most exciting and most disturbing of all. Many innocent people have fled through the dark passages, often crawling in muddy water to emerge to the warm and silent welcome of those who have dug these paths to freedom. Always they have been near the armed Vopos who were listening and waiting to shoot them or their helpers. Always they faced fear and danger to seek a new life in the free West.

Many tunnels were built and many were discovered and flooded or walled up. Students from the Free University were anxious to keep digging even after the technical methods for discovering the tunnels were perfected to a high degree. Many lost their lives in futile attempts when walls fell in and water mains broke. Many were shot in trying to gain the entrance to some escape route.

The best-known tunnel was the one that was begun in May, 1962. This was planned and financed in large measure by the Berlin staff of NBC [National Broadcast Company, a British TV news channel]. A beginning point was established in an unused but normal looking workshop on the Bernauer Strasse. Here small Volkswagen buses went in and out bringing electrical tools, lumber, and other things needed for the work. The dirt was stored in the cellar. Some fifty young men worked in shifts for a period of six months.

A Dangerous Project

The greatest problem was of course secrecy. With so many working and over such a long period of time, the possibility of betrayal or of inadvertent acts that would give the undertaking away was alarming. The tunnel was not discovered, however, even after the first escapees crawled through the dark passage. The main threat to completion was flooding. At one point the workers broke into a cracked water main. They told the city authorities, who mended the leak without knowing how it had been found or why it was important to the informants.

The initial shaft that was driven down was fifteen feet deep and took three nights to build. The workers had to keep pumping and pulling the earth out in little containers for which they laid a track. In the digging, they crouched low, their feet in water. A stark electric bulb which they had wired themselves gave dim light to the workers who were in constant danger of caveins until they built a wooden frame with a supporting ceiling to lessen the risk. During the five months of construction there were two floods, one in June and another in July. Both threatened complete failure to the undertaking. Eventually the pumping succeeded and, with only a few inches of mud, the digging went on. The man at the far face of the 450 feet of excavation usually lay on his back with the shovel between his legs. Sometimes he had to use his hands to scoop out the sand and dirt. The tin basin, used when the hole was small, was dragged back by the men at the tunnel opening in the cellar. Space was limited because there must be no activity outside that could be noticed in either West or East Berlin. The Vopos were constantly patrolling above, as the tunnelers penetrated into the sector. They had always kept a careful watch at Bernauer Strasse, a frequent escape point. Their pacing could be heard by the men working far under the pavement. There was no talking in the tunnel because of fear that the East German police might hear.

The long task was not over until October 1962. During those

months dozens of shorter tunnels had been dug; some had been discovered and blocked up, some had caved in. There had been cases of shooting at the point of the reception centers. Some of the "passengers" had collapsed in the narrow tunnels, some, bleeding from shots before their escape, had died after they reached the West and safety. The methods of detecting the work of the tunnels constantly improved. The Vopos and Grepos drove stakes into the shafts when they found them. They probed likely points along the sector border. The tunnel-digging enterprise became constantly more perilous.

Crawling into the West

In mid-October a few people assembled, alerted by a youth with a West German passport who had been permitted to cross at Checkpoint Charlie, coming in twos and threes at spaced intervals. They gathered in a small cellar near the border. The Vopos walked up and down the streets not noting any special gathering and not interested in the silent couples in dark clothing with small packages or suitcases. In the tunnel from the West side the leader came out at the East and led the first of some twenty-eight persons through the long dark passageway to safety. These men and women had to crawl most of the way on hands and knees. They came out trembling, weeping but still silent, for the escape route must not be betrayed. They grouped in the dark cellar where they were embraced and given hot coffee. A few of the babies and children were dragged along in the tin basins that had been used for bringing out the earth. The mission was a success. The joy among the escapees was still mingled with a kind of nightmare of fright, but the reunion of the families was a reality that grew in its wonder.

A second, similar crossing and a third were carried out at short intervals, but with each episode and more people involved, the danger of discovery increased. Too many on both sides of the Wall knew of the operation. There was also the prospect of increasing water seepage as pumping became more difficult. The total who used the tunnel to come to the West was reported as fifty-nine. The tunnel was never discovered by the East Zone authorities, but the increasing risk, with repetition and spreading knowledge of what had been done, led the leaders to flood the shaft in late October to prevent loss of life. The story was out in *Newsweek* on October 22, in *Time* on October 18.

Controversy over the Documentary

A controversy arose over the plan to show a television documentary on the tunnels. Both CBS and NBC were involved in the early stages of the plan. Then NBC secured control and, for a price, was permitted to film the construction and the escape. The State Department for days objected to the release of the film for television. Finally, they realized it could not be prevented. So it came about that this remarkable documentary of ninety minutes has been seen by millions—only after the possibility of using the tunnel was over and with the knowledge that the East German authorities had already perfected the listening devices and electronic equipment to aid in the detection of such activities. From the outset tunnels were not safe and they became ever more perilous.

The considerable cost of lumber, digging equipment, electricity, and wages paid to some of the excavators was met by NBC. Several of their top officers in Berlin worked over the blueprints and the plans and followed the digging in detail, advising and helping to administer the pumping that went on for several weeks during each of the two floodings. They agreed that, in the film, only the faces of those who gave their permission would be shown. Thus as one watches the dramatic moment when the first escapees climbed the ladder and were pulled up to the cellar by waiting West Berliners, many of their faces are blacked out in the picture. On some of the other faces the strain and emotion is deeply etched and the silence is broken only by low murmurs in the murky shadows of the small reception area in the cellar. The watcher, thinking of the hours of uncertainty, shares the tension as one person after another comes through, and the relief when the leader finally says, "They have all made it."

The Opening of East Germany

By Tom Heneghan

The following article, written by Tom Heneghan, describes the final few weeks before the East German border was opened to the West. Heneghan explains how increased resistance among the East German population coupled with East German president Erich Honecker's unwillingness to implement reforms created an explosive atmosphere in the late 1980s. But tensions rarely flared into violence. Instead, the reform-minded Soviet president, Mikhail Gorbachev, proved that East German hard-liners could not count on Russian support if revolution came. Without Soviet backing, the East German government had no idea how to control its intractable population. As popular outcry grew, the government crumbled and tried unsuccessfully to recast itself as a progressive force willing to make change. By then the will of the people won out and the restrictive borders of the nation were thrown open on November 9, 1989. Heneghan, a journalist and long-time observer of East German politics, was in Berlin when the Berlin Wall—the symbol of divisiveness between East and West—fell. The following year, free elections were held in East Germany and the Communist leaders were deposed. In October 1990, East and West Germany merged back into one nation with its capital at the once-divided city of Berlin.

Mikhail Gorbachev came, saw, conquered and teased. On his first visit to West Germany in June 1989, the dynamic Soviet President added a new word to the political vocabulary — "Gorbyrnania". Cheering crowds met him wherever he went. The fresh breeze that Gorbachev's *perestroika* [Russian for rebuilding, standing for economic reform] and *glasnost* [Russian for openness, standing for cultural and political reform] had brought to Soviet politics seemed to promise a new era of peace and cooperation in Europe. He and his attractive wife

186   Germany

Raisa were worlds away from the *apparatchiks* [Russian term for party officials who execute the interests of their organization disregarding the general good] who used to reign in the Kremlin. "Gorby" ended his triumphal tour with a tantalising little hint. Asked at a news conference about the Berlin Wall, he said, "The Wall could disappear once the conditions that created the need for it disappear." A follow-up question about reunification brought the Delphic answer: "Everything is possible . . . time will decide."

Perestroika was already bringing changes throughout the Soviet bloc. Only a month before Gorbachev's visit to Bonn, Hungarian border guards began dismantling the Iron Curtain along the Austrian frontier and handing out bits of the barbed wire as souvenirs. A free election in Poland in June brought in the Soviet bloc's first non-communist government to office. In July, Gorbachev announced the end of the Brezhnev doctrine of limited sovereignty in Eastern Europe. The mood of change and hope sweeping the communist world was so strong that even the bloody Tienanmen Square massacre in June, which crushed China's democracy movement, could not dampen it.

But where was democracy in the German Democratic Republic? The old hard-liners in the Politburo [the highest committee in the dominating socialist party] refused to drop their ideological guard. The leadership feigned indifference to the new trends coming from Moscow. As the party ideologist Kurt Hager put it, "If your neighbour put up new wallpaper in his apartment, would you feel you had to paper your apartment over again as well?" When East Germans began reading about reform in the rejuvenated Soviet press, censors banned the popular weekly *Sputnik*.

East Germans Want Out

Parallel to this, the number of East Germans applying to leave for the west rose dramatically. East Berlin let 10 to 20 thousand people leave every year in the 1980s. Those applying to leave were usually fired from their jobs and shunned by colleagues. Many sought help from the Protestant churches, which formed support groups and provided some work while they waited—sometimes for years—to be allowed out. They also started organising protests. In March 1989, when foreign businessmen flocked to the Leipzig Spring Fair, several hundred people marched through the city chanting "We want out."

It was one of the great banalities of life in the communist world that provided the final spark. On 7 May 1989, East Germany held local elections, and official candidates officially chalked up a 98.85 per cent "yes" vote. The dissidents, in an unprecedented move, filed official complaints about vote-rigging. Attendance at Leipzig's Monday peace prayers, a late afternoon service started by the Nikolai Church in 1982, swelled from 800 in early May to around 2,500 by late June. "Worshippers" (many of whom had never seen the inside of a church before) had to file past plain-clothes men from the hated Stasi security police to get in. On their way out, they would shout, "Stasi pig" and "Stasi out." For them, free elections and the right to travel would be a little piece of heaven on earth.

When summer vacation time came, thousands of East Germans flocked to Hungary hoping to cross the border into Austria. They could get West German passports at Bonn's embassy in Budapest, but Hungarian border guards often refused to let them out. Desperate, the East Germans returned to the embassy in the hope that it would help them emigrate. By the beginning of August, about 130 East Germans were holed up in the embassy in Budapest and hundreds more camped out elsewhere. At the same time, another 80 had fled into the West German permanent mission in East Berlin a further 20 were in the embassy in Prague. The crowds grew steadily during the month.

The Floodgates Burst Open

Throwing in its lot with the West, Hungary flung open its border at the stroke of midnight on 10 September. Long lines of Trabis, Wartburgs and Ladas poured out and raced through the night across Austria. When the first cars reached the West German border, relief agencies were ready with free petrol, drinks and food. Local businessmen searched for skilled labourers. Television reports of the enthusiastic reception prompted another wave of East Germans to pull up stakes and leave. The new arrivals were overwhelmingly young and mostly male. Most had been trained in a traditional German apprenticeship, making them the kind of skilled workers the communist state was supposed to favour These were people with the most comfortable life the Soviet bloc could afford, yet they were ready to bolt from home at the first opportunity. Three-quarters said the lack of free speech or the right to travel drove them to quit the country.

Even while so many were leaving, over 16 million others

stayed put. In many cases, that decision was just as challenging to the government. Those who did not go west wanted a better east. It made no difference whether they stayed behind out of political conviction, for family reasons or simply because they didn't want to move. Each departure tore holes in the very private networks of family, friends and colleagues, the "niches" that made life in East Germany liveable.

As the departures mounted, official East Berlin wavered between speechlessness and denial. The controlled press ignored the exodus. Honecker spent the summer recovering from a gall bladder operation. In his absence, the Politburo rigidly ignored the rising discontent. When [Honecker's representative Egon] Krenz suggested staying in East Berlin because of the tension, Honecker was so annoyed at the suggestion that things were not under control that he ordered him to take four weeks' vacation. The crown prince obeyed.

The denial could not endure. East Germany's fortieth anniversary was coming up on 7 October and the malcontents would not be allowed to steal the show. By coincidence, the fortieth anniversary of China's communist state was due one week earlier. This led to an outpouring of solidarity messages from East Berlin to Beijing, a name now synonymous with the Tienanmen massacre.[1] The ailing Honecker made his first major public appearance of the season at a ceremony in East Berlin's State Opera House to mark China's anniversary. The message was not lost on loyal communists. On 6 October, a workers' militia unit in Leipzig threatened a "Chinese solution" to end the swelling weekly demonstrations after the Monday peace prayers. "We are ready and able to defend our achievements effectively to stop these counterrevolutionary actions once and for all. If needed with weapons in our hands," it said in a statement in the local newspaper.

Political Opposition Grows

It was in this overheated atmosphere that the opposition began to form. Just after Hungary opened its border, 30 activists met outside East Berlin to found New Forum as a nation-wide platform for public dialogue on reform. Its leading figures were living examples of how East Germany had gone wrong. Bärbel

1. On the 3rd and the 4th of June 1989, thousands of pro-democratic student protesters on Tienanmen Square in Beijing were killed by troops of the Communist government.

Bohley, an East Berlin artist who became the group's spokeswoman, was a feminist and peace campaigner. She and two other dissidents were expelled to Britain in early 1988 after demonstrating for free speech at a ceremony honouring the legendary Communist Rosa Luxemburg. They returned six months later. Another founder, Jens Reich, was a soft-spoken molecular biologist. For about 20 years, he and other East Berlin intellectuals had met privately for weekly talks on politics, philosophy, history and any other taboo topic. When the time came, many became charter members of the New Forum.

In the weeks that followed, other groups launched political parties to rival the Socialist Union Party (SED). Many were led by Protestant pastors, a reflection of the relatively independent role enjoyed by their church under communism and their activism in sheltering dissidents during the 1980s. Some of the most active pastors formed Democratic Awakening on 2 October as a reform socialist opposition. Others founded the Social Democratic Party on 7 October.

Within weeks, 200,000 people had signed the New Forum manifesto. Bohley started a media blitz with a unique German–German twist. Her calls for reform went out over crackling telephone lines to radio stations in West Berlin, Cologne and Hamburg, which beamed them back to East Germans astonished by her courage. A new breakfast show on West Berlin's RIAS-TV gave East Germans a daily round-up of the previous night's protests, and tips about what to expect next.

Honecker returned to work in late September determined to bear up the exodus mess. On 29 September, he agreed to allow the 5,490 East Germans occupying Bonn's embassy in Prague to leave for West Germany. But they had to travel in East German trains through the GDR and be stripped of their citizenship en route. Another 809 refugees in the West German embassy in Warsaw would cross their homeland in another train. Two days after the Prague embassy was emptied, 4,500 new arrivals had crowded into the building waiting to emigrate. Desperate, East Berlin suspended visa-free travel to Czechoslovakia at 5 P.M. on 3 October. In a secret report to the Politburo on 4 October, Erich Mielke, the head of the Stasi, said that even communists were threatening to quit the party and apply for an exit visa.

The embattled government rounded up more "freedom trains" to ferry another 7,600 refugees from Prague and 600 others from Warsaw. In Dresden, some 3,000 youths chanting "We want out" and "Gorby! Gorby!" stormed the railroad station hoping to hop onto a passing train. Blocked by riot police, they fought a three-hour battle in vain. About 400 blocked the tracks further down the line. In the confusion, one man had both legs cut off by a passing train and many others were injured.

Teenagers Squeal: "Gorby! Gorby!"

When Gorbachev arrived in East Berlin on 6 October for the anniversary, he found the same Brezhnev-style stagnation he was battling against back home. That evening, the Soviet bloc's old guard lined up along Unter den Linden to watch an FDJ torchlight parade. [The Free German Youth (FDJ) was the only official youth organization in East Germany.] Honecker pumped the night air with his traditional clenched fist salute. Poland's Wojciech Jaruselski stood at ramrod attention. Romanian dictator Nicolae Ceausescu grumpily tried to ignore the boos wafting up from the crowd when he was introduced. As every FDJ group passed the reviewing stand, the parade slowed down. Teenage girls in blue FDJ shirts and jeans squealed "Gorby! Gorby!" Other youths echoed dissident slogans. Poland's former Prime Minister Mieczyslaw Rakowski leaned over and asked, "Mikhail Sergeievich, do you understand what they're saying?" Gorbachev nodded, but Rakowskl translated the slogans anyway. "They're saying 'Gorbachev, save us.' This is the end."

A Politburo meeting after the military parade on anniversary day got nowhere. Gorbachev addressed the group first, spelling out his policies and hinting that East Berlin should do likewise. Unruffled, Honecker sang his country's praises in communist clichés. When he finished, Gorbachev looked up in amazement, then got up and left the room without saying a word.

At their final reception that evening in the East German parliament, the communist elite had a front-row seat on the spreading unrest. Just outside, across a canal, about 3,000 protesters in Marx Engels Park were shouting "Gorby, come out!" and "Freedom! Freedom!" One of the guests watching the scene from inside recalled, "It was spooky. The mood was depressed, there was a touch of *Götterdämmerung* [the end of the world in old Germanic mythology] about.... It was like being on the *Titanic*." Police and Stasi men tried to haul away the ringleaders, prompting scuffles with the young crowd. Once riot police had dispersed the crowd, it snaked instead through the dark streets of East Berlin, swelling as it progressed. Phalanxes of truncheon-wielding police, some with attack dogs, swept along the main boulevards while smaller units chased demonstrators down side streets where they were beaten and arrested.

Ten Thousand at the Peace Prayers

The spectre of a "Chinese solution" hung over Leipzig as the Monday Peace Prayers neared on 9 October. Local army units and special mobile police joined the city police, workers' militia and Stasi units in a security force of at least 8,000 men. Extra blood supplies were distributed to hospitals. Workers in the city were let off early and parents were told to pick up their children from school by 3 P.M. SED members were warned of a looming counter-revolution. In the early afternoon, riot police took up position near the four churches in central Leipzig that were holding peace prayers at 5 P.M.

Up to 9,000 people turned up for the prayer sessions, far more than could fit into the churches. One participant, Susanne Rummel, later recalled seeing her church ringed by police and Stasi. "None of us wanted to say the words civil war or bloodletting aloud, but it seemed tangibly near to everyone." After the services, at least 20,000 people gathered on Karl Marx Square. As they advanced around the Ring Road in a sea of flickering candles, the crowd swelled to 70,000. "For me, the greatest moment came when I marched in that crowd and started calling, first softly and then louder and louder, 'We are the people! We are the People!'" said 58-year-old housewife Eva Günther. "I saw police, but I was not afraid. I felt strong and I threw my arms into the air and screamed my heart out."

Most marchers had never dreamed of protesting in public before. They were bitter over the exodus that put relatives and friends beyond a border they might never be able to cross. The sight of so many frustrated neighbours shouting out political demands that normally brought instant arrest broke down the wall of fear and taboo that was crucial to keeping East Germany under control.

Another invisible pillar of the state, the threat of violent repression, also crumbled that night. No tanks rumbled over the cobblestones to replay the bloody suppression of the 1953 workers' uprising. There were no beatings or arrests. In fact, the riot police withdrew during the evening. "We had a plan of operation for everything," parliament speaker Horst Sindermann said later. "We just weren't prepared for candles and prayers." Both Krenz and Honecker subsequently tried to claim credit for averting a bloodbath, but it seemed that Leipzig security authorities had no clear guidelines from East Berlin as to whether to shoot or not.

The victory in the churches and on the streets of Leipzig that night marked the decisive turning point in the grass-roots struggle for democracy. It forced the once omnipotent SED into a retreat that seemed less dramatic than it was only because the protesters were so disciplined. It began the first successful and peaceful revolution in Germany.

Life Punishes Those Who Come Too Late

During his East Berlin visit, Gorbachev coined the phrase of the year when he said, "Life punishes those who come too late." It was a warning to Honecker, but he failed to get the message. Others understood it, however. Fearing they might go down with Honecker's sinking ship, Krenz and the East Berlin SED chief Gunter Schabowski began plotting to oust him. They lined up about half of the 26-member Politburo behind them. Gorbachev was informed in advance and sent his best wishes for the conspiracy's success. When Honecker opened the Politburo session on 17 October, Prime Minister Willi Stoph promptly broke in and proposed that he be fired. Honecker looked stunned but agreed to allow a discussion. One by one, his colleagues all turned against him. In the end, Honecker joined in the unanimous vote to relieve him of his duties. His protégé Krenz was named to replace him. When it was announced the next day, the news of Honecker's resignation caused as much surprise as the appointment of his hard-line deputy did consternation.

Krenz did his clumsy best to keep up with the pace of change. The new party leader proclaimed a policy of *"Wende"* ("turnaround"), coining the name East Germans came to use for the tumultuous autumn of 1989. He visited factories to hear workers' complaints. He met Protestant church leaders and announced an amnesty for those who had fled to the west. He let the dull grey media come to life. By early November, Krenz was frantically jettisoning almost every piece of unpopular ballast he could. He fired targets of public wrath such as Margot Honecker, the former leader's wife and hard-line education minister, and later sacked five elderly leaders including Mielke and chief ideologist

Kurt Hager. He promised a new travel law, a constitutional court and alternative service for conscientious objectors. "Trust our policy of renewal," he begged in a televised address. "Your place is here. We need you."

By now, who was listening? The news that Prague had opened its border to West Germany that evening drowned out Krenz's speech. East Germans were soon racing through Czechoslovakia into Bavaria at the rate of two to three hundred an hour. When half a million protesters massed at East Berlin's Alexanderplatz on 4 November, the SED was the target of public ridicule. Posters full of wit and satire bobbed up and down in a sea of banners calling for free elections and democracy. "Put Asterix in the Politburo" one demanded. One of the best depicted Krenz as the Big Bad Wolf over the words, "Grandmother, why do you have such big teeth?"

Waiting for the Highpoint

Forty years of fear were forgotten. Chinese solutions and Soviet invasions were history. If Leipzig won the decisive battle for democracy, East Berlin got to stage the victory parade. The Leipzigers had shown that the emperor had no clothes. The Berliner were now laughing at his nakedness. Reform-minded communists were booed when they joined dissidents to address the crowd. The legendary former spymaster Markus Wolf, who secretly pictured himself as the best hope for *perestroika* in East Germany, saw his dreams collapse within minutes of starting to speak. Chants of *"Aufhören!"* ("Stop!") gave way to scattered calls of *"Aufhängen!"* ("Hang him!"). "People's power" was on the verge of victory. Anything could happen.

From then on, each day seemed to bring the highpoint of the drama, only to be surpassed by events the next day. On the Monday, the press published the draft of a new travel law that granted East Germans 30 days in the West annually but made no provision for hard currency. This was as good as telling the unemployed they were allowed to windowshop for a Mercedes. The government of Willi Stoph, prime minister since 1976, resigned on Tuesday. The Politburo was the next to fall at a special session of the Central Committee on Wednesday. Trying to put a convincing face on its plans for reform, the SED nominated Dresden party boss Hans Modrow—another supposed "East German Gorbachev"—as the next prime minister.

9 November 1989

On the morning of Thursday, 9 November, four senior officials met at the Interior Ministry to draft a new law to legalise emigration. About 225,000 people had left so far that year and there was no end in sight if East Berlin didn't act decisively. These officials were no closet liberals. Two were from the Ministry of State Security (MfS), the other two were "unofficial collaborators" (IMs) of the Stasi. But they sensed there would be trouble if they legalised emigration without also permitting day trips to the west. So they decided to tackle the problem head-on by allowing private travel without any conditions or delay. None of them thought things would change quickly, since travellers would still need to apply for passports and visas.

That afternoon, Krenz interrupted a Central Committee session on economic reform to mention the travel law. "Whatever we do in this situation, we're bound to make a mistake," he said. "But this is the only solution that spares us the problem of dealing with this through third countries, which harms the international image of the GDR." Only three officials had any comments, all of them minor. When Schabowski, who was due to meet journalists later, turned up to be briefed, Krenz handed him the short text of the draft law and said, "Announce this. It will be a bombshell." Without even reading it, Schabowski decided to announce it at the end of his news conference.

The day's excitement seemed to be drawing to an end when Schabowski met the media at 6 P.M. After an hour of wandering questions and answers about the Central Committee, he announced in passing that a new law would allow East Germans to travel abroad or emigrate freely. "When does that go into force?" a voice called out from the hall. Looking baffled, Schabowski thumbed through his papers and said, "As far as I know, right away . . . immediately." Suddenly all ears, reporters asked if this applied to trips to West Berlin. Schabowski frowned, shrugged his shoulders and wondered in silence whether the Soviets had been informed of all this. But he found the relevant passage and read it aloud: "Permanent emigration can take place at all GDR border crossing points to the Federal Republic and West Berlin." On his way out, RIAS-TV cornered Schabowski and asked if he expected an exodus. "I hope it doesn't come to that," he remarked.

THE HISTORY OF NATIONS
Chapter 6

Future
Challenges

Germany's Foreign Policy

By Theo Sommer

This article by Theo Sommer, a writer for the weekly German newspaper Die Zeit, discusses the development of German foreign policy from the time after the Second World War through the Cold War and Reunification to the present. Sommer shows how in the 1990s it became more and more difficult for Germany to avoid becoming involved in international military actions, even though the Allied forces had insisted, after World War II, that Germany's military be for defense alone. Sommer also discusses Germany's role within NATO and the building of the European Union, which abolished border and custom controls and created the euro, a new currency shared by twelve European countries.

G erman foreign policy over the last fifty years has been a long journey to normality whose starting point was 1949 amidst a pile of rubble i.e. amidst absolutely nothing, which was all the Nazis had left behind. The victors were the sole decision-makers in Germany's future and it was they, too, who set up a West German central power base in Bonn at which point the Soviets installed the East German Communist regime, the Party of Socialist Unity at a time when the East-West conflict was just starting to escalate. The Federal Republic of Germany and the German Democratic Republic on the other side of the iron curtain arose out of the Cold War and they remained, until the end of that war in 1989, a potential battlefield.

A Long Way to Normality

The Federal Republic's overriding state policy was, consequently, a result of this situation. Accordingly, the first "initiation" law passed by the newly-founded state was aimed at regaining sovereignty, the second at the country's integration in an overall European structure, the third at asserting itself in the hostile new world order, and the fourth at overcoming the division of Germany. Konrad Adenauer, Germany's first chancellor, made these four initiation laws the cornerstones of his foreign policy. They become mandatory for all his successors, too. Adenauer managed, piece by piece, to wrest sovereignty for the Federal Republic from the western allies. His aim was to make Germany an equal partner among free nations.

Steadfast relations with the West were a vital part of this. Most of the barriers to sovereignty fell in 1955 when the Federal Republic joined NATO [North Atlantic Treaty Organization]. However, the Allies retained the right to have the last word on issues relating to "Germany as a whole." At the same time, the process of European integration began in 1950/51, bringing with it the opportunity for Bonn to gain respectability and influence in a wider partnership perspective once the European Economic Community (EEC) had been created in early 1958. Self-confidence grew after West Germany was allowed to re-build its armed forces in 1955. Things came to a halt, however, at Adenauer's efforts at re-unification. He was forced to witness how the Berlin crisis of November 1958, which Khrushchev had provoked, ended in the building of the Berlin Wall on August 13, 1961, tearing Germany apart and extinguishing all hopes at that point for a restoration of German unity. The four initiation laws, which had determined the beginnings of the Federal Republic, remained mandatory for all Adenauer's successors. This was a continuous thread throughout successive governments, from 1969 through 1982 right up to 1998. Changed times brought new trends, yet these basic principles remained untouched. However, Germany only really finally arrived at normality at the beginning of the new century as a state which will always be mindful of its past but whose chief concern is now with the future.

The Reunification

Two of the main tenets of German state policy are now obsolete. On October 3, 1990, divided Germany became re-united once more. At the same time, the re-united country regained its full sovereignty. Various other restrictions on sovereignty which still exist—especially those connected with the increasing powers of an expanding EU—belong to those which were relinquished voluntarily and which serve a higher purpose: namely, to make our continental nations fit for future survival within a greater united Europe.

Asserting the country's interests is still the main object of German foreign and security policy. Yet diplomats and politicians have always kept to the "one for all and all for one" motto whereby Germany's strategic interests are best represented as part of a bigger organization i.e. the North Atlantic Treaty (NATO) or the Western European Union (WEU). In that respect, nothing has changed. On a military level, Germany can do nothing on its own, yet within NATO a European Security and Defence Identity is becoming more and more important. At the same time, a European Security and Defence Policy is starting to emerge within the EU. The most obvious sign of this is the Rapid Reaction Force currently being set up, designed to enable the EU to act in a crisis without American assistance, if necessary.

With communism at an end, German policy in both foreign affairs and security has, inevitably, undergone a fundamental change. Germany's existence is no longer threatened, as was the case during the Cold War. These days, there are other challenges to be faced: ethnic and religious rivalries outside the NATO area, the decline of nation states, violation of human rights and terrorist attacks. All these new dangers also force the Bundeswehr (German armed forces) to adapt to new tasks.

West Germany's Humanitarian Aid Missions

By the time re-unification came in 1990, the Bundeswehr had taken part in over 120 humanitarian aid missions throughout the world without ever having taken part in any military action under the UN [United Nations] flag since the most common interpretation of the Basic Law still prohibited this at the time. Consequently, Germany did not get involved in the Gulf War in 1991; the [Helmut] Kohl government bought its way out by contributing ten billion dollars. Even then, a "policy of restraint" continued to dominate German politics. But it became increasingly difficult for Germany to back away from its partners' expectations. After re-unification, the country was obliged to assume more responsibility at a global political level. Bundeswehr medical orderlies ran a field hospital in Cambodia in 1992/93 while Bundeswehr helicopters flew UN disarmament inspectors on control missions to Iraq from 1991 to 1996. Marine troops took part in monitoring the arms and trade embargo against Milosevic's Yugoslavia from 1992 to 1996; German Luftwaffe [Air Force] soldiers flew AWACS [Airborne Warning and Control System] planes on behalf of NATO from 1993 to 1995, monitoring the air traffic ban in Yugoslavia's air space. Around 1,800 Bundeswehr soldiers were stationed in Somalia from 1992 to 1994 in order to give the UN troops logistic back-up. In the course of nearly 2,000 flights between 1992 and 1996 the Luftwaffe transported 13,000 metric tonnes of relief goods to Bosnia and Herzegovina. After the Federal Constitutional Court ruling of July 12, 1994 the military operations got more dangerous or "more robust" as the term is nowadays. Following that, in late 1995, the Bundeswehr dispatched a contingent of around 3,600 soldiers in order to support the IFOR [Operation Joint Endeavour] in Croatia. Since late 1996 the troops have been part of the SFOR [Operation Joint Guard] troops in Bosnia and Herzegovina. In 1999, from March to June, the Luftwaffe took part in NATO air strikes against Serbia, using 14 Tornados. Since then, the Luftwaffe has been administering a section of Kosovo as part of the Kosovo Force (KFOR). In summer 2001 the Bundeswehr assumed the role of "lead nation" in Macedonia as part of the "Amber Fox" operation, aimed at helping the Slavs and Albanians to live peacefully together. Since 1994 almost 100,000 Bundeswehr soldiers have been in the Balkans.

The Bundeswehr were just getting used to their mission in the Balkans when the war against bin Laden's terrorism and his militant al-Quaeda group pushed them once more into an unexpected role. The Federal Chancellor put a total of 3,900 men at the USA's disposal for a possible mission in the geostrategic area around Afghanistan: for ABC [atomic, biological, and chemical] missile defence, securing maritime traffic, evacuating the wounded and providing air transportation. In so doing, he was following the maxim which he had uttered directly after the attacks of September 11th; namely, Germany would need to assume more responsibility on a global political level since it was not only declarations of "unlimited solidarity" which counted but also "a willingness to provide appropriate military skills in order to combat international terrorism."

The European Imperative

Alongside the self-assertion imperative the European imperative continues to have an unabated effect. 20th century Europe: 75

years of bloodshed and terror. However, this terror has been overcome as European states have grown closer together. In 1979
Helmut Schmidt created the European currency system; in 1990
the Common Market came into force and in Maastricht—one
year after German re-unification—the stage was set for the common currency and political union. It was to Helmut Kohl's credit
that he did not turn his back on the European idea after the
restoration of Germany unity and that he chose in fact to support the unification process more than ever. The EU now com-
prises 15 members and after eastern expansion it could comprise
27 members by the middle of this century. Moreover, the Schen-
gen Agreement, which has abolished border and customs controls between 13 EU countries, has been in force since the spring
of 1995. On January 1, 1999, Europe's common currency was
introduced and in . . . [since January 1, 2002] people in 12 EU
countries will have the new common currency, the euro, in their
pockets. The euro offers the Brussels union a promising launch-
ing pad into the 21st century. For some time now discussions
have been under way about an even more ambitious project: a
European constitution. The birth of such an idea will not be devoid of complications and a unified vision is still a long way off.
Yet there is a greater need than ever before for a better definition
of overlapping areas of responsibility and jurisdiction between
regions, states and community institutions; perhaps in the form
of a new constitution? Like all EU achievements to date it will
not be easy and it will take time but it will come in the end. The
German foreign minister Joschka Fischer sparked off the discussion with his Humboldt speech in May 2000. And one thing's
for sure: the EU has to integrate more than ever, not just at economic or foreign policy and security levels but also, just as important, at a political level.

Guidelines for the Future

Germany must continue to dedicate itself to the European idea
which, in turn, should strive to achieve that old goal of a feder-
alist—not centralist!—Europe. In the short term, Europe can aim
for a United Europe of States but it should not lose sight of its
long-term aim: the United States of Europe. As regards asserting
itself, Germany should continue to seek this within an organization; for example, NATO in its present and future form as well
as the military potential that the EU is striving to set up. In this

respect it will continue to be of vital importance for the Germans to keep their relations with Washington intact. The threat posed by international terrorism will remain a constant challenge. In the end, it could be a question of weighing up at the start what crises Germany should get involved in, what ones it should not and in what situations it should keep an open mind; not least, in order to avoid unreasonable demands. Can we in fact afford to translate words into action? Should we limit ourselves from the outset—as regards manpower, finances and geography? Or should we, conversely, follow the English maxim: "Put your money where your mouth is"? Both solutions would be preferable to an unpredictable foreign policy based on the state of the finances.

Yet there is more to German foreign policy than merely continuing the Europeanization process and an unabated determination to assert itself. The one lesson to be learned from "Afghanistan" is that it would be criminal, indeed foolhardy, to ignore the fact that while bin Laden manipulates the feelings of hundreds of millions of people for his own false ends, these feelings nevertheless do exist. There is a connection between the alienation of many Muslims and the unresolved Palestine issue in the same way as there is a connection between the misery of countless people and their readiness to pin the blame for their situation on the industrialized nations. Globalization improved many people's prospects, whether in the North or the South. Yet many people could not keep up and are now limping along, without hope, behind those who are storming ahead. There must be greater efforts to give them specific help. After ten years of unity the Federal Republic of Germany is currently in the process of grasping its own historical significance. It has built up traditions, must assimilate new experiences. History has put Germany out to sea in the uncertain waters of global politics. The country's leaders must now redefine—or define more clearly than before—how they propose to turn tradition and experience into guidelines for the new century.

The Need for Economic Reform

BY JACK EWING, ANDREA ZAMMERT, CHRISTINE TIERNEY,
AND FREDERIK BALFOUR

The following is an article that was published in the magazine
BusinessWeek in November 2001. The article begins by arguing that
the German chancellor Gerhard Schröder wants to create a new era for
Germany, one in which its geopolitical role matches its economic strength.
The German economy is the largest in Europe and the third largest in
the world, yet in the long shadow of the Second World War, the article
notes, Germany had been hesitant to assert itself politically upon the
world stage. The authors concur that Germany deserves a stronger role in
international politics, but they argue that such a role will depend on the
country's continued economic strength, about which they express concerns.
Although the quality and efficiency of German production is without
parallel, they argue, the economy as a whole needs reform. In particular,
they point to the high unemployment rate and its connection to an in-
flexible job market, and they argue that a more forceful sense of innova-
tion and entrepreneurship is needed. The text is by four BusinessWeek
writers: Jack Ewing in Frankfurt, Andrea Zammert in Offenbach,
Christine Tierney in Paris, and Frederik Balfour in Islamabad.

German Chancellor Gerhard Schröder spent only about four hours in Islamabad, Pakistan, on Oct. 28, 2001. After stepping from his Luftwaffe Airbus A310, Schröder met with Pakistani President Pervez Musharraf to promise $50 million in aid and repeat his support for U.S. military action [against terrorists and a repressive government] in Afghanistan. Then Schröder flew on to India, whose leaders, suspicious of Pakistan's motives, badly needed a pep talk.

A Western head of state visits a frontline nation in the war against terrorism. In these scary times, that hardly seems significant—until you consider the decades of history Schröder was trying to shed with his shuttle diplomacy. In the 52 years of the German Federal Republic's existence, chancellors have made a point of avoiding war zones. The stamp of Nazi boots, after all, still echoed in the ears of the world, so even a hint of militarist zeal by a German leader was *verboten* [forbidden].

But Schröder, a former peace activist and the son of a Wehrmacht soldier who died in combat, is trying to create a new epoch for Germany, an epoch where the nation's geopolitical strength matches its economic force. That means asserting Germany's "unlimited" solidarity with the U.S. in the current crisis. On Nov. 6, Schröder said he will send up to 3,900 German troops to help the U.S. fight the war against terrorism. "It is a new phase," says Karsten D. Voigt, coordinator for German-American cooperation in the German Foreign Office. "It's our chance to contribute to a cohesive Western response" to terrorism. There's more to it than that, though. Schröder's stance is also a declaration of strength, of the essential role Germany must play in the West.

It certainly is time Germany played a larger role on the world stage. The nation has spent half a century apologizing for Nazi crimes and making financial reparations to victims. Now virtually all of its political and business leaders were children during World War II or not even born. As the biggest country in Europe, Germany should lead the Continent to a new era of statecraft.

But Schröder is pursuing his geopolitical dreams at a risky moment. Any wider influence that Germany will wield rests squarely on its economic might—the financing power of its well-capitalized banks, the intelligence of its highly trained workforce, the exceptional quality of its manufactured goods. Yet this huge machine is slowly but surely falling into disrepair. German economic growth, which hit 3% last year, is once again reverting to the subpar rates of the 1990s. If this keeps up, then over the long term Germany cannot develop into the global player Schröder envisions. And if Schröder neglects the economy, he does it at Germany's—and Europe's—peril. Germany accounts for 24% of the gross domestic product of the entire European Union. If Europe goes into recession, as now looks likely, only Germany can lead it out.

Tax Cuts

Just a year ago, Schröder thought his pace of reform was right on target and would help Germany avert the recession that stalked the U.S. After all, he cut taxes, took the first steps towards mending the broken pension system, and encouraged the immigration of foreigners with needed skills. He made it easier for companies to sell unwanted assets, setting the stage for far-reaching corporate restructuring. He even convinced the nation's factory workers, the world's best paid, to keep wage demands in check.

There was indeed a growth spurt, but it didn't last. This year growth will slip to 0.7%. Unemployment, at 9.5%, remains far ahead of the U.S. rate of 5.4%, and business confidence is at an eight-year low. The downward lurch shatters any idea that Germany can quickly recover the economic dynamism of the 1960s and 1970s.

Schröder should consider the grim news a wake-up call. Sure, he faces reelection next year and doesn't want to anger voters with unpopular spending cuts or pension reforms. But a lot more needs to be done. Some of the tasks are longstanding ones: loosening up the labor market, redesigning social welfare to get the long-term unemployed back in the workforce, cutting red tape, and slashing taxes further.

But the Chancellor should try thinking out of the box, as well. As the economy slows dangerously, he's got to find a way to stimulate growth without fueling inflation. Schröder could reduce taxes for personal corporations, cut capital gains levies for smaller companies to encourage restructuring, and exempt smaller firms from some of the more onerous provisions of German labor law. Most important, though, Schröder needs the courage to face up to interest groups and push through the most difficult reforms, such as changes in job-protection laws.

"A Brake"

Besides, although times are tough all over, signs are mounting that Germany's place in the world economy could be eroding. The nation just fell again in the Geneva-based World Economic Forum's rankings of national growth competitiveness—from 14th to 17th. That means Germany's potential for five-year growth lags such places as Hong Kong and New Zealand. Among other things, the World Economic Forum (WEF) faulted Germany for its inflexible job market. Meanwhile, personal wealth in Germany has declined from 80% of the U.S. level in 1991 to 70% in 2000. "Germany used to be one of the growth motors of Europe," says Peter Müller, prime minister of the western state of Saarland and a member of the opposition Christian Democrats. "Now we're a brake."

Many economists and business leaders doubt Germany can sustain growth much above 2%, even in good times. That's not enough to pay for Germany's generous social welfare system, which still bankrolls free university education and such luxuries as health-spa stays and has to support a growing number of retirees. And it's not enough to ensure Germany a leadership role among Western nations. "Germany will be a dying star if it fails to adapt to the new world economic order," University of Chicago economist James J. Heckman warned a Berlin audience earlier this year. Nor is that kind of growth enough to power Europe, especially as the EU [European Union] takes on the burden of expanding to the East. Long term, Germany must be able to sustain growth of 3% or more to protect its privileges and lead the Continent.

Hard Hats

Like it or not, Germany sets the tone for reforms elsewhere in Europe, as well. Last year, when Germany cut corporate and income taxes, France and Italy followed—however reluctantly. German Foreign Minister Joschka Fischer has framed the debate for the future of the European Union with his call in May for a United States of Europe with stronger federal powers. Germany has the most influence over expansion of the EU to Central European states. "Germany's essential," says Noël Goutard, chairman of the supervisory board of French auto-parts maker Valeo. "Europe can't prosper without Germany."

Schröder, for all the bad news, has allies he can call on. In every sector in Germany, companies and individuals are trying to figure out a way to recapture the growth rates of 30 years ago. Many of them are drawing on Germany's core strengths in designing and assembling complex products. "Germans are by nature engineers and not entrepreneurs," says Ulrich Steger, a former member of the management board of Volkswagen who is now a professor at the International Institute of Management Development in Lausanne, Switzerland.

The massive factories of steelmaker ThyssenKrupp in the Ruhr Valley city of Duisburg offer some clues on how that engineering strength can transform companies. The complex, which has produced steel since 1891, exemplifies both old and new Germany. Yellow cranes unload rust-colored ore from river barges. Workers in hard hats and tan work suits bicycle past corrugated metal factory buildings covered in brown soot.

That's the old Germany. The new Germany lies inside a factory that's as clean as any office building. Here, with the help of Siemens electronics, steel ribbon is squeezed to the exact thickness required for the roof of, say, a Volkswagen Golf. The brand new factory, known as the Beeckerwerth cold strip mill, requires just eight workers per shift to produce 172,000 tons of steel a month.

That's called productivity. And it's one reason why Thyssen-Krupp, even though it is still weighed down by older, overstaffed mills, is still eking out a profit while Bethlehem Steel Corp. and other U.S. steelmakers face bankruptcy. Even with the highest manufacturing wages in the world, Germany remains among the world's most productive countries.

Cautious

But even under the most optimistic scenarios, ThyssenKrupp and other big companies won't create the jobs the country needs. For that, Germany needs fast-growing new companies. When it comes to new-business creation, Germany falls in the middle of 21 countries surveyed by the Global Entrepreneurship Monitor, a consortium of researchers managed by Babson College in Boston and the London Business School. Germany ranks behind countries such as Argentina and South Korea, not to mention the U.S.

Risk-takers are starting to emerge from the corporate canyons. Management consulting firms such as Munich's Roland Berger Strategy Consultants report losing up to a quarter of their consultants during the dot-com boom. One was Hendrik Gottschlich, a former Berger partner who in 1999 founded Advanced Commerce, a Munich-based provider of software, services, and consulting for companies that want to market products online or via catalog. "It was always my dream to start a company," says Gottschlich, 36. Today, his company has 22 employees. He's not the only brave entrepreneur. Even after the catastrophic collapse of share prices, companies listed on Frankfurt's Neuer Markt, the bourse for many startups, employed 139,000 people in Germany as of July. That's about double the number a year earlier. The total is sure to decline as some Neuer Markt companies go under or lose their stock listing, but the net effect will still be positive.

Surprisingly, some of the most promising signs of entrepreneurship are in East Germany, where hard-pressed executives, government officials, and workers are determined to undermine the inflexible system inherited after reunification from the West. One of the most ambitious efforts is taking shape in Frankfurt/Oder, a city of 71,000 on Germany's eastern border. In a field outside the city, so close to Poland that cell phones switch back and forth between Polish and German providers, Klaus Wiemer is pouring concrete for a $1.5 billion semiconductor factory.

Chip Shot

With backing from Intel Corp., the former Texas Instruments Inc. executive plans to create 1,500 jobs, enough to make a dent in the region's 18% unemployment. Using new technology developed by a local research center, Wiemer plans to build a foundry to make custom chips for the communications industry. He's gambling that the current chip downturn will be over by the time the factory starts producing in 2003. In fact, he expects to have a cost edge, because he's extracting big discounts from makers of chip-manufacturing equipment.

This must be how Germany felt in the "Economic Miracle" years after World War II, when the collapse of the old order drove a tidal wave of entrepreneurship. Something similar is happening in Frankfurt/Oder, once the capital of East Germany's semiconductor industry. Desperate city officials nag Wiemer to submit forms faster so they can approve them. Labor unions are staying out of his way. Locals are already lining up for jobs—three for every opening. "These people have fire in the belly," says Wiemer, who speaks English with a trace of Texas twang. "Some of them are in their 50s. This is the last chance they have to do something with their lives."

Elsewhere in Germany, other bureaucrats are fighting the country's formidable forces of inertia. The Saarland is littered with depleted coal mines and abandoned factories. Since winning election as state prime minister in 1999, Peter Müller has tried to get things moving. Besides cutting bureaucracy, Müller's government has trimmed a year from the time it takes to finish secondary school, so most students are eligible for university at 18. Seems like a small thing. But it helps address business complaints that Germans are too old by the time they enter the workforce. Business has taken note of Saarland's friendly attitude. "We have easy access to the economics minister and prime minister," says Hans Schardt, director of European vehicle operations for Ford of Europe, which builds Focus cars in Saarland.

Can the spirit of reform blossom nationwide? It's easy to be pessimistic. Sometimes Germans seem to be in the grip of complacency brought on by 50 years of prosperity. When Darmstadt-based pharmaceutical maker Merck looked for a site to build a $200 million protein-production facility, it received pitches from the U.S., Singapore, Ireland, Spain, and Taiwan. One country that didn't bother to make a pitch: Germany. "So far, Germany hasn't tried very hard to get us to invest here," says Merck CEO Bernhard Scheuble. "There's still a certain hostility to innovation."

Schröder seems to embody the nation's ambivalence. After chasing Helmut Kohl from office in 1998, the former prime minister of Lower Saxony got off to a good start. Schröder, a lifelong socialist, pushed through steep corporate- and income-tax cuts. Business rates of 38.6% are competitive with the U.S.

Schröder still pals around with top business leaders, such as Jürgen Schrempp of DaimlerChrysler or Jürgen Weber of Lufthansa, and they are urging him to pick up the pace. But with elections in less than a year, Schröder seems fearful of any move that might upset organized labor and other elements of his party's left wing. With the opposition Christian Democrats in disarray, insiders say, Schröder is less worried about them than about dissenters within his own center-left Social Democratic Party, or SPD.

The threat of recession is bolstering those voices on the left. Economists such as Gustav Horn of the German Institute for Economic Research in Berlin now question whether Europe's tough job-protection laws are really so bad. "I consider that argument highly exaggerated," says Horn, head of macro analysis and forecasting for the institute. It doesn't help that the U.S. model looks tarnished in the current downturn.

Yet ordinary Germans may be more willing to change than their leaders give them credit for. For example, 56% of Germans believe unemployment benefits are too generous, according to a poll by the Allensbacher Institute. "People voted for Schröder in the expectation that he would modernize the country," says pollster Manfred Güllner, CEO of the Forsa Institute in Berlin. Timid leaders, not reluctant citizens, are the biggest obstacle, he says. Especially timid leaders who are uninformed about business. In Schröder's cabinet, just 1 out of 14 members, Economics Minister Werner Müller, has experience in business management. The demographics are similar in parliament. There's a "fundamental readiness to reform" among the populace, says Güllner. "But the members of Schröder's party are telling him to step on the brakes."

Staying Put

Waffling on reform has not done anything to stem the rising tide of the jobless, now 9% of the workforce. A third haven't worked in at least a year. More exasperating is the fact that even in the downturn, businesses still report problems finding enough skilled workers. "We have trouble getting qualified people, especially engineers," says Hans-Ulrich Lindenberg, a member of the management board of ThyssenKrupp Steel. Some candidates refuse to move 50 miles to take a job in Duisburg, he says.

Critics say the current benefit system encourages lethargy. Hans-Jürgen Ott, a 48-year-old father of two who lives in Offenbach, a city near Frankfurt, has been out of work for nearly 10 years, ever since arthritis in his knees forced him to give up his job as a municipal truck driver. Ott says he's capable of doing lighter work but has never undergone retraining. His only offer in a decade: a government-sponsored job as a gardener. Ott said he wasn't healthy enough. "What prospects do I have? Not many, not many," Ott says. Ott is trying to qualify for full disability so he can collect retirement benefits, a move that would put him on the dole for good.

So far, Schröder has been reluctant to make major changes in the welfare system that supports Ott and others. That may finally change, perhaps even before the election, one government source says. Schröder probably has enough public support to introduce a so-called negative tax that would reward the working poor. The French government already is doing so, paying a tax credit of up to $500 to workers who earn minimum wage or a little more. "The design of these transfer systems is what we really have to think about," says Jürgen von Hagen, director for economic and social issues at the Center for European Integration Studies in Bonn. "We have to make working more worthwhile."

Economists at the European Central Bank also urge Germany, as well as France and Italy, to make it easier for companies to hire and fire people. Schröder is unlikely to tamper with the system until after elections in fall 2002. But quietly, his government already has eased enforcement of laws that make it harder to hire people as outside contractors, a way of getting around labor rules. That suggests that Schröder, if re-elected, may be open to easing work protections.

But government isn't the only problem. Plenty of people in Germany pay lip service to reform. Action is something else, and in this regard Germany Inc. has a lot to answer for. Industry associations are gung-ho for tax cuts and less regulation. But threaten their interests, and they clamor for protections like any line worker. Earlier this year, for example, German business torpedoed reforms that would have created Europe-wide takeover rules and made hostile bids easier to pull off.

Corporate Germany also doesn't know what to do with a massive gift from Schröder. At the urging of CEOs such as Deutsche Bank's Rolf Breuer, the government eliminated the capital-gains tax for companies that sell their stakes in other companies. That was supposed to allow banks and insurance companies to sell their stakes in industrial companies. The law takes effect on Jan. 1, so companies should already be announcing deals structured to close in the new year.

So far, there's no sign of a big bang. Deutsche Bank, which owns stakes in such companies as DaimlerChrysler and builder Philipp Holzmann, will take up to five years to unwind its holdings, predicts Supervisory Board Chairman Hilmar Kopper. Prices are depressed. But tradition also plays a role. "There's an emotional connection to some of these assets," he says.

To their credit, German companies have changed plenty in the past decade. As they have pushed abroad, companies learned from their counterparts in the U.S. Munich-based electronics giant Siemens copied General Electric Co., selling off units that weren't tops worldwide in their field. In the current downturn, German companies have reacted much more quickly than they used to, cutting costs and breaking the old taboo of laying off workers. Siemens has announced 17,000 job cuts, more than half in Germany. Layoffs are still more costly than in the U.S. because companies are required to pay severance. But, with the help of pragmatic workers' councils, German companies have become more adept at swiftly cutting staff. While painful, job cuts set the stage for low-inflation growth later on.

Still, there's something missing—the kind of hustle people

have when they really want to change something. Then again, Germans handle change differently. After the strife of two wars, they treasure consensus. They debate for years. When some magical degree of popular assent is reached, though, change can happen like an avalanche. John Kornblum, former U.S. ambassador to Germany and now the chairman of Lazard Frères in Germany, recalls that in the 1970s Germany opposed the policy of détente toward the Soviet Union. Later the Germans became some of the most zealous advocates of tighter ties with the Russians. Kornblum senses a similar shift in attitudes about Germany's economy. "You're seeing a near-critical mass among the elite," says Kornblum. "I think we're on the verge of major change." For Germany's sake —and Europe's—he had better be right.

The Turkish Minority

BY JOHN ARDAGH

A discussion of the situation of Germany's largest minority group, the Turks, is the focus of this article. After giving an overview of the immigration of foreign workers into West Germany after World War II, the article's author, John Ardagh, discusses some of the problems Turks face living and working in Germany today. As Ardagh points out, Turks still face discrimination and legal insecurity and are often stuck with the kinds of jobs that Germans do not want. Ardagh also discusses the situation in the Kreuzberg quarter of Berlin, the city with the largest Turkish population of any city outside of Turkey. According to Ardagh, Turks in Kreuzberg are often hesitant to integrate into German culture. John Ardagh is the author of the book Germany and the Germans, *from which this piece is drawn.*

Y ou can see them in their hundreds at the weekends in the vast halls of the German railway termini, which they take over as informal meeting-places and endow with the ambience of some Mediterranean town square. Here shops and stalls sell them kebabs and pizzas, or their national newspapers such as *Hurriyet* and *El Pais*, while the trains coming and going from Istanbul, Athens or Naples provide nostalgic hints of home. Or you notice them in the streets of the poorer quarters, outside cafés and groceries with strange names and spicy smells—spare dark-eyed Sicilians, moustachioed Montenegrins, and dumpy Anatolian peasant women in headscarves. Including their families, these foreign workers total well over 4 million: about one-third are Turkish, with Italians, Yugoslavs, Greeks and Iberians as the next most numerous. They were invited so pressingly to Germany during the years of fast economic growth, when labour was in short supply: but, though some have now been here for decades, few have integrated into German society or have felt encouraged to do so. Today, in a time of high unemployment, they have become something of an embarrassment—especially the Turks, whose culture, life-style and religion are so different. They live in run-down housing that the Germans don't want, their children swell the classes of German schools, and they smart under the resentments they arouse. It is all quite a problem. As the liberal writer Max Frisch has put it, 'We called for a labour force but we got human beings.'

Much has been written about the plight of the immigrant workers in Europe, especially in West Germany. Sometimes the newspapers carry reports of Turks committing suicide in desperation; or the slogans aerosolled on walls, 'Türken raus!' (Turks out), bring echoes of the 'Juden raus!' [Jews out] of the 1930s. So, when I myself began to explore this subject, I feared the worst. However, after much research in the main cities and talks with Turks, Germans and others, I reached the conclusion that although of course the problem exists it has tended to be exaggerated. For there is a positive side to the picture. First, one comes across countless examples of personal friendships and good neighbourly relations, while innumerable German organisations and individuals of all kinds devote their time generously to helping the immigrants. Secondly, there is much less violence or open conflict than in a country such as Britain with a higher degree of integration; the average Germans attitude is one of polite indifference, or grumbling contempt, rather than active hostility. But of course the foreigners chafe at their treatment by a society that takes their labour but does not make them feel accepted—in a Germany that, unlike the United States or the ex-colonial powers, has virtually no experience of absorbing alien cultures. And this complex problem of the Gastarbeiter (guest workers)—as they have long been called unofficially, with what today seems a touch of irony—has come to trouble the conscience of the more liberal Germans. Does it not cast a shadow over the new Germany's bright ideals of 'Europeanism' and 'internationalism'?—or even raise basic questions about just how kind and tolerant this new German society is?

The Hiring of Foreign Workers

In the first years after the war, the arrival from the east of some 14 million refugees, nearly all of them German, provided the reborn economy with the extra labour it needed. But by the later 1950s this supply had become inadequate (in 1961 there were some 500,000 unfilled job vacancies): so the Federal Government began to look abroad, to the poorer countries of southern Europe. And they poured in very readily, these Italians, Yugoslavs and others: most of them at that time were single men without their families, attracted by the opportunities to learn some skills and above all to earn far higher wages than was possible back home, and thus buy a house or land or start a business. The governments of the 'donor' countries happily supported the emigration too, for it eased their own unemployment, it brought in foreign currency, and it provided free training for workers who in modern factories picked up techniques that their homelands could never have given them. Therefore several nations, including Turkey in 1961, signed treaties allowing Germany to set up recruiting offices in their cities for use by German firms. The arrangement suited all sides. Some *Gastarbeiter* were even welcomed with bouquets at railway stations by grateful mayors; the millionth to arrive officially, a Portuguese, in 1964, was fêted as a hero by the German media and given a motorbike as a present. Those were the days. . . .

Around 1970, German industry was making another leap forward, and even more immigrants were needed. But by now the Spanish and Italian economies had so far improved that the supplies from those quarters were drying up, and many Spaniards and Italians were returning home. So the Bonn Government turned to the best other source available: the Turks, already present in modest numbers. Whereas many of the south European workers were by now semi-skilled or even skilled, the Turks were most of them poor peasants from Anatolia; and they have always proved quite ready to take on the more menial jobs—in the mines, on building sites, as sweepers and refuse-collectors—that the Germans spurn. They arrived intending to remain just a few years, but most have stayed on far longer—'finding German money sweeter than Turkish honey' (as one Turk said to me), and often deterred by the acrid taste of that honey in a Turkey of high unemployment, great poverty and political severity. And yet, like most other *Gastarbeiter*, they have not really put down roots in Germany. All foreign workers legally employed are entitled to the same pay as Germans; they have full welfare and social rights and most employers treat them fairly. But hardly any have even applied for German citizenship. They retain their ties with home and their dream of returning to live there one day, and so in Germany they remain in a kind of limbo between two cultures. There is little of an American-style 'melting-pot'.

The "Guests" Stayed

Ever since the first signs of world recession at the end of 1973, the Government has imposed a virtual ban on new recruitment from outside the European Economic Community (EEC). But this has had a paradoxical effect. Knowing that they might lose their work permits if they left Germany for more than three months, many hitherto itinerant *Gastarbeiter* simply decided to settle there and to get their wives and children to join them; the Turks in particular, so family-minded, were also unhappy at remaining as single men in an alien Christian culture so far from home. So the Turkish families have blossomed and bred: despite the ban, the overall Turkish population rose from 1,028,000 in 1974 to 1,581,000 in 1982. Other figures are equally striking: whereas the ban did succeed in reducing the numbers of active foreign workers from 2.6 million in 1973 to 1.9 million a decade later, the overall foreign population continued to rise in this period, from 4.0 to 4.6 million (it has since been dropping slightly, to about 4.3 million in 1985). Family dependents today account for 60 per cent of the total, whereas in the 1960s some 90 per cent of the workers were single men—living in the sad dormitories of cramped hostels and chasing German girls (or at least, the Italians did; the Turks, whatever their other 'faults' in German eyes, are much less lecherous). Today (1985 figures) the Turks number 1,425,000, while the other main communities are the Yugoslavs (600,000), Italians (545,000), Greeks (287,000), Spanish (158,000) and Portuguese (83,000), with some 200,000 others also in the *Gastarbeiter* category (such as the Moroccan in Fassbinder's *Fear Eats the Soul*, or redundant Glasgow shipyard workers). Today the general German view, alike governmental and popular, is that there are too many of these foreigners for the good either of society or of the economy. And so, with unemployment rising, resentment has been growing—ironically, just at a time when integration, especially of the non-Turks, has finally been making some progress....

Of all these nationalities, Yugoslavs tend to be the best liked, and are much appreciated by employers for their intelligence, politeness and hard work. Spaniards are popular too; but there is still some prejudice against south Italians, thought of as feckless and noisy.... Ever since the inception of the EEC's free labour market, the Italians have been at liberty to live and seek work in Germany much as they please: but this has not led to any flood, for the reasons I gave earlier. The Greeks, who joined the EEC in 1980, have since then been acquiring a similar freedom during a

A DEMOGRAPHIC PROBLEM

In this article, published in the London Daily Telegraph *on April 7, 2001, Toby Helm describes his personal experiences with the German reluctance to have children. Helm also discusses some of the costs of this attitude, including the fact that Germany's population is expected to decrease by 14 to 20 percent in the next fifty years.*

When a French neighbour announced to our street that she was expecting her seventh child, she was piqued to discover that not all her German acquaintances shared her delight.

If she had spoken to my wife she wouldn't have been so shocked. At a cocktail party recently a woman inquiring whether my wife was expecting her first child went pale and yelped "Are you Catholic?" when told it was (shock!) our third.

Germans have a very distinct attitude to childbirth. Broadly put, to have more than two children means either that you are a scrounger (child benefits are generous), you don't know how to use birth control, or there is some sort of religious reason for your productivity.

Large families tend to be regarded as rather "antisocial". There is no equivalent to the British middle-class clan stuffed into its Volvo estate. The trend here is for women to have one child and maybe a second fairly late in life. Having given birth, they devote all their energies to the offspring in the best Mutti (mother) tradition. Never mind if Mutti is a high-flying lawyer or highly paid neurosurgeon.

The focused but often unsmiling way that German moth-

seven-year transitional period; and since January 1986 the same has begun to be true of Spaniards and Portuguese too. Again, no flood is expected. So these nationalities are not regarded as posing any great threat—and when a German today says, 'I hate *Gastarbeiter*', he usually means, 'I hate Turks'. Some 80 per cent of all Turks in EEC countries are in Germany. . . .

If they were all from the Istanbul middle classes, there would

---

ers observe their offspring in the playgrounds of Berlin is evidence of the grim seriousness with which parenthood is approached. These attitudes have a price. The attendant problems are currently the subject of heated debate in the media and among politicians.

A recent decision by the country's favourite newsreader, Gabi Bauer, to quit her job for a year or two because, at the age of 38, she is expecting twins has been the catalyst for an intense public debate, and has belatedly focused attention on a looming crisis. The problem is that Germany, Europe's largest economy, is running out of hands to keep it going. There are fewer young people to honour what is known as the "generation contract" under which those of working age are expected to fund the generous pensions of their parents and grandparents, who live ever longer.

Among northern nations in the European Union, Germany has the lowest fertility rate—1.33 children per woman, as opposed to 1.70 in Britain, 1.73 in France and 2.04 in America. In the 1990s, in what was East Germany, the rate dropped to well under 1.0 child per woman. The country's population is expected to plunge by between 14 per cent and 20 per cent in the next five decades. . . .

The major parties are all looking at how to get more mothers to work and be mums, but attitudes will be hard to change. Most German women believe that only they can raise their children. If there were more creches and tax breaks, there is no guarantee they would take them up.

Toby Helm, "Worldwide: Why Germany Is Fretting over a Lack of Breeding," *Daily Telegraph,* April 7, 2001.

be much less of a problem. But they have tended to come from rural Anatolia, often illiterate; and in so many ways they are so 'different' that inevitably the mutual culture shock has been far greater than in the case of the European immigrants. Reacting with blind prejudice rather than trying to understand, many ordinary Germans fear and despise the Turks for their 'alien' Muslim religion, their seclusion of their womenfolk, their teeming kids, their 'dirt' and 'noise', their garlicky breath and cooking smells (not necessarily worse than those of Greeks or Sicilians) and the more bizarre of their household practices. I heard tales of sheep and goats kept tethered on tenement landings. . . . Usually it is the newly-arrived ones who have behaved like this: after a while they learn to 'adapt', so today such incidents are much more rare.

It is not easy to draw a fair and balanced picture, for much of Turkish peasant custom and behaviour (concerning more serious matters than sheep-ritual) does seem genuinely shocking to the very same European liberals who plead for kinder treatment of Turks. . . .

Efforts to Help the Turks

But I must again stress that many Germans of all kinds do make great efforts to help the Turks and other immigrants. Not only do the Churches run welfare centres and kindergartens, but in 1984 they successfully campaigned to kill a callous project by Kohl's hard-line Interior Minister, Friedrich Zimmermann, that would have reduced from 16 to six the maximum age at which children remaining abroad should be allowed to join their *Gastarbeiter* parents in Germany. The *Bund* [federal] and *Land* [state] governments and city councils, though certainly they could do much more (see below), at least have social affairs departments staffed by well-meaning liberals who wield sizeable budgets and generally do their bit—as witness the city-funded local street festival I found one Sunday in Munich, where a troupe of Turkish youths and blonde local *Mädchen* [girls] gave a display of folk-dancing.

Individuals are active too: in Bavaria alone, there are some 30 German volunteer organisations who help Turkish children with their homework. The unions, in defiance of the racist element in their rank-and-file, also have a good record: *Gastarbeiter* make up 10 per cent of DGB [Association of German Labor Unions] membership, and a few have even been elected to factory works-councils. As for employers, most of the larger firms at least treat their immigrants well and will seldom dismiss a Turk if he is a good worker. Some companies have even made efforts to come to terms with the Turks' religious customs: a Turkish leader in Berlin told me that he had persuaded Siemens and some other firms to instal little Islamic prayer-rooms in their factories, as well as to provide special canteens serving Oriental food. As for the old Koranic rule that even a man must not be seen washing naked, for some years this caused problems in the big communal shower-rooms of the mines and steelworks, for the Turks demanded separate cubicles, but were refused. Finally, a senior 'liberal' mullah came from Istanbul and explained to the workers (who in Germany tend to be under the sway of reactionary mullahs) that the new modernised Koran had lifted the ban on male nudity. So all ended happily....

Berlin's Turkish Quarter

In Stuttgart, and in Munich or the Ruhr, nearly all the Turks are in more-or-less working-class jobs; likewise in Frankfurt, where tensions are much the worst and 22 per cent of the population are *Gastarbeiter*. Berlin is the one German city where the Turks, like the coloured minorities in London or New York, have their own educated elite, playing some part in local intellectual life. Here you find Turkish writers and lawyers, and exhibitions by Turkish artists, while the number of Turkish university students is far higher than elsewhere. This city with its 115,000 Turks (the biggest Turkish town outside Turkey) also has much the best municipal record of trying to help them: this was due quite largely to Richard von Weizsacker, Federal President, who as CDU [Christian Democratic Union] governing mayor in 1981 poured funds and staff into a new *Land* welfare centre for immigrants, and also plastered the city with propaganda posters of happy young Turks and Germans, hand-in-hand together.

This was not the picture ten or fifteen years ago, after the Turks ... had first settled en masse in the slums of the Kreuzberg district, near the Wall, and the startled Germans had reacted angrily. This was the 'Kreuzghetto' of the tabloid headlines, where rival gangs of youths were reported to be assaulting each other nightly. But today this image of Kreuzberg is out-of-date. All has become fairly amicable. First, the Turks are now numerous enough (35,000, or 25 per cent) to feel reasonably secure and at

home, in a 'town' of their own of some two square miles
(though by no means a ghetto). Secondly, Kreuzberg since the
mid-'70s has become a true Greenwich Village, filling up with
middle-class Greeks, Leftish intellectuals and the kind of *radical-
Schickeria* who, unlike working-class Germans, actually think it
smart to live in a racially-mixed area, where they can have Turks
as neighbours and get friendly with them. Kreuzberg is 'in'. During the squatter period, young radicals eagerly helped Turkish
families to settle in empty buildings; and nowadays the local Turks
seem to be almost outnumbered by the sociologists, media Left-
ies and assorted do-gooders who have come to scrutinise them
like some rare wild-life species. True, this idyll is sometimes shattered by the *Schlägerbanden*, gangs of young neo-Nazi skinheads,
usually out-of-work, who bash up Turks—and the young Turks
bash back. But such incidents are far rarer than they used to be.
By contrast, in some tenements the Turks have finally become
friends with their poor and elderly German neighbours, the original inhabitants, and mutual help has developed: the Turks haul
up coal and wood for the oldies, who in turn do baby-sitting
when the Turkish wives are at work.

I visited the city-funded Turkish social centre in Adalbert-
strasse, right by the Wall. It is run by and for Turks. . . . There was
folk-dancing, an engagement party, and a more emancipated atmosphere than in Stuttgart. Here I met Emine Altiok, a dazzling
young woman from Adana who had studied at Berlin University
and was now with the state *Rundfunk*, making radio programmes
for local Turks: 'I'm second generation. I came here as a small girl
with my father, who makes furniture. I'm married to a Turk, who
is culturally "integrated", so he doesn't try to dominate me: I'd
never stand for that. Most second-generation Turkish marriages
split up, however, simply because the women have become emancipated in Germany, they earn their own living and won't accept
the usual role of a Turkish wife.' Turning to the general position
of Turks in Germany, she went on: 'In every way, things were far
tougher for my father's generation: they had language problems,
and the Germans were more xenophobic in those days. For us it's
easier, but we have a new problem of identity. Are we Turkish or
German? We cherish our own culture and religion, but we see
positive things in European society especially for women. Many
women who go back to Turkey just can't cope any more with
the restrictions, at least not in the provinces—it's easier in Istan-

bul or Ankara. We, who plan to stay in Germany, intend to work out a middle way between Turkish female subservience and German excess of liberty.'. . .

The Turks and German Unemployment

It is ironical that just when Turkish/German personal contacts seemed to be improving, and the Turks were at last starting to feel more at home, so now the rise in unemployment has increased German prejudice against them. Generalisation is not easy: but broadly the pattern seems to be that, on the one hand, friendliness and neighbourly good-will have increased among those who know each other personally, but at the same time there has been a growth in indiscriminate ill-feeling towards foreign workers as a whole—'Kemal next door, he's a good chap—but what of all the other Turks?'—is a common German attitude. And, since *Gastarbeiter* are supposed to be stealing jobs from Germans, the facile equation can be made, 'Two million foreign workers = two million German unemployed, so send them all home!' Sensible people realise that this is nonsense, for most out-of-work Germans are not seeking the same jobs as Turks, too often relegated to the most menial chores. And if they *were* sent home, who could be found to do this kind of work? In Düsseldorf, the SPD [Social Democratic Party]-led city council commissioned a study which showed that, if the 36,000 immigrant workers departed, rubbish disposal services and public transport might well collapse, and hospitals and the building industries would be seriously short of labour. . . .

Radical Turkish Views

Though the Turks in Germany would certainly like to feel more secure and better accepted, most of them remain wary of integration. Here they are under powerful pressure from fundamentalist Islamic forces which, strangely enough, are stronger in Germany than in Turkey itself, and are also linked with the Turkish extreme-Right political movement, the Grey Wolves. These groups exert considerable influence over a bewildered peasant population in a strange land: they preach that integration into this 'infidel' society is wicked, and that Turks should not adopt 'decadent' European habits such as alcohol or freedom between the sexes. The mullahs in Koranic schools sometimes tell their pupils not to believe what they are taught in German classes. Here I

quote a leading article in *The Times* of September 5, 1983, about
the North Africans in France as well as Turks in Germany: 'In
both countries, fundamentalist Islamic groups, suppressed by their
home governments, are exploiting the relatively free and plural
nature of West European society, as well as the alienation and dis-
orientation felt by many of the immigrants, to try to impose on
the immigrant communities a totalitarian and intolerant world
view, with the result that the most well-meaning attempts by the
French and Germans to assimilate, emancipate or simply educate
the immigrants sometimes encounter a discouragingly hostile response.' Hence, for example, the difficulty in persuading Turkish
parents to permit their teenage daughters any leisure life outside
the home. And the few families who dare to step out of line and
Germanise are often rejected by their own people—'There's a
growing dichotomy,' I was told by Carla Baran, a psychologist
from Istanbul who works for the official Bavarian welfare service
for Turks, in Munich; 'some families are growing more liberal,
others more traditional. And it can be the same inside families: I
get visits from girls of 14 who've run away from home, or attempted suicide, because they can't stand their parent's strictness.
These tensions are worse here than back in Turkey, because of
the German influence and the fears of Germanising. It's a tough
situation: but I think integrating is bound to come within another
generation or so. The fanatics will lose in the end.' . . .

Remaining Problems

'Integration' is the current catchword—but what does it really involve? The German authorities claim that it is official policy for
Gastarbeiter to integrate into German society: but the Turks say,
'This is hypocritical. If they were sincere, they would make it easier for us to stay. They do not give us enough security of residence.' Here the legal position is that a foreigner is first given a
short-term permit; after a few years he can acquire a permanent
one, as well as an indefinite residence permit. He does not lose his
work permit if he loses his job; but if he commits a crime he is
likely to forfeit his rights of residence and be expelled. A German
also by law has preference over a foreigner for filling a job vacancy.
German officials claim that today some 85 per cent of foreign
workers have unlimited work permits, and that in the present employment climate it would not be politically feasible to grant them
fuller rights. And yet, many Turks claim that they still feel inse-

cure. One factor may be that anyone with a dark face is vulnerable to the frequent random identity checks by the police who are trying to hunt down the large number of illegal immigrants. . . . The question 'Just how xenophobic are the Germans?' is not an easy one to answer. Certainly horror-stories can be quoted by the score, but these may not give a fair picture. First we must distinguish between xenophobia, i.e. dislike of all foreigners, and racism, which is more selective. The Germans today are one of the least chauvinistic of major Western countries: they positively fawn over Scandinavians, Britons or even French . . . But, when it comes to darkerskinned or more alien folk, matters are different: probably the Germans *are* on average more racist than the British, or even the French, but they are well behind the Swiss, European champions in this field. In Germany, there is little actual violence towards immigrants, as we have seen. Neo-Nazi thugs try to whip up hatred, and some have been jailed for it: but these tiny extremist groups have little popular following, and their slogans (e.g. 'We finished off the Jews: Turks, it's your turn next'), though nauseating, are not representative. The average German may not warm towards *Gastarbeiter*, but he shows little residue of the old Aryan super-race mentality of the Nazi creed: it is significant that the Allensbach polls, though recording plenty of xenophobia in other respects, found only 8 per cent of respondents saying 'yes', and 69 percent saying 'no', to the crucial question, 'Are German children more intelligent than those of foreign workers?'. . .

However, in this law ridden country, one surprising and serious lacuna remains, the absence of effective laws against racial discrimination. Small ads for job vacancies or flats to let often stipulate, *'Nur für Deutsche'* [Only for Germans] or *'Nur Europäer'* [Only Europeans]; many pubs refuse *Gastarbeiter* and one in Frankfurt even had a notice up, *'Kein Zutritt für Hunde and Türken'* (No Entry for Dogs and Turks); some public discos in Frankfurt deny entry to coloured people (except if a white man brings a coloured girl—that's quite chic). In Britain, under the Race Relations Act, all this would simply be illegal. In Germany, to pass such a law would require huge political courage; and it might take many years, for it would involve the amendment of 40 existing laws.

In the meantime, could not the media and the authorities play a firmer role in trying to educate people away from prejudice?

Weeklies such as *Die Zeit* and *Der Spiegel*, it is true, have an excellent record of anti-racist articles, while any average regional daily is usually quite free from xenophobia. But this positive side is counterbalanced by the pernicious influence of the mass-selling tabloid *Bild Zeitung* it is not openly racist in its editorials, but with their shrieking headlines its new stories do endlessly sensationalise the 'misdoings' of Turks and others (e.g. stories about child-beating), and this whips up popular prejudice. The public television channels give a balanced news coverage: but they provide too few background programmes about the lives and problems of *Gastarbeiter*, the nature of Islamic religion, and so on. So potent a medium could certainly be playing a stronger educative role. And, as I have already suggested, the Federal and *Land* governments could do more to lead opinion and set a positive example. As all politicians know well, the treatment of immigrants remains one of the most crucial tests of the new German democratic ethos. The *Gastarbeiter's* very presence forces the Germans to look at themselves more closely.

CHRONOLOGY

A.D. 9

At a battle in the Teutoburg Forest, Germans under Arminius halt the expansion of the Roman Empire.

370–410

The Huns penetrate into German settlement areas and push the Germans into the Roman Empire; German invasions into Roman territory contribute to the downfall of the Roman Empire.

768

Charles the Great (Charlemagne) ascends the throne.

800

The pope crowns Charlemagne emperor of the Holy Roman Empire.

843

The Treaty of Verdun divides Charlemagne's empire; his grandson Louis the German becomes the ruler of the eastern half, the East Frankish Empire.

1315

A major famine kills many Germans.

1351

The plague kills about a third of Germany's population.

1450

Johann Gutenberg, the inventor of the printing press, prints the Bible.

1517

Martin Luther writes his ninety-five theses, which criticize practices of the Roman Church.

1555

The Treaty of Augsburg gives princes the right to determine the religion practiced in their territory.

1618

The Thirty Years' War begins.

1648

The Treaty of Westphalia concludes the Thirty Years' War and grants local princes almost full sovereignty in their territories.

1740

Frederick the Great comes to power in Prussia and greatly increases Prussian territory and influence.

1806

Napoléon conquers Germany.

1813

Napoléon is defeated in the liberation wars.

1814–1815

The map of Germany is radically redrawn at the Congress of Vienna; before the intrusion of Napoléon, hundreds of independent states had existed; after the Congress, only thirty-nine remained, mostly the larger ones.

1834

A Prussian initiative, the *Zollverein* (trade customs union), is founded and considerably increases German economic power.

1848

Revolution spreads through Germany.

1862

Otto von Bismarck becomes the Prussian prime minister.

1864

The Prussian and Austrian military defeats Denmark; Prussia annexes the territory of Schleswig and Holstein, which Denmark had sought.

1866

Prussia defeats Austria.

1871

After Germany's defeat of France, William I is coronated as the German emperor in the Hall of Mirrors of Versailles, outside of Paris.

1914

On June 28 the Austro-Hungarian heir to the throne, Archduke Francis Ferdinand, is assassinated in Sarajevo; shortly thereafter, World War I begins.

1918

On November 11 Germany concedes defeat and agrees to an armistice, ending World War I.

1919

In January the Spartacus Revolutionaries proclaim a socialist republic and occupy parts of Berlin; three months later Munich is the scene of a leftist coup attempt; the Treaty of Versailles is signed.

1920

In Berlin parts of the military try to overthrow the republic; the government has to flee to the city of Weimar.

1933

On January 30, President Paul von Hindenburg appoints Adolf Hitler chancellor; after a fire in the parliament building in Febuary, the Emergency Decree allows the Nazis to abolish laws that protect civil rights; the Enabling Law passes in parliament in March, allowing the Nazis henceforth to pass laws without parliamentary participation; Propaganda Minister Joseph Goebbels declares an official boycott of Jewish shopkeepers, doctors, and lawyers; Jewish civil servants and teachers are fired; universities and the arts are "cleansed" of Jewish influence; Germany leaves the League of Nations.

1935

In violation of the Versailles treaty, Germany renews conscription; the Nuremberg Laws declare that Jews are not German citizens.

1938

Germany annexes Austria; on the night of November 9, synagogues and Jewish shops across the country are burned or vandalized.

1939

Germany invades Czechoslovakia and Poland.

1940

Germany invades Denmark, Norway, Holland, Belgium, Luxembourg, and France; German troops march into Paris; the Battle of Britain begins; the Auschwitz concentration camp is established.

1941

Germany invades Yugoslavia, Greece, and Russia and declares war on the United States; the Birkenau and Chelmno extermination camps open.

1942

Extermination of Jews begins in Sobibor, Belzec, Auschwitz, and Treblinka; Germans lose the Battle of Stalingrad, halting advance into Russia.

1944

Germany occupies Hungary; a group of German officers tries to assassinate Hitler.

1945

The Russian army enters Germany from the east; troops from France, Britain, the United States, and Canada enter from the west; Hitler commits suicide; Germany surrenders on May 8; the Nuremberg War Crimes Trials begin on November 20.

1948

The airlift for the supply of West Berlin starts; the Marshall Plan, along with currency reform, helps stimulate the rebuilding of Germany.

1949

The Western occupation zones turn into the German Federal Republic (BRD) while the Soviet occupation zone becomes the German Democratic Republic (DDR).

1955
West Germany becomes a member of NATO.

1961
On August 16 East German Communists build the Berlin Wall.

1973
East Germany and West Germany establish a formal diplomatic relationship.

1989
On November 9 the Berlin Wall falls; unimpeded travel is possible between East and West Germany.

1990
Germany is officially reunited on October 3.

1991
The Maastricht Summit leads to the creation of the European Union, a central banking system, and a common currency scheduled for 1999, and it commits twelve European nations, including Germany, to implementing a common foreign and security policy.

1993
Heads of state ratify the Maastricht Treaty; the European Union is formed, with union citizenship for every person who is a citizen of a member state; union citizens are free to live and work without restriction in other union countries.

1998
The European Commission recommends eleven countries participate in the new currency; in addition to Germany are Austria, Belgium, France, Finland, Luxembourg, Ireland, the Netherlands, Spain, Italy, and Portugal; the European Central Bank is inaugurated in Frankfurt.

1999
The euro comes into effect for all electronic transactions; in Kosovo, the German military undertakes its first combat role outside of its borders since World War II.

2002
Euro currency hits the streets on January 1.

FOR FURTHER RESEARCH

General

Tristam Carrington-Windo, *A Dictionary of Contemporary Germany*. London: Hodder and Stoughton, 1996.

Martin Kitchen, *The Cambridge Illustrated History of Germany*. Cambridge: Cambridge University Press, 1996.

Eva Kolinsky and Wilfried van der Will, eds., *The Cambridge Companion to Modern German Culture*. Cambridge: Cambridge University Press, 1998.

John Sandford, ed., *Encyclopedia of Contemporary German Culture*. New York: Routledge, 1999.

Early History

Roland H. Bainton, *Here I Stand: A Life of Martin Luther*. New York: Mentor Books, 1950.

Marshall Dill Jr., *Germany: A Modern History*. Ann Arbor: University of Michigan Press, 1961.

H.W. Koch, *A History of Prussia*. London: Longman, 1978.

Martyn Rady, *The Emperor Charles V*. London: Longman, 1991.

E.A. Thompson, *The Early Germans*. Oxford: Clarendon Press, 1965.

The 1848 Revolution and the German Empire

David Blackbourn and Geoff Eley, *The Peculiarities of German History: Bourgeois Society and Politics in Nineteenth-Century Germany*. New York: Oxford University Press, 1984.

Jonathan Sperber, *Rhineland Radicals: The Democratic Movement and the Revolution of 1848–1849*. Princeton, NJ: Princeton University Press, 1991.

Hans-Ulrich Wehler, *The German Empire 1871–1918*. Leamington Spa, Warwickshire, UK: Berg, 1985.

Bismarck

Otto von Bismarck, *Reflections and Reminiscences*. New York: Harper & Row, 1968.

Lothar Gall, *Bismarck: The White Revolutionary*. Boston: Allen & Unwin, 1986.

George O. Kent, *Bismarck and His Times*. Carbondale: Southern Illinois University Press, 1978.

World War I

Volker Berghahn, *Germany and the Approach of War in 1914*. New York: St. Martin's Press, 1973.

Martin Gilbert, *The First World War: A Complete History*. New York: Henry Holt, 1994.

Holger Herwig, *The First World War: Germany and Austria-Hungary, 1914–1918*. New York: St. Martin's Press, 1997.

Stuart Robson, *The First World War*. New York: Longman, 1998.

The Weimar Republic

Eberhard Kolb, *The Weimar Republic*. London and Boston: Unwin Hyman, 1988.

Walter Laqueur, *Weimar: A Cultural History 1918–1933*. New York: Putnam, 1974.

Anthony James Nicholls, *Weimar and the Rise of Hitler*. New York: St. Martin's Press, 1979.

Detlev Peukert, *The Weimar Republic: The Crisis of Classical Modernity*. New York: Hill and Wang, 1992.

The Third Reich and the Holocaust

Wolfgang Benz and Walter H. Pehle, eds., *Encyclopedia of German Resistance to the Nazi Movement*. Trans. Lance W. Garner. New York: Continuum, 1997.

Martin Broszat, *The Hitler State*. New York: Longman, 1981.

Anne Frank, *The Diary of Anne Frank*. Ed. Otto H. Frank and Mirjam Pressler. Trans. Susan Massotty. New York: Doubleday, 1995.

Ian Kershaw, *The "Hitler Myth": Image and Reality in the Third Reich*. New York: Oxford University Press, 1987.

Michael L. Morgan, ed., *A Holocaust Reader: Responses to the Nazi Extermination*. New York: Oxford University Press, 2001.

Louis L. Snyder, *Hitler's Elite: Biographical Sketches of Nazis Who Shaped the Third Reich*. New York: Hippocrene Books, 1989.

Eli Wiesel, *Night*. Trans. Stella Rodway. New York: Bantam Books, 1986.

Christian Zentner and Friedemann Bedurftig, eds., *Encyclopedia of the Third Reich*. Trans. Amy Hackett. 2 vols. New York: Macmillan, 1991.

Postwar

Jerry Bornstein, *The Wall Came Tumbling Down*. New York: Arch Cape Press, 1990.

Desmond Dinan, *Ever Closer Union: An Introduction to European Integration*. 2nd ed. Boulder, CO: Lynne Rienner, 1999.

William S. Ellis, "The Morning After: Germany Reunited," *National Geographic*, September 1991.

Norman Gelb, *The Berlin Wall: Kennedy, Khrushchev, and a Showdown in the Heart of Europe*. New York: Times Books Division of Random House, 1986.

Simon Hix, *The Political System of the European Union*. New York: St. Martin's Press, 1999.

Life, "The Boy Who Died on the Wall," August 31, 1962.

Peter Marcuse, *Missing Marx: A Personal and Political Journal of a Year in East Germany, 1989–1990*. New York: Monthly Review, 1991.

Adrian Webb, *The Longman Companion to Germany Since 1945*. New York: Longman, 1998.

Charles Wighton, *Adenauer: A Critical Biography*. New York: Coward-McCann, 1964.

INDEX

10/03